TELEKOLLEG MULTIMEDIAL

TRAIN YOUR ENGLISH!
GRAMMATIK- UND WORTSCHATZÜBUNGEN ZUM GRUNDKURS ENGLISCH

BERNARD BROWN

TELEKOLLEG MULTIMEDIAL

TELEKOLLEG MULTIMEDIAL wird veranstaltet von den Bildungs- bzw. Kultusministerien von Bayern, Brandenburg und Rheinland-Pfalz sowie vom Bayerischen Rundfunk (BR). Der Rundfunk Berlin-Brandenburg (RBB) unterstützt das TELEKOLLEG MULTIMEDIAL.
Dieser Band enthält das Arbeitsmaterial zu den vom Bayerischen Rundfunk produzierten Lehrsendungen.

Nähere Infos zu TELEKOLLEG MULTIMEDIAL:
www.telekolleg.de
www.telekolleg-info.de

Das Buch „Train your Englisch! Grammatik- und Wortschatzübungen zum Grundkurs Englisch" ist eine kompetenzorientierte Einführung in das Fach Englisch, und richtet sich an alle an Grundbildung interessierte Lernende der verschiedenen Schulstufen und Schulformen.

1. Auflage 2012
© BRmedia Service GmbH
Alle Rechte vorbehalten
Umschlag (Konzeption): Heike Collip, München
Umschlag-Hintergrund: Christine Meder, München
Satz und Grafik: SMP Oehler, Remseck
Gesamtherstellung: Print Consult GmbH, München
ISBN: 978-3-941282-46-9

INHALTSVERZEICHNIS

EINFÜHRUNG .... S. 7

CHAPTER 1: PRONOUNS, PLURALS AND THE VERB TO BE .... S. 9
The personal pronouns (Die Personalpronomen) .... S. 9
The possessive pronouns (Die Possessivpronomen) .... S. 10
The reflexive pronouns (Die Reflexivpronomen) .... S. 12
The plural of nouns (Die Pluralbildung von Substantiven) .... S. 14
The verb *to be* (Das Verb „sein") .... S. 15
Let's look at words .... S. 16

CHAPTER 2: ARTICLES, MORE PRONOUNS, NUMBERS AND A FEW PREPOSITIONS ... S. 18
The indefinite article (Der unbestimmte Artikel) .... S. 18
The definite article (Der bestimmte Artikel) .... S. 19
The demonstrative pronouns (Die Demonstrativpronomen) .... S. 20
The numbers (Die Zahlen) .... S. 21
Let's look at words .... S. 22
Do you still remember? .... S. 23

CHAPTER 3: WORD ORDER, ASKING QUESTIONS (1) AND AUXILIARIES .... S. 24
Word order (Wortstellung) .... S. 24
Asking questions (Fragebildung) (1) .... S. 27
Auxiliaries (Hilfsverben) .... S. 29
Let's look at words .... S. 31
Do you still remember? .... S. 32

CHAPTER 4: THE PRESENT SIMPLE, THE PRESENT CONTINUOUS, IMPERATIVES AND ASKING QUESTIONS (2) .... S. 34
The present continuous (Die Verlaufsform der Gegenwart) .... S. 34
The present simple (Die einfache Form der Gegenwart) .... S. 35
Imperatives (Befehlsformen) .... S. 38
Asking questions (Fragebildung) (2) .... S. 39
Let's look at words .... S. 41
Do you still remember? .... S. 44

CHAPTER 5: QUESTION TAGS AND SHORT ANSWERS .... S. 46
Question tags (Frageanhängsel) .... S. 46
Short answers (Kurzantworten) .... S. 48
Let's look at words .... S. 50
Do you still remember? .... S. 53

Chapter 6: The Past Simple and Past Continuous .... S. 56
The past simple (Die einfache Form der Vergangenheit) .... S. 56
The past continuous (Die Verlaufsform der Vergangenheit) .... S. 60
Let's look at words .... S. 62
Do you still remember? .... S. 63

Chapter 7: The Future Tenses .... S. 66
The future tenses (Die Zukunftsformen) .... S. 66
    a) The present continuous .... S. 66
    b) The future simple (will future) .... S. 66
    c) The "going to" future .... S. 67
    d) The present simple .... S. 68
    e) The future continuous .... S. 69
Let's look at words .... S. 70
Do you still remember? .... S. 72

Chapter 8: The Present Perfect Simple and Present Perfect Continuous ..... S. 75
The present perfect simple (Die einfache Form des Perfekts) .... S. 75
The present perfect continuous (Die Verlaufsform des Perfekts) .... S. 80
Let's look at words .... S. 81
Do you still remember? .... S. 82

Chapter 9: Adjectives and Adverbs, the Position of Adverbs and Comparisons ..... S. 85
Adjectives and adverbs (Adjektive und Adverbien) .... S. 85
The Position of adverbs (Die Wortstellung der Adverbien) .... S. 87
Comparisons (Steigerung/Vergleiche) .... S. 88
Let's look at words .... S. 93
Do you still remember? .... S. 95

Chapter 10: The Past Perfect Simple, the Past Perfect Continuous and the Future Perfect .... S. 97
The past perfect simple (Die einfache Form der Vorvergangenheit) .... S. 97
The past perfect continuous (Die Verlaufsform der Vorvergangenheit) .... S. 99
Another future form: the future perfect (Eine weitere Zukunftsform: the future perfect) .... S. 100
Let's look at words .... S. 102
Do you still remember? .... S. 104

Chapter 11: The Passive, Relative Pronouns and Clauses .... S. 107
The Passive (Das Passiv) .... S. 107
Relative pronouns and clauses (Relativpronomen und -sätze) .... S. 110
Let's look at words .... S. 115
Do you still remember? .... S. 117

CHAPTER 12: INDIRECT SPEECH .... S. 119
Indirect speech I: statements (Indirekte Rede I: Aussagesätze) .... S. 119
Indirect speech II: questions (Indirekte Rede II: Fragen) .... S. 122
Indirect speech III: requests and commands (Indirekte Rede III: Bitten und Aufforderungen) .... S. 123
Let's look at words .... S. 126
Do you still remember? .... S. 127

CHAPTER 13: INFINITIVES AND GERUNDS .... S. 130
Infinitives (Infinitive) .... S. 130
Gerunds (Gerundien) .... S. 136
  a) Gerunds after verbs (Gerundien nach Verben) .... S. 136
  b) Gerunds after prepositions (Gerundien nach Präpositionen) .... S. 138
  c) Gerunds as verb nouns (Gerundien als Verbalsubstantive) .... S. 139
  d) Gerunds after special expressions (Gerundien nach bestimmten Ausdrücken) ...... S. 140
  e) Gerunds and two subjects (Gerundien und zwei Subjekte) .... S. 140
Infinitive or gerund (Infinitiv oder Gerundium)? .... S. 141
Let's look at words .... S. 141
Do you still remember? .... S. 143

CHAPTER 14: PARTICIPIAL CONSTRUCTIONS .... S. 145
Shortened relative clauses (Verkürzte Relativsätze) .... S. 145
Participial constructions to express reasons
(Partizipialkonstruktionen zum Ausdruck des Grundes) .... S. 147
Participial constructions as a substitute for *and* or *and so*
(Partizipialkonstruktionen als Ersatz für *and* und *and so*) .... S. 148
Participial constructions to express time (Partizipialkonstruktionen zum Ausdruck der Zeit) ...... S. 148
Let's look at words .... S. 150
Do you still remember? .... S. 152

CHAPTER 15: CONDITIONAL SENTENCES .... S. 157
If-clauses (*If*-Sätze/Wenn-Sätze) .... S. 157
  a) *If*-clause type 1 (*If*-Satz Typ 1) .... S. 157
  b) *If*-clause type 2 (*If*-Satz Typ 2) .... S. 158
  c) *If*-clause type 3 (*If*-Satz Typ 3) .... S. 160
  d) *If*-clause – other types (*If*-Satz – andere Typen) .... S. 163
Let's look at words .... S. 164
Do you still remember? .... S. 165

TEST YOUR GRAMMAR! .... S. 168
TEST YOUR VOCABULARY! .... S. 173

KEY TO EXERCISES .... S. 178

Einführung

„Grammatik ist zu schwer für mich – und außerdem sehr langweilig."
„Um Gottes willen – das habe ich in der Schule schon nicht verstanden – besser wird es sicherlich nicht werden."
„Ich habe bloß einen Quali – Englisch – das wird sehr schwer."
„Grammatik und Wortschatz? Das mache ich immer nach Gefühl. Leider trügt mein Gefühl meistens!"
„Englische Grammatik? Die werde ich in 100 Jahren nicht verstehen."
„Ich bin so vergesslich – ich schaffe es einfach nicht, englische Wörter in meinem Gedächtnis zu behalten."

Falls Sie das Gefühl haben, dass diese Aussagen oder eine davon Ihrem Gemütszustand entsprechen, dann ist das Buch, das Sie in den Händen halten, gerade das richtige für Sie.

Das Buch versteht sich als Trainer, der Lücken – sogar sehr große Lücken – in Ihren Englischkenntnissen schließen soll. Dabei werden Sie sicherlich häufig Grund zum Lachen und Schmunzeln haben, wenn Sie die vielen Witze in den Erklärungen und Übungen lesen. Auch wenn Ihre „Ausgangsbasis" nicht der Mittleren Reife entspricht oder wenn Sie sehr, sehr viele englische Strukturen und Vokabeln vergessen haben: Dieses Buch möchte Sie an der Hand nehmen! Wenn Sie die Kapitel und Übungen in diesem Buch regelmäßig und gewissenhaft durcharbeiten, werden Sie selbst über Ihre vielen Fortschritte überrascht sein. Damit Sie erfolgreich sind, hier einige Tipps:

- Wenn Sie sich einigermaßen „fit" im Bezug auf englische Strukturen und englischen Wortschatz fühlen, empfehle ich Ihnen die zwei Tests am Ende von Kapitel 15 zu machen. Wenn Sie Lücken feststellen, dann nehmen Sie sich die entsprechenden Kapitel in diesem Buch vor.

- Wenn ein Arzt Ihnen eine Medizin verschreibt, wären Sie schlecht beraten, die ganze Flasche in zwei Tagen einzunehmen! Ähnlich verhält es sich mit dem Lernen! Es ist effektiver jeden Tag 20–30 Minuten für das Lernen zu investieren, als fünf und mehr Stunden am Ende der Woche mit den Übungen zu verbringen.

- Wiederholung: In jedem Kapitel finden Sie Übungen, die dazu dienen, Strukturen und Aspekte aus früheren Kapiteln zu wiederholen. Es ist jedoch zu empfehlen, die einzelnen Kapitel und die darin enthaltenen Übungen regelmäßig zu wiederholen. Auch wenige Minuten „diagonales Lesen" helfen, die Strukturen sich noch einmal ins Gedächtnis zu rufen und sie zu verfestigen.

- Damit Sie sich die Strukturen und Vokabeln ins Gedächtnis einprägen, ist zu empfehlen, selbst Sätze unter Verwendung der entsprechenden Struktur zu bilden. Überlegen Sie sich Sätze, die Ihr eigenes Leben, Ihre Freunde und Ihre Verwandten beschreiben:

    My wife has been working in Rosenheim since 2004.
    I have been learning English for the last five years.
    My girlfriend enjoys skiing, but I'm not good at skiing.
    The staff in my firm are very friendly.
    My son's T-shirt looks weird.

Es ist uns bewusst, wie beschäftigt viele von Ihnen sind. Jedoch lässt sich diese Übung leicht in den Alltag integrieren. Immer wieder hat man einige Minuten, in denen man für sich einige Sätze unter Berücksichtigung der einzuübenden Struktur formulieren kann.

In diesem Trainer finden Sie auch einige Übungen zum Wortschatz der Sendungen, um Ihnen zu helfen, sich wichtige Wörter merken zu können. Diese Übungen können aber nicht als Ersatz für den Aufbau eines Grundwortschatzes dienen.

Die Tipps, die wir zum Thema Grammatik und Strukturen gegeben haben, gelten auch für den Wortschatz:

- Bitte nehmen Sie sich nicht zu viele Wörter in Ihrem Lernpensum vor: Denken Sie daran, dass man in der Regel ein Wort fünf, sechs Mal gesehen haben muss (am besten in verschiedenen Zusammenhängen), um das Wort dem Passivwortschatz eingliedern zu können. Um das Wort in den Aktivwortschatz aufnehmen zu können, müssen Sie es in mehreren Sätzen selbst anwenden. Wenn Sie nur acht bis zehn Wörter am Tag lernen, haben Sie in einem Monat Ihren Wortschatz um viele Wörter erweitert. Wiederholung ist auch beim Wörterlernen unabdingbar – es ist viel einfacher, ein Wort zu vergessen, als es im Langzeitgedächtnis zu verankern!

- Es ist oft besser, Wörter nicht einzeln zu lernen und im Gedächtnis zu speichern, sondern sich diese zusammen mit den dazugehörenden Verben, Präpositionen etc. einzuprägen. Dies ist insbesondere dann zu empfehlen, wenn der englische Sprachgebrauch vom deutschen abweicht:
    to go by train; to do your homework; to attend school; to belong to someone

- Versuchen Sie beim Lernen der Wörter, zwei oder mehrere der neuen Wörter in einen Satz einzubauen. Auf diese Weise werden sie leichter im Gehirn „vernetzt".

    I put the ragged trousers in the fridge.
    His ragged trousers look weird.
    Although my fridge isn't worth much I still like it.

Auch diese Übung kann man während des Alltags machen.

- Zum Schluss: Seien Sie bitte geduldig mit sich selbst: „Rome wasn't built in a day." Lassen Sie dieses Buch zu Ihrem ständigen Begleiter in den nächsten Monaten werden. Vor über 2500 Jahren hat angeblich Laotse seinen Schülern den Ratschlag gegeben: „Lernen ist wie Rudern gegen den Strom. Hört man damit auf, treibt man zurück." Mit häufiger Wiederholung – auch wenn manchmal nur wenige Minuten dazu zur Verfügung stehen – werden Sie sicherlich Ihr Ziel erreichen.
  Bei den meisten Übungen ist Platz für die Lösung vorgesehen. Bitte verwenden Sie bei den anderen Übungen z. B. Übersetzungen ein gesondertes Blatt.

I wish you all the best on your way to success!

Bernard Brown

CHAPTER 1: PRONOUNS, PLURALS AND THE VERB *TO BE*

In diesem Kapitel beginnen wir unsere Reise durch die englische Grammatik mit folgenden Themen: mit den Pronomen, der Pluralbildung von Substantiven und dem Verb *to be* (sein). Dazwischen werden Sie gelegentlich etwas zum Schmunzeln haben.

THE PERSONAL PRONOUNS (DIE PERSONALPRONOMEN)

Ein Schwerpunkt der ersten Sendung sind die *pronouns* (Fürwörter). Das sind Wörter, die <u>für</u> andere Hauptwörter im Satz stehen können. Let's begin with the *personal pronouns*: ***I, you, he, she, it, we, you, they***. Sie stehen für das Subjekt eines Satzes (ich, du, er etc.). The only problem here is: In English, dog, cat, butter … are all *it* – don't forget!

EXERCISE A.

Write *I, you, he, she, it, we, they*:

1) (Diane) __She__ lives in the Hamptons.
2) (Kirk) __He__ lives in Kent.
3) (My sisters) __They__ work in Munich.
4) (My sisters, my brother and I) __We__ all meet once a year either in Yorkshire or in the Hamptons.
5) (The cat) __It__ can't speak English.
6) (The cat and the dog) __They__ like English fish and chips.
7) "Hello Mary! __You__ look very tired."
8) "__I__ am tired. __I__ have so much work."

Wie wir in der Sendung gesehen haben, können Pronomen auch als Objekt im Satz stehen, aber im Gegensatz zur deutschen Sprache gibt es nur ein Objektpronomen (me, you, him, her, it, us, them) und nicht zwei (mir – mich, dir – dich, ihm – ihn, ihr – sie etc.).

EXERCISE B.

Write in the *object pronouns*:

1) "Look, there's your brother!" "Really? I can't see __him__."
2) "Mr Kear, I have a letter for __you__."
3) "This bag is heavy. Mary, can you help __me__?"
4) "Where are Stuart and Malcolm? I have a job for __them__."

5) "My brother and sister are so noisy." "Yes, I can hear __them__."

6) "Why isn't Mrs Simmonds here? I must phone __her__."

7) "Hello Bill. Susan and I can't do the maths homework. Can you help __us__?"

8) "Betty and Cedric, where are you? I can't see __you__."

9) "This table is heavy. I can't lift __it__."

10) "This fish is too big. I can't eat __it__ all!"

> **WATCH OUT! (1)**
> Gelegentlich haben Deutsche Probleme mit der Übersetzung des kleinen Wortes „sie" bzw. „Sie".
> Im Englischen gibt es unterschiedliche Pronomen für das deutsche „sie/Sie": you, she, her, it, they, them.

EXERCISE C.

Write in the right translation for "Sie/sie".

"Look! There's Mary! Can you see (1) __her__?"

"Yes, I can. I know (2) __her__ quite well. (3) __She__ has got two little daughters.

(4) __They__ go to Beulah nursery school."

"Beulah nursery school? Is that a good school?"

"(5) __It__ certainly is. The problem is that poor Mary has to take (6) __them__ there before she goes to work every day."

THE POSSESSIVE PRONOUNS (DIE POSSESSIVPRONOMEN)

In der Sendung haben wir gesehen, dass Possessivpronomen, die angeben, wem etwas gehört, in zwei Formen vorkommen können: mit einem Substantiv (my book, his wife, etc.) oder anstelle eines Substantivs.
    That's mine. This car is ours (= our car).
This exercise can help you with the *possessive pronouns*:

EXERCISE D.

Write in the *possessive pronouns* in these jokes:

"(1) __Your__ boyfriend looks great in (2) __his__ new pullover," says Julia to (3) __her__ friend Christine.

"That's not a new pullover," says Christine. "That's (4) __my__ new boyfriend."

A man is walking in the park. A boy and a girl with a dog are also walking in the park. The man looks at the big dog and asks the boy. "Does (5) **your** dog bite?"

"No," replies the boy, "(6) **My** dog doesn't bite."

The man goes to the dog and the dog bites (7) **his** finger.

"Ouch!" he cries, "You said (8) **your** dog doesn't bite!"

"That's right," says the boy. "But that's not (9) **my** dog. You see that girl there? That's (10) **her** dog."

Two children are talking about (11) **their** friend George.

"He bites (12) **his** nails," says Mary.

"But," says Tom, "my sister bites (13) **her** nails, my two brothers bite (14) **their** nails and I bite (15) **my** nails."

"Yes," says Mary, "but George doesn't bite (16) **his** fingernails – he bites (17) **his** toenails."

"Goal!" says the referee (Schiedsrichter). "For which team?" one of the players asks.

"For (18) **our** team," says the referee.

The man on the operating table is very nervous.

"I'm so nervous, doctor," he says. "This is (19) **my** first operation."

"That's interesting," says the surgeon to (20) **his** patient. "It's (21) **mine**, too."

Mr Smith: "Is this ball (22) **yours** ?"

Peter: "Did it do any damage?"

Mr Smith: "No, it didn't."

Peter: "Then it's (23) **mine** ."

> **WATCH OUT! (2)**
> In German we say: Das ist ein Freund von mir (dir, ihm, ihr, uns, Peter).
> In English we say: That is a friend of <u>mine</u> (yours, his, hers, ours, Peter's).

> **WATCH OUT! (3)**
> In German we say: Er hat ein eigenes Auto.
> In English we say: He has <u>his</u> own car. Or: He has a car of <u>his</u> own.

THE REFLEXIVE PRONOUNS (DIE REFLEXIVPRONOMEN)

Gleich in der ersten Folge des Grundkurses Englisch „The Barbecue – Meat and Meet" hat uns Carolin ausführlich über die meisten englischen *pronouns* aufgeklärt. Es ist Zeit, die letzten *pronouns* zu besprechen: die sogenannten *reflexive pronouns*. In der deutschen Sprache ist es etwas einfacher als in der englischen – meistens nimmt man das direkte Objekt (mich, dich, uns etc.). Nur in der 3. Person Einzahl und Mehrzahl (er, sie, es, sie) nimmt man **sich** und **sich selbst**: Ich schaute **mich** im Spiegel an. Wir schauten **uns** im Spiegel an. Er schaute **sich** im Spiegel an. Sie schauten **sich** im Spiegel an. Das Subjekt spiegelt sich (reflects itself!) sozusagen im Objekt! In der Übersicht sehen Sie, wie diese Sätze im Englischen gebildet werden. Man benutzt *reflexive pronouns*, wenn eine Person sowohl Subjekt als auch Objekt einer Handlung ist:

Mike cut **himself** yesterday. He looked at **himself** in the mirror and said to **himself**: "Mike, even with all that blood on your face, you still look wonderful."

THE REFLEXIVE PRONOUNS

Singular
I looked at **myself** in the mirror.
You looked at **yourself** in the mirror.
He looked at **himself** in the mirror.
She looked at **herself** in the mirror.
It looked at **itself** in the mirror.

Plural
We looked at **ourselves** in the mirror.
You looked at **yourselves** in the mirror.
They looked at **themselves** in the mirror.

each other/one another
We write to **each other/one another**.   They help **each other/one another**.

Wichtig ist in unserem Zusammenhang, dass es eine ganze Reihe von Verben gibt, die im Deutschen ein Reflexivpronomen (mich, dich, sich, uns, euch) verlangen. Im Englischen folgt aber auf diese Verben kein Reflexivpronomen.

Ich kann es mir leisten, es zu kaufen. = I can afford ~~myself~~ to buy it. = I can afford to buy it.

Hier sind weitere wichtige Verben, die normalerweise keine *reflexive pronouns* benötigen. Viele haben wir schon eingeführt, einige sind neu:

apologize	complain	get ready	look forward to
argue	concentrate on	get washed	move
be interested in	feel	hurry (up)	relax
change	get annoyed	imagine	remember
rest	shave	worry	

apologize = sich entschuldigen; complain = sich beschweren; get ready = sich vorbereiten; look forward to = sich freuen auf; argue = streiten; concentrate on = sich konzentrieren auf; get washed = sich waschen ; move = bewegen; be interested in = interessiert sein an; feel = fühlen; hurry (up) = sich beeilen; relax = sich entspannen; change = sich ändern; get annoyed = sich aufregen; imagine = sich vorstellen; remember = sich erinnern; rest = sich ausruhen; shave = sich rasieren; worry = sich sorgen;

Wenn wir eine wechselseitige, gegenseitige Beziehung zwischen Menschen ausdrücken wollen, benutzen wir *each other* bzw. *one another*:
>They talked to **themselves** (mehrere Selbstgespräche!).
>They talked to **each other/one another** (ein Gespräch zwischen den beiden!).

Now try this exercise.

EXERCISE E.

Write in *reflexive pronouns* or *each other* if it is necessary.

1) The patient in the waiting room is very nervous.
   The dentist introduces _himself_: "I'm Dr Wilson, your dentist. Now, don't worry _—_," he says. "It won't hurt you."
   "I don't believe you," says the other man, "I'm a dentist _myself_."

2) "Please hurry _—_ and open the door," Bill says to his friend Fred.
   Fred complains _myself_: "Can't you open the door _yourself_?"
   "Of course I can open the door _myself_," says Bill, "but the paint is still wet."

3) Helen and Robert have got a telephone love affair: They talk to _each other_ eight hours a day on their mobile phones. They can't, of course, really afford _—_ it, but they feel _—_ so happy!

4) Rachel and Tom looked at _each other_ in the eyes. "I love you Rachel," Tom said.
   "I love _myself_, too," Rachel replied, as she looked at _herself_ in her pocket mirror.

5) Tim and his sister Sue are feeling _—_ hungry. "Look at the biscuits on the table!" Tim says. Let's help _ourselves_."
   "We can't," says Sue. "They're dog biscuits."

In dieser Übersicht sind die Pronomen noch einmal zusammengestellt:

Subject Pronouns	Object Pronouns	Possessive Pronouns	Possessive Determiner
I	me	my	mine
you	you	your	yours
he	him	him	his
she	her	her	hers
it	it	its	(its)
we	us	our	ours
you	you (pl.)	your (pl.)	yours
they	them	them	theirs

THE PLURAL OF NOUNS (DIE PLURALBILDUNG VON SUBSTANTIVEN)

Für Lernende der deutschen Sprache ist die Pluralbildung äußerst kompliziert, da es in der deutschen Sprache so viele Formen gibt: Brüder, Frauen, Parks, Kühe etc. Wie Sie in der Sendung gesehen haben, bilden wir in der englischen Sprache die Mehrzahl in der Regel, indem wir ein -s anhängen. Allerdings gibt es bei der Pluralbildung einiger Wörter etwas zu beachten. Erinnern Sie sich an die FOXY-Regel?
F: wife – wives; O: tomato – tomatoes; X: glass – glasses; Y: lady – ladies, aber boy – boys.
Es gibt außerdem sieben wichtige unregelmäßige Formen:

man – men	foot – feet	tooth – teeth
woman – women	person – people	
child – children	fish – fish	

Falls Sie über die Landwirtschaft reden wollen, können Sie vielleicht auch ox – oxen und sheep – sheep zur Liste hinzufügen.

WATCH OUT! (4)
Viele Substative im Deutschen, z.B. Fremdwörter aus dem Englischen, haben dieselbe Form in der Einzahl wie auch in der Mehrzahl: Fenster, Manager, Teenager. Dies verleitet den Lernenden der englischen Sprache dazu, das -s bei der Pluralbildung von Substantiven wegzulassen. Bitte begehen Sie diese Sünde nicht!
Also: two teenagers, two managers, etc.

EXERCISE F.

Write down the *plurals* of the following words:

school	schools	life	lives	child	children
student	students	city	cities	diet	diets
toy	toys	man	men	family	families
brush	brushes	knife	knives	woman	women
difficulty	difficulties	industry	industries	steak	steaks
foot	feet	sheep	sheep	fish	fish

THE VERB TO BE (DAS VERB „SEIN")

In all languages the verb *to be* is a very important verb!

EXERCISE G.

Put in: *am/are/is*

On the telephone.

"Hello, __are__ you Johny's teacher?"

"Yes, I __am__ ."

"Well, Johny __is__ very ill and so he can't come to school today."

"Oh dear, I __am__ very sorry. And who __are__ you?"

"This __is__ my father."

We often use *short forms* in English:
I'm/I'm not;   you're/you aren't (you're not);   he's/he isn't (he's not);
she's/she isn't (she's not);   it's/it isn't (it's not);   we're/we aren't (we're not);
they're/they aren't (they're not);   who's; how's; Bill's; etc.

EXERCISE H.

Put in the *short forms*:

1) This is Mr Hartley. __He's__ a teacher in Telekolleg.
2) Hello Mr Hartley. __I'm__ pleased to meet you.
3) Tom and Sue __aren't__ at work today – __they're__ ill.
4) I __'m__ sorry. __I'm__ late.
5) "Where are you, Tony and Helen?" "__We're__ here in the garden, mum. __It's__ so sunny."
6) "Where's Samantha?" "Well, she __isn't__ here in the flat. She __is__ in the garden."

EXERCISE I.

Do you remember? Translate these sentences:
1) Können Sie meine Schwester hören? Nein, ich kann sie nicht hören. Aber deine Brüder sind im nächsten Zimmer und sie sind sehr laut. Sie können sie hören.
2) Das ist ein Buch von uns.
3) Wir haben unsere eigene Methode, Wörter zu lernen.

LET'S LOOK AT WORDS

Well, that's enough grammar for today! New Zealand is an interesting country. My sister Miriam lives on the North Island and is very happy there. In this text you can read about the schools there:

Dr Miriam Brown is <u>extremely</u> enthusiastic about New Zealand. When she came to this country some years ago, she only wanted to work in the <u>medical</u> <u>service</u> for a year or so and then <u>return</u> to England. Now five years have gone by and Dr Brown is still in New Zealand.

Her three children are one of the reasons why she is still in New Zealand. They really love the school system
5 there. Teachers have a lot of freedom to be <u>flexible</u> in New Zealand and it can happen that the teacher says one day: "It's such a lovely day, we'll have our lesson outside today – on the beach. We'll have the <u>maths</u> lesson on Friday." In a country where it is sunny seven months of the year, this can happen very often!

Dr Brown says that the New Zealand philosophy is that no one is <u>unsporty</u> or <u>uncreative</u>. Every pupil can find a sport or form of art that he likes and can do well.

10 When the family was in England, her daughters Leah and Feya were <u>written off</u> as unsporty and only interested in <u>purely</u> <u>theoretical</u> subjects. In her school in Taurange (near Auckland) Leah is still <u>excelling</u> academically, but she is also good at long distance running, hockey and swimming. Most schools in New Zealand have their own swimming pools, so it is easy to practise after school.

Schools in New Zealand are quite <u>multicultural</u>. In the class of Emile, Dr Brown's son, there are pupils from
15 South Korea, the Fiji Islands, Belgium, Denmark, Samoa, England and, of course, pupils who were born in New Zealand – of British or Maori <u>origin</u>. And the teacher? He's from Zimbabwe! The country sounds very interesting – I must visit my sister soon!

EXERCISE J.

Many students worry (machen sich Sorgen) when they see new words in English. However (jedoch) when you look at many words you can often guess their meaning from similar (ähnlichen) words in German or from the context (Kontext!) of the words. Can you write down the meaning of the underlined words?

extremely = äußerst (The German words "extrem"/"Extremist" are helpful.)

EXERCISE K.

Words like people come in families! Remember the text about New Zealand that you heard in the programme and read in the chapter "The Barbecue – Meat and Meet" and write in the right forms of the words. What do the words in brackets mean?

1) The land on the hills on the North Island is very __fertile__ (fertility).
2) New Zealand is __famous__ (fame) for its __natural__ (nature) wonders.
3) The high sky tower in Auckland is an __important__ (importance) landmark.
4) Geysers, sleeping volcanoes, beautiful hills and fields: The landscape in New Zealand is very __varied__ (vary).
5) __Countless__ (count) numbers of tourists visit New Zealand every year.

EXERCISE L.

Crossword puzzle:
And now for some relaxation! This crossword puzzle has got some words from the programme and from the chapter "The Barbecue – Meat and Meet". Can you find them?

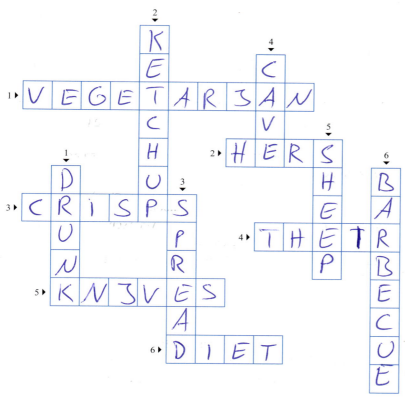

Across:
1) A _vegetarian_ does not eat meat.
2) You know Norma. Well, Peter is a friend of _hers_ .
3) People often eat _crisps_ at the cinema.
4) Peter and Mary have ~~~~~~ _their_ own car.
5) This plural form is interesting.
6) I can't eat too much chocolate – I'm on a _diet_ .

Down:
1) Some people think the duke got _drunk_ and fell down.
2) This is the American word for tomato sauce.
3) Fred's family is _spread_ out all over the United Kingdom.
4) They found the duke in a _cave_ .
5) There are more _sheep_ than people in New Zealand!
6) You can have a _barbecue_ in your garden in summer, but not in winter.

CHAPTER 2: ARTICLES, MORE PRONOUNS, NUMBERS AND A FEW PREPOSITIONS

In diesem Kapitel beschäftigen wir uns als Erstes mit drei kleinen englischen Wörtern: *a*, *an* und *the*.

THE INDEFINITE ARTICLE (DER UNBESTIMMTE ARTIKEL)

Wie in der zweiten Sendung erklärt, gibt es im Englischen zwei Formen des unbestimmten Artikels, je nachdem, ob das Substantiv mit einem Konsonanten (b, c, d, f, g etc.) oder einem Vokal (a, e, i, o, u) anfängt. Bei Wörtern, die mit u, e oder h beginnen, müssen wir auf der Hut sein: Das u in *uncle* ist ein Vokal. Deshalb sagen wir *an uncle*. Dagegen wird das u in *university* nicht wie ein Vokal ausgesprochen, sondern wie das y in *yellow*. Deshalb sagen wir *a university*. Ähnlich verhält es sich mit dem h in *house* und *hour*. Wir sagen *a house*. In *hour* wird das h nicht ausgesprochen, daher sagen wir *an hour*. Wir sagen auch *a European*, aber *an elephant*. Die gute Nachricht ist, dass es nur wenige solche Ausnahmen gibt! Schreiben Sie bitte in der ersten Übung die passenden unbestimmten Artikel in die Lücken.

EXERCISE A.

Write in *a* or *an*:

1) _an_ Italian
2) ____ English word
3) ____ barbecue
4) ____ umbrella
5) ____ organization
6) ____ computer
7) ____ useful book
8) ____ French town
9) ____ octopus
10) ____ European city
11) ____ address
12) ____ apple
13) ____ honour (Ehre)
14) ____ happy TK student
15) ____ office
16) ____ insect

WATCH OUT! (1)

Im Gegensatz zum deutschen Sprachgebrauch benutzen wir *a/an* bei Berufsbezeichnungen und bei Zugehörigkeit zu einer Gruppe, Konfession, politischen Partei etc.:
   She's **a** doctor. He's **a** vegetarian. She's **a** catholic. Tom is **a** member of the Labour Party.

WATCH OUT! (2)

A/an wird bei bestimmten Ausdrücken verwendet. In der entsprechenden deutschen Redewendung fehlt meistens der Artikel. Hier sind einige der wichtigsten Redewendungen:

for **a** change	zur Abwechslung	as **a** rule	in **der** Regel
to have **a** cold	Schnupfen haben	to be in **a** hurry	in Eile sein
it's **a** pity	schade	once **a** month	einmal **im** Monat
for **a** long time	lange Zeit	fifty miles **an** hour	fünfzig Meilen **pro** Stunde
to have **a** holiday	frei haben		
They cost two pounds **a** kilogram.		Sie kosten zwei Pfund **pro** Kilogramm.	

Exercise B.

Translate the sentences:
1) Er ist immer in Eile.
2) Er ist Raucher.
3) Sie ist Engländerin und Lehrerin.
4) Zur Abwechslung können wir hier essen.

Wie die deutsche Sprache unterscheidet die englische zwischen dem unbestimmten Artikel und dem bestimmten Artikel:

THE DEFINITE ARTICLE (DER BESTIMMTE ARTIKEL)

Eric: Hi, Jenn, I'm looking for **an** apartment.
Jenn: **The** apartment you want is on our website.

Wenn ein Substantiv in einem allgemeinen Sinn verwendet wird, verzichtet man normalerweise auf den Artikel *the*. Dies gilt auch für abstrakte Begriffe (Graham is interested in philosophy) oder stehende Begriffe (z. B. modern society, pop music, etc.) Nur wenn das Substativ näher erläutert wird, verwendet man den Artikel *the* (**The** philosophy of Hegel is not easy to understand).

> ### WATCH OUT! (3)
> Es gibt eine Reihe von Wendungen, die mit *the* gebildet werden oder umgekehrt ohne *the*. Im Deutschen verhält es sich oft anders. Die meisten englischen Ortsangaben werden z. B. ohne *the* gebildet:
> St Paul's Cathedral, Buckingham Palace, Windsor Castle
> Es gibt aber keine Regel ohne Ausnahme. Bei Flüssen, Museen und Kunstgalerien wird der bestimmte Artikel verwendet:
> **the** National Gallery, **the** Science Museum, **the** River Thames
> Im Moment genügt es, wenn Sie folgende wichtige Wendungen lernen:
>
> | | | | |
> |---|---|---|---|
> | with the help of | mithilfe von | from the beginning | von Anfang an |
> | it's the custom | es ist Brauch | in February | im Februar |
> | at the expense of | auf Kosten von | on Tuesday | am Dienstag |
>
> | | |
> |---|---|
> | I have breakfast/lunch/dinner | ich frühstücke, esse zu Mittag/zu Abend |
> | he goes to (is at) school/university/work | er geht zur Schule/Universität/Arbeit; er ist in der Schule/Universität/Arbeit |
> | he goes to (is in) bed | er geht ins Bett/er ist im Bett |
> | Where is Oxford Street? | Wo ist die Oxford Street? |
> | Windsor Castle is nearby ... | Das Schloss Windsor ist in der Nähe von ... |

Exercise C.

Put in *the* where necessary.

1) He reads about __-__ history, especially _the_ history of Bavaria in the twentieth century.

2) I liked George right from _____ beginning.

3) We need _____ water to live. _____ water here is very rich in minerals.

4) I must go to _____ bed early tonight.

5) Munich is _____ city which I live in.

6) Not everybody likes _____ city life.

7) John is still at _____ school. _____ school in our town is very big.

8) What can we eat for _____ breakfast?

9) _____ second meal of the day is _____ lunch.

10) _____ breakfast that they serve in this restaurant is not cheap.

11) I live in _____ Lenham Road, near _____ Jessam Avenue.

12) _____ Westminster Abbey is near _____ Trafalgar Square and _____ Hyde Park.

13) In _____ March we want to go to New York and see Central Park.

The demonstrative pronouns (Die Demonstrativpronomen)

Ein Beispiel für englischen schwarzen Humor (sick humour):
Mary: "Mum, I don't like **this** meat. Can I give it to our dog?"
Mum: "Sorry, **that** is our dog."

Wir benutzen *this* und *these* (Mehrzahl), um Gegenstände, Tiere oder Menschen zu bezeichnen, die in der Nähe des Sprechers liegen. *That* und *those* (Mehrzahl), um Gegenstände, Tiere oder Menschen zu benennen, die vom Sprecher eher entfernt sind.

Exercise D.

Write in *this*, *these*, *that* or *those*:

1) Can you see _that_ man over there?

2) _____ houses in the next street are all very old.

3) _____ book here is very interesting.

4) Oh dear! Look at _____ black clouds. We can forget our picnic!

5) Hey – who left _____ letters here on my desk?

6) _____ car here is mine, but _____ car is hers.

THE NUMBERS (DIE ZAHLEN)

Wahrscheinlich bereiten Ihnen die Zahlen, Daten und Uhrzeiten im Englischen wenige Schwierigkeiten. Aber zur Kontrolle können Sie die folgenden Übungen machen:

EXERCISE E.

Write out these *dates*:

1) 10. 06. 1674   the tenth of June sixteen seventy-four
2) 21. 03. 2010
3) 15. 10. 1993
4) 31. 12. 1884
5) 05. 02. 1773
6) 11. 07. 2008
7) 23. 01. 1970
8) 09. 11. 1989
9) 12. 05. 1871
10) 22. 09. 2005

EXERCISE F.

"Telling the time". Write out these *times* in English:

1) 4.15   (a) quarter past four (in the morning)*
2) 8.55
3) 10.30
4) 11.35
5) 15.45
6) 19.40

7) 5.59 _____

8) 17.09 _____

9) 12.00 _____

10) 13.27 _____

* Wie im Deutschen ist es im Englischen unüblich zu sagen: fifteen minutes past seven

LET'S LOOK AT WORDS

In German we have many words that often come with a preposition (Präposition): auf, in, zu, an, von etc.

For example:
im Schnitt   **on** average
das hängt **vom** Wetter ab   that depends **on** the weather
ich gehe **zu** Fuß   I'm going **on** foot

In English, as you can see, these prepositions are often different. Sie sparen sich Zeit, wenn Sie Wort und Präposition zusammen lernen. Wählen Sie in der folgenden Übung das jeweils passende Verb mit Präposition (siehe Kasten darunter), um die Ausdrücke aus den ersten zwei Sendungen zu übersetzen.

EXERCISE G.

Choose the right verbs and prepositions from the box below:

1) We must _carry out_ _____ (durchführen, in die Tat umsetzen) our plan.

2) New Zealand and Australia _____ (gehören zu) the Commonwealth.

3) The number of tourists here _____ (hört nicht auf) rising every year.

4) The region is _____ (gekennzeichnet durch) sleeping volcanoes.

5) Every year I _____ (sich darauf freuen) my holiday in Brighton.

6) London is _____ (berühmt wegen) its many sights.

7) The Commonwealth _____ (besteht aus) many countries in four continents.

8) Education is _____ (aufgeteilt in) four different types of education: primary, secondary, further and higher education.

| keeps | consists | famous | divided | | to | ~~out~~ | into | to |
| belong | look forward | ~~carry~~ | characterized | | by | on | of | for |

DO YOU STILL REMEMBER?

Here are two exercises to check!

EXERCISE H.

Choose the right pronouns from the box below.

1) Mrs Smith's son comes home with dirty shoes. She looks at _him_ and says: "Look at those dirty shoes. Why can't you clean _____ before you come in?"

   "Mummy," _____ son asks _____: "You mustn't be angry with _____. You've got a vacuum cleaner (Staubsauger). Why can't you get _____, clean the floor _____ and laugh like the woman in the TV commercial for vacuum cleaners?"

2) The customs official (Zollbeamter) sees the two passengers and asks _____: "Cognac? Whisky? Cigarettes?" The man says: "That's very nice of _____, but no thank you." "Yes," says _____ wife. "_____ have already got _____ _____. Look at this bag. _____'re in _____."

| we | them | it | ~~him~~ | them | ourselves | his | her | her | you | they |
| it | me | yourself | them |

EXERCISE I.

Please translate these sentences:
1) Stuart ist ein guter Freund von uns.
2) Wir schreiben uns jeden Tag.
3) Ist dieses Buch deins?
4) Carol hat ein eigenes Zimmer.
5) Ich mache mir Sorgen um meine alte Tante. Sie kann sich nicht an mich erinnern.

Chapter 3: word order, asking questions (1) and auxiliaries

Let's begin this chapter with a joke:

A zoo keeper at the zoo says to the visitors:
"Ladies and gentlemen, come and watch this! A sheep and a lion in the same cage!"
A little boy is very impressed (beeindruckt): "That's fantastic! How do you do it?" he asks.
The zoo keeper replies: "Oh, it's easy.
    We   put   another sheep   into the lion's cage   every two minutes."

Word Order (Wortstellung)

Wie wir in der dritten Sendung gesehen haben, unterliegen die Satzteile in der englischen Sprache einer bestimmten Ordnung.

(Zeit) Subjekt	Prädikat (Verb)	Objekt	Ort	Zeit
⇩	⇩	⇩	⇩	⇩
We	put	another sheep	into the lion's cage	every two minutes.

Die Zeitangabe kann man an den Anfang oder an das Ende des Satzes stellen. Unser Zoowächter könnte deshalb auch sagen:

| Every two minutes | we | put | another sheep | into the lion's cage. |

Auch der deutsche Satz unterliegt einer bestimmten Ordnung:

Maria	trinkt	im Büro	jeden Tag	eine Flasche Cola.
Im Büro	trinkt	Maria	jeden Tag	eine Flasche Cola.
Jeden Tag	trinkt	Maria	eine Flasche Cola	im Büro.

Die allerwichtigste Regel für den Bau des deutschen Satzes (so lernen es die Engländer!) ist: Das Verb steht an zweiter Stelle. Auch wenn wir mit einem anderen Wort den Satz beginnen, z. B. oft, müssen wir uns an diese Regel halten:

| Oft | trinkt | Maria | eine Flasche Cola | im Büro. |

Im Englischen **ist** **es** jedoch sehr wichtig, das Subjekt vor das Prädikat (Verb) zu stellen.
            ⇩   ⇩
           Prädikat Subjekt

Der letzte Satz auf Englisch:
However **it** **is** very important to put the subject before the predicate (verb).
        ⇩   ⇩
    Subjekt Prädikat

Im Gegensatz zum deutschen Sprachgebrauch könnte der Zoowächter deshalb nie sagen:
~~Another sheep put we into the lion's cage every two minutes.~~

WATCH OUT! (1)
Wichtig ist auch, dass wir im Gegensatz zum Deutschen die Hilfsverben etc. normalerweise nicht von den Hauptverben trennen:

We **will see** John tomorrow. (Wir **werden** John morgen **sehen**.) I **must go** now. (Ich **muss** jetzt **gehen**.)

WATCH OUT! (2)
Wie Sie in der Sendung gesehen haben, gibt es einige Wörter, die angeben, wie oft eine Handlung oder ein Ereignis stattfindet. Dies sind die wichtigsten: always (immer), sometimes (manchmal), occasionally (gelegentlich), usually (gewöhnlich), seldom (selten), never (niemals), hardly ever (kaum). Diese Wörter stehen unmittelbar vor dem Hauptverb, aber nach dem Verb *to be*:

"Do you **often find** the questions in maths exams difficult?"
"No, I don't. I **usually understand** the questions, but the answers **are always** difficult to find."

Don't worry. These three exercises will help you to understand English sentence structure:

EXERCISE A.

Which of the sentences is correct?

1) a) He's the phone connecting to the power supply now. ☐
   b) He's connecting the phone to the power supply now. ✓
   c) He's connecting now the phone to the power supply. ☐

2) a) Now need I to update the software. ☐
   b) Now I need the software to update. ☐
   c) Now I need to update the software. ☐

3) a) Could you please the last step repeat? ☐
   b) The last step could you repeat please? ☐
   c) Could you please repeat the last step? ☐

4) a) We can buy the laptop in this shop tomorrow. ☐
   b) We can buy tomorrow the laptop in this shop. ☐
   c) Tomorrow we can buy in this shop the laptop. ☐

5) a) Tom works usually from Monday to Friday in London. ☐
   b) Tom usually works in London from Monday to Friday. ☐
   c) Tom from Monday to Friday usually works in London. ☐

Exercise B.

Put the words in brackets into their correct places in the sentences:

1) Mrs Finch   works   at the weekend   (in her firm)

   Mrs Finch works in her firm at the weekend.

2) Mr Smith   doesn't   eat   cornflakes   for breakfast   (always)

   _____

3) We   play   table-tennis   together   (after work)

   _____

4) I   can   a red light   on the router   (see)

   _____

5) Our colleague   is   downloading   onto the computer   (the software)

   _____

6) The secretary   sends   her reports   by e-mail   (hardly ever)

   _____

7) Our partner Ms Maunders   must   send   the catalogue   (today)

   _____

8) My girlfriend   usually   takes   out of her mouth   before she kisses me   (her cigarette)

   _____

9) I   can   use   the laptop   now   (on Ray's desk)

   _____

Exercise C.

Put these words in the right order to make correct sentences:

1) are / rising / at present / prices

   Prices are rising at present.

2) an apple / every day / eat / I

   _____

3) are / Peter and Mary / breakfast / making / now

   _____

4) can't / Mark / the new program / install

_____

5) need / we / the program / update / to

_____

6) don't / I / here / the latest version of the software / have

_____

7) can / always / read / from the front / the labels / you

_____

8) of the firmware / I / have / the latest version / don't

_____

9) don't / in the office / they / on Saturdays / usually / work

_____

10) goes / Peter / every summer / on a diet / always

_____

ASKING QUESTIONS (FRAGEBILDUNG) (1)

Im nächsten Kapitel werden wir zwei wichtige Zeitformen (*tenses*) näher kennenlernen: *the present simple* und *the present continuous*. In einem späteren Kapitel werden wir die Zeitform *past simple* behandeln. Hier wollen wir uns darauf beschränken, Fragen in der Gegenwart (*present simple*) und in der Vergangenheit (*past simple*) zu bilden. Wie wir in der Sendung und in diesem Kapitel gesehen haben, erfolgt der englische Satzbau nach diesem Muster:

AUSSAGESATZ				
Ort/Zeit	Subjekt	Prädikat	Objekt	(Ort) Zeit
Now	I	need to update	the firmware	(now).

Um die Frageform in der Gegenwart (*present simple*) oder in der Vergangenheit (*past simple*) zu bilden, bleiben wir bei derselben Struktur: Aber anstatt die Zeit an den Anfang des Satzes zu setzen, verwenden wir im Englischen ein *do* (bei *he*, *she* oder *it* ein *does*) bzw. in der Vergangenheit ein *did*.

FRAGESATZ				
Subjekt	Prädikat	Objekt	(Ort)	Zeit
Do	I	need* to update	the firmware	now?
Did	I	need* to update	the firmware	then?

* siehe WATCH OUT! (4)

> **WATCH OUT! (3)**
> Bei Fragen mit *do, does* und *did* steht das zweite Verb immer **im Infinitiv (in der Grundform), ohne -s:**
> Does he **speak** English? Did he **go** to work yesterday?

Wichtig ist, dass in der englischen Sprache die Frageform – bis auf wenige Ausnahmen – mit *do* gebildet wird. Vergleichen Sie diese Sätze:

Spielt dein Mann Fußball? Englisch: **Does** your husband **play** football?

Allerdings wird beim Verb *be* für die Bildung von Fragen und negativen Aussagesätzen keine Umschreibung mit *do* verwendet.

Nach diesen Übungen werden Sie die Frageform besser verstehen.

EXERCISE D.

Miriam is asking Rachel about her new flat. Match her questions with Rachel's answers:
1) I hear that you've got a new flat. What's it like?
2) Are the rooms very large?
3) Do you like your neighbours?
4) How old are they?
5) Do you need to buy a lot of furniture for the flat?
6) What's a "wardrobe"?
7) How expensive is the flat?
8) Is it far from your work?

(a) I'm not sure, but they both still go to the kindergarten.
(b) Oh yes – about 24 square metres. And the windows are huge, so there's always lots of light.
(c) Oh, it's quite cheap really. The rent is only £ 260. The utility costs are £ 120.
(d) Oh of course, you're American, so that's a new word for you. I think you say "closet" in the States.
(e) Oh it's wonderful – it's a lovely two-roomed flat right here in the neighbourhood.
(f) Not at all. It's only a ten minute drive by car or I can use public transport: There's a bus stop just outside the flat.
(g) They're very helpful. They live in the flat on the ground floor and have two lovely children – a boy and a girl.
(h) Oh no – it's already furnished – there's a wardrobe, a bed, bookshelves and a little table.

Now look at the dialogue and see if you are right!

Miriam: I hear that you've got a new flat. What's it like?
Rachel: Oh it's wonderful – it's a lovely two-roomed flat right here in the <u>neighbourhood.</u>
Miriam: Are the rooms very large?
Rachel: Oh yes – about 24 square metres. And the windows are <u>huge</u>, so there's always lots of light.
Miriam: Do you like your neighbours?

Rachel: They're very helpful. They live in the flat on the ground floor and have two lovely children – a boy and a girl.
Miriam: How old are they?
Rachel: I'm not sure, but they both still go to the kindergarten.
Miriam: Do you need to buy a lot of <u>furniture</u> for the flat?
Rachel: Oh no – it's already <u>furnished</u> – there's a wardrobe, a bed, <u>bookshelves</u> and a little table.
Miriam: What's a "wardrobe"?
Rachel: Oh of course, you're American, so that's a new word for you. I think you say "closet" in the States.
Miriam: How expensive is the flat?
Rachel: Oh, it's quite cheap really. The rent is only £ 260. The <u>utility costs</u> are £ 120.
Miriam: Is it far from your work?
Rachel: Not at all. It's only a ten minute drive by car or I can use public transport: There's a bus stop just outside the flat.

Now its time for you to make questions!

Exercise E.

Make questions for these sentences:

1) They live in a nice neighbourhood.   *Do they live in a nice neighbourhood?*
2) You always eat a big breakfast.   _____
3) You need my help.   _____
4) Tom has the updated version of the software.   _____
5) Miriam works with the new program.   _____
6) The children in this English class read Harry Potter stories.   _____
7) Mrs Jenkins and Mr Finch work in this room.   _____
8) I need to download the software.   _____

Auxiliaries (Hilfsverben)

Einen weiteren Schwerpunkt in der dritten Sendung bilden die *auxiliaries*: Hilfsverben.
Hilfsverben „helfen", Zeiten zu bilden: I **have** seen him. They **are** drinking coffee.)
Und sie helfen, eine ganze Reihe von Sprechabsichten zum Ausdruck zu bringen.
Beispiele:
Fähigkeit: I can repair the car. Bitte: May/Could I use your computer? Forderung/Vorschlag: You should/ought to finish the work first. Notwendigkeit: We must finish the work before Monday.
Fragen, die diese Hilfsverben enthalten, werden nicht mit *do* gebildet.

EXERCISE F.

Write in *can*, *could*, *may*, *is*, *are*, *would* and *have*:

1) __Could/Would__ you please connect the phone?

2) _____ you install the latest software?

3) _____ Tom connecting the computer to the power supply?

4) _____ you see a red light on the Router?

5) _____ you installed the T-Box program?

6) _____ I help you?

7) _____ you connect the extension cord to the T-phone for me, please?

8) _____ you like a cup of coffee?

9) _____ those two colleagues flying to New York?

Sehr wichtig sind folgende drei Ersatzformen:
can (Fähigkeit) = to be able to;   must = to have to;   may/can (Erlaubnis) = to be allowed to

"I'm **not able to** sleep at night."
"Oh dear! You must be very tired."
"No, I'm not. I sleep in the office in the morning and afternoon."

"Do I **have to** speak English?"
"Well, half the world speaks English."
"Well, isn't that enough?"

"Why do you always play with those terrible children from the other street? Why don't you play with the nice children next door?" "Because they **aren't allowed to** play with me."

EXERCISE G.

Which sentences are correct?
1) a) My 14 year-old daughter isn't allowed to stay out late on Saturdays.   ✓
   b) My 14 year-old daughter has to stay out late on Saturdays.
2) a) Quick, our train leaves at 5 o'clock. We have to leave now.
   b) Quick, our train leaves at 5 o'clock. We're allowed to go now.
3) a) Some people are allowed to remember a hundred numbers in five minutes.
   b) Some people are able to remember a hundred numbers in five minutes.
4) a) Many doctors have to work at night.
   b) Many doctors are allowed to work at night.
5) a) My brother isn't allowed to read Spanish.
   b) My brother isn't able to read Spanish.

Später werden wir wieder auf die Hilfsverben zu sprechen kommen. Hier begnügen wir uns mit einer Schwierigkeit, die Englischlernende (mit deutscher Muttersprache) oft haben:

> **WATCH OUT! (4)**
> „Er muss nicht kommen"/„Er braucht nicht kommen" wird im Englischen so wiedergegeben:
> He **needn't (doesn't have to/hasn't got to/doesn't need to)** come.
> Um das Leben nicht unnötigerweise zu verkomplizieren, schlage ich vor, dass Sie nur eine dieser Formen in Ihren aktiven Wortschatz übernehmen, z.B. **need**.
> He **mustn't** come dagegen bedeutet: Er **darf nicht** kommen!

Exercise H.

Which sentences are correct?
1) a) You needn't drink water. You can drink coffee. ✓
   b) You mustn't drink water. You can drink coffee.
2) a) Bill mustn't forget to buy a ticket for the train. I haven't got a ticket for him.
   b) Bill doesn't have to buy a ticket for the train. I haven't got a ticket for him.
3) a) Bill mustn't forget to buy a ticket for the train. I've got a ticket for him.
   b) Bill doesn't have to buy a ticket for the train. I've got a ticket for him.
4) a) Yvonne hasn't got to park here. She's next to the bus stop!
   b) Yvonne mustn't park here. She's next to the bus stop!
5) a) We can eat here, but we mustn't. There's another good restaurant in the next street.
   b) We can eat here, but we needn't. There's another good restaurant in the next street.

Exercise I.

Translate these sentences into English:
1) Wir müssen keinen neuen Computer kaufen/Wir brauchen keinen neuen Computer zu kaufen.
2) Wir dürfen nicht zu spät nach Hause kommen.
3) Darf ich morgen wieder kommen?
4) Sie dürfen den Laptop nicht anschließen.
5) Könnten Sie bitte zu mir kommen?

Let's look at words

When you read a text in English, you will usually find some words that are new for you. Don't worry! You know that you can often work out the meaning of these words without a dictionary. In Übung D. fragt Miriam z. B. nach *furniture* in der Wohnung. Rachel spricht in ihrer Antwort von *wardrobe*, *bed*, *bookshelves* und *table*. Auch wenn uns die Wörter *wardrobe* oder *bookshelves* nicht geläufig sind, können wir mithilfe der Wörter *bed* und *table* erschließen, dass *furniture* – falls wir die Bedeutung des Wortes nicht mehr wissen – „Möbelstück(e)" bedeutet. Daraus können wir ableiten, dass *furnished* „möbliert" heißt.

Exercise J.

Word guessing:
Versuchen Sie, die Bedeutung der anderen unterstrichenen Ausdrücke in Übung D. auf ähnliche Art und Weise zu ermitteln!

Exercise K.

This time just a short exercise on some of the words in the third programme. Choose the right words from the box below:

1) Scotland, Wales and Northern Ireland have their own __independent__ parliaments.

2) With a computer you _____ one problem after the other every day!

3) The Scottish kilt bears _____ to the Scottish love of tradition.

4) _____ Scotland, three other countries – England, Wales and Northern Ireland make up the United Kingdom of Great Britain.

5) The most _____ parts of Scotland are the cities and towns.

6) Bars and cafés in Edinburgh are often old _____ houses.

7) Not everybody drinks alcohol in _____.

8) Life for the Scottish was often a life full of _____.

9) Not many people in Scotland try to _____ the traditional Scottish language, Gaelic.

10) The United Kingdom was _____ over three hundred years ago.

cultivate   populated   independent   moderation   encounter
hardship   founded   witness   converted   apart from

Do you still remember?

Before you relax with a few jokes another revision test!

Exercise L.

Which is right?
1) We see (us/each other/ourselves) once a year.
2) George has a book of (mine/me/myself).
3) Tamara has (an/her) own car.

4) Nobody in New Zealand is written (on/off/up) as unsporty.
5) John has (a/an/--) cold.
6) With (a/the/--) help of my Spanish wife, I am learning Spanish.
7) (These/That/Those) flowers in the next garden are lovely.
8) I'm looking forward (to/on/in) the next programme on TV.
9) I love most music but (the/a/--) music which my teenage son plays is terrible.
10) The car industry in this country is very strong. (She/He/It) is important for the economy.

Well, after all that hard work it is time to relax! Here are some jokes for you with some of the *auxiliaries*:

It's midnight and Michael goes to his dad's bed.
"Dad, **can** you write in the dark?" he asks.
"Yes, I **can**," his dad says.
"Good," says Michael, "**can** you write your name here on my school report*, please?"

A man is driving in a one way street.
"Excuse me, sir," says a policeman, "are you going in the right direction?"
"I'm sure that I am," says the driver, "but I **must** be late – the others are all coming back."

"Stop!" Petra says to her friend. "We **mustn't** eat those mushrooms*. They're poisonous*!" "It's OK" says Jane. "We **needn't** eat them. We **can** sell them."

*report = Zeugnis; mushrooms = Pilze; poisonous = giftig. Could you guess these words?

Chapter 4: The Present Simple, the Present Continuous, Imperatives and Asking Questions (2)

I hope that you are still enjoying the preparatory course. Don't forget: learning English is like taking medicine. When we have a cold, it is not good to drink the whole bottle of medicine in one day! It is better to take a teaspoonful of medicine every day! Similarly (in ähnlicher Weise) it is better to do a little English every day than to do nothing from Monday to Friday and then work for six hours on English at the weekend!

In this chapter we want to talk about two *present tenses* and *questions with question words*.
As usual at the end there is an exercise on vocabulary and some revision tests.

The Present Continuous (Die Verlaufsform der Gegenwart)

Im Mittelpunkt der vierten Sendung stehen die zwei Gegenwartsformen des Verbs. Die Engländer erlauben sich den Luxus zweier Gegenwartsformen, übrigens zusammen mit den Italienern und Spaniern. Wie Carolin in der Sendung erklärt hat, beschreibt die Verlaufsform der Gegenwart eine Handlung, die zum Zeitpunkt des Sprechens nicht abgeschlossen ist – die also weiter andauert. Carolin hat uns informiert, dass *now*, *right now*, *just now*, *at the moment*, *at present*, *look* und *listen* Signalwörter sind, die uns oft darauf aufmerksam machen, dass das *present continuous* angesagt ist. Die Form wird mit *to be* in der Gegenwart gebildet und das Hauptverb mit einem *-ing* versehen:

A policeman **is standing** near an angler. There is a sign near the angler: "Fishing prohibited!"
(„Angeln verboten!")
"**Are** you **fishing** here?" he asks the angler.
"No," says the fisherman, "I**'m washing** my worm."

Bei einigen Verben ändert sich bei der Bildung der Verlaufsform die Schreibweise:
waste (verschwenden) – He's wast**ing** my time.
ru**n** – Look! John's ru**nn**ing very fast.
d**ie** – These flowers are d**y**ing.

> **WATCH OUT! (1)**
> Sehr oft verwenden wir im Deutschen die Gegenwartsform, um ein Ereignis oder eine Handlung in der Zukunft zu beschreiben:
> Morgen kommen wir früh. Nächsten Sommer fahren wir nach Irland.
> Im Englischen nehmen wir normalerweise in solchen Zusammenhängen die Verlaufsform der Gegenwart:
> We**'re coming** early tomorrow. Next summer **we're going** to Ireland.

Exercise A.

Put the verbs in brackets into the right form of the *present continuous*.

1) Your child Patricia __is making_____ (make) so much noise.
2) I _____ (have) breakfast now.
3) Today we _____ (not work) in the office. We _____ (swim) in the sea.
4) "That machine is so noisy." "It's OK – I _____ (stop) it right now."
5) Hey Terry – you _____ (not do) your homework!
6) Look at Harold and Meg: They _____ (lie) on the wet grass.
7) We _____ (see) the client next week.

The Present Simple (Die einfache Form der Gegenwart)

Die einfache Form der Gegenwart ist uns schon im letzten Kapitel begegnet, als wir die Bildung der Fragen mit *do* behandelt haben. Im Gegensatz zum *present continuous* wird das *present simple* benutzt, um Handlungen, Ereignisse, Vorgänge etc., die nicht in der unmittelbaren Gegenwart stattfinden, zu beschreiben. Dabei werden die bereits erwähnten *adverbs of frequency* (Adverbien der Häufigkeit) *always*, *often*, *usually*, *sometimes*, *occasionally*, *seldom*, *hardly*, *hardly ever*, *never* oder Ausdrücke wie *every day*, *once a week*, *on Mondays*, *at five o'clock* etc. oft verwendet. Wie in der dritten Sendung und im letzten Kapitel gezeigt, wird die Frageform mit *do* bzw. *does* gebildet, ebenso die Negativform (*do + not*).

Do you **work** here? No, I **don't work** here. Yes, I **work** here.

> ### Watch out! (2)
> Beim Gebrauch dieser Zeitform machen Lernende der englischen Sprache häufig drei große Fehler. Daher merken Sie sich bitte:
>
> a) Das -s in der dritten Person Singular darf nicht vergessen werden: *He, she, it – das -s muss mit.*
>   Beispiele:
>   he swim**s**, she swim**s**, it swim**s**, Tom swim**s**, the dog swim**s**. Mary watche**s** TV.
>   Wenn wir *do* als Hilfsverb einsetzen, kommt kein -s am Ende des Hauptverbs:
>   Peter **loves** football. He **doesn't love** you.
>
> b) Negativsätze werden mit *do* bzw. *does* umschrieben.
>   Es heißt nicht: ~~He speaks not Italian~~.   Sondern: He **doesn't** speak Italian.
>
> c) Bei den Verben *can*, *must*, *should*, *ought to*, *to be*, *could*, *may* wird keine Umschreibung mit *do* bzw. *does* angewandt.
>   He **cannot** come tomorrow. You **shouldn't** get up early.

Exercise B.

Use the *present simple form* of the verbs in brackets.

1) I _live_____ (live) in a small town in Scotland, but my brothers _____ (not live) near me. They _____ (live) in Oxford.

2) Betty _____ (not be) very happy in her new job. She _____ (like) to have a lot of colleagues around her.

3) _____ you _____ (drive) an old car?

4) We _____ (not/can) come to the party tomorrow.

5) Malcolm _____ (not get) home early during (während) the week. He seldom _____ (get) home before eight o'clock in the evening.

6) We _____ (not/usually/eat) in fast food restaurants.

7) _____ you _____ (speak) French?

8) Gerry _____ (still/play) tennis, although (obwohl) he _____ (be) 94 years old!

9) David and I _____ (not go) out very often but once a month we usually _____ (watch) a film at the local cinema. Jane sometimes _____ (watch) the film with us.

10) Alison always _____ (brush) her teeth before she _____ (kiss) me, but I _____ (not/often/brush) my teeth.

11) _____ your wife _____ (smoke) cigarettes in bed? No, she _____ (not/smoke) cigarettes in bed – she _____ (smoke) a pipe.

12) Bill and Sue _____ (should/not/go) on a diet. They only _____ (weigh) fifty kilograms each.

Die Unterschiede zwischen den zwei Gegenwartsformen sind wichtig:

"My daughter **is** very clever. She **speaks** three languages and now she'**s learning** algebra. Sally, tell Mrs Thomas the word for 'hello' in algebra."

Sally spricht zwar drei Sprachen, aber <u>sie spricht diese nicht im Moment</u>, als ihre stolze Mutter über sie redet. <u>Zur Zeit</u> aber lernt sie Algebra (das ihre Mutter irrtümlich für eine Sprache hält).

Es gibt eine Anzahl von Verben, die nie in der Verlaufsform benutzt werden, weil sie einen permanenten Zustand zum Ausdruck bringen:

    I **love** (**hate/dislike**) fish and chips. I **know** Tom.

Vermutlich werde ich auch morgen, übermorgen oder auch im nächsten Jahr die wunderbare englische Köstlichkeit immer noch mögen (hassen, nicht mögen). Genauso ist es wahrscheinlich, falls ich nicht einen schlimmen Gedächtnisverlust erleide, dass ich auch in der Zukunft Tom weiterhin kennen werde. Zu den Verben, die nicht in der Verlaufsform benutzt werden, gehören:

to belong to	gehören	to want	wollen
to consist of	bestehen aus	to believe	glauben
to contain	beinhalten	to know	kennen, wissen
to have	im Sinne von „besitzen"	to need	brauchen
to hate	hassen	to mean	bedeuten
to like	mögen	to think	im Sinne von „meinen"
to love	lieben	to understand	verstehen
to own/to possess	besitzen		

Siehe auch: stative verbs (Zustandsverben) in „Into the English World", Kap. 4.

> ### WATCH OUT! (3)
> Einige dieser Verben können in beiden Zeitformen benutzt werden, wobei sich die Bedeutung verändert. Hier greifen wir nur zwei wichtige Beispiele heraus:
> a) **have:** I have (besitzen) a wonderful $56,000 bath and I'm having a shower (ich dusche mich) now. After that, I'm having a five course breakfast (nehme ich ... ein) at the Italian restaurant.
> b) **think:** I'm thinking (ich denke an) of my lovely girlfriend Mavis now. I think (Ich meine) that the tattoo on her nose is wonderful.

Bitte entscheiden Sie in der nächsten Übung, welche der beiden Zeitformen jeweils benötigt wird:

Exercise C.

Put the verbs in these jokes into their right forms (*present simple* or *present continuous*).

1) "Why _do_ birds _fly_ (fly) south in winter?"

    "Because they _____ (not want) to walk."

2) "Waiter! What _____ this fly _____ (do) on my ice cream?"

    "I _____ (think) it _____ (learn) to ski, sir."

3) "What _____ that woman _____ (do)?"

    "She _____ (look) for a one pound piece."

    "How _____ you _____ (know)?"

"Because I _____ (hold) it here in my hand."

4) Mrs Simmonds: "Doctor, it's terrible. My husband _____ (blow) smoke rings every day."

   Doctor Dobbin: "That's OK, Mrs Simmonds. Many smokers _____ (do) that."

   Mrs Simmonds: "But my husband _____ (not smoke)!"

5) Little four-year-old Tania and her dad are in New York for the first time.

   They _____ (stand) in a lift in a skyscraper and the lift _____ (go) higher and higher.

   Tania asks her father: "Dad, _____ God _____ (know) that we _____ (come)?"

6) "How many hours _____ you _____ (sleep) every day?"

   "Four to five." "That isn't enough!"

   "It's enough for me. I _____ (sleep) ten hours every night."

7) "You _____ (need) glasses," the optician says.

   "But," says the patient, "I _____ (wear) glasses now."

   "Then I _____ (need) glasses," says the optician.

IMPERATIVES (BEFEHLSFORMEN)

Eric hat uns in der Sendung gezeigt, wie höfliche Aufforderungen (*requests*) oder Befehle (*imperatives*) im Englischen formuliert werden. Dazu ein Beispiel:

Mrs Tomly is walking down the road. A man asks her: "Excuse me, but do you know the way to Jessam Street?" "I'm sorry, but I don't," Mrs Tomly says.
"Well," says the man, "you **go** down this street and **turn** left at the traffic lights (Ampel). **Don't cross** the road, but **go** down the next street on your right – Morseby Road and you're there in Jessam Street."

EXERCISE D.

Translate these sentences into English.
1) Bitte rauchen Sie nicht im Badezimmer.
2) Sam! Nimm deine Katze aus dem Kühlschrank!
3) Norma, spiel nicht mit den Tigern – das ist gefährlich!

Asking Questions (Fragebildung) (2)

Die Liebe kann oft, wie wir alle wissen, große Enttäuschungen bereiten. Humphrey z. B. verdient unser großes Mitleid:

"You're looking so unhappy Humphrey," his friend Tom said.
"I am," Humphrey said. "I write ten love letters to my girlfriend Agatha before breakfast every day. And now she wants to marry the postman!"

Armer Humphrey – er hätte das Problem sicherlich nicht gehabt, wenn er seiner Angebeteten E-Mails statt Briefe geschickt hätte. Vergessen wir aber für einen Moment seine große Enttäuschung und kommen wir auf ein wichtiges Grammatikthema zurück, das wir schon im letzten Kapitel angesprochen haben: Die Bildung von Fragesätzen.

Es ist möglich, dass wir durch Humphreys Schluchzen Teile seiner Aussage nicht ganz verstanden haben. Kein Problem – durch gezielte Fragen und die passenden Fragewörter können wir die fehlenden Informationen erfragen:

I	write	ten	love letters	to my girlfriend Agatha	before breakfast	every day.
↑	↑	↑	↑	↑ ↑	↑	↑
			What?	**Who (Whom)?**		
Who?		**How many?**		**Whose?**	**When?**	**How often?**

Who writes ten love letters to his girlfriend before breakfast every day?
How many love letters **do** you **write** before breakfast every day?
What do you **write** before breakfast every day?
Whose girlfriend **do** you **write** to?   (Bitte merken Sie sich die Stellung der Präposition!)
Whom do you **write** to?   (In informellem Englisch kann man auch *who* benutzen: Who do you write to?)
When do you **write** to her?
How often do you **write** to her?

Es fällt sofort auf, dass wir es mit zwei unterschiedlichen Satzbauarten zu tun haben:
        Who **writes** ten letters to his girlfriend before breakfast every day?
Aber: How many love letters/What/When/How often etc. **do** you **write** …?

Bei Fragen nach dem Subjekt eines Satzes gibt es keine Änderung in der Wortstellung. Wir brauchen bei der Frage nach dem Subjekt (Humphrey) den Satz nicht umstellen.

Bei Fragen nach allen anderen Teilen des Satzes müssen wir Subjekt und Verb umstellen und uns beim *present simple* (und – wie wir später sehen werden – auch beim *past simple*) der berühmten „Umschreibung mit *do*" bedienen.

Nehmen wir Humphreys zweiten Satz: She wants to marry the postman.

Die Frage nach dem Subjekt – Agatha – verlangt, wie wir wissen, keine Umstellung des Satzes:
>	**Who wants** to marry the postman?

Die Frage nach dem Objekt – Agathas Begierde – dagegen verlangt eine Umstellung des Satzes und die Umschreibung mit *do*:
>	**Who(m) does** she **want** to marry?

Bei allen anderen Zeitformen oder Hilfsverben wie *can*, *should*, *must* usw. brauchen wir die Umschreibung mit *do* nicht:
>	Can you call the mechanic?

Auch bei *to be* brauchen wir keine Änderungen vorzunehmen:
>	My father is a mechanic. **Who is** a mechanic? **What is** your father?

To help you "get the hang of it" (den Dreh heraus bekommen) here are a few exercises.

Exercise E.

Choose the correct sentences.
1) a) ~~How you are?~~
    b) How are you? ✓
2) a) Where can go we now ?
    b) Where can we go now?
3) a) What are you doing at the moment, Bill?
    b) What are doing you at the moment, Bill?
4) a) Why we must leave so early?
    b) Why must we leave so early?
5) a) Which student can give me the answer?
    b) Which student can me give the answer?
6) a) Who is to your party coming tomorrow?
    b) Who is coming to your party tomorrow?
7) a) Which country does attract the most tourists?
    b) Which country attracts the most tourists?
8) a) Who speaks Russian here?
    b) Who does speak Russian here?
9) a) How many people attended the knitting course last weekend?
    b) How many people did attend the knitting course last weekend?
10) a) Who plays golf in your family and how often does he play?
    b) Who does play golf in your family and how often plays he?
11) a) Where do all these people come from?
    b) From where come all these people?

Exercise F.

Translate these sentences.
1) Wer besucht Herrn und Frau Meier jedes Wochenende?
2) Wie oft besucht Claudia ihre Eltern?
3) Wer spricht gerade mit Fred?
4) Worüber sprechen sie?
5) Wie viele Kollegen arbeiten hier jeden Tag?
6) Wie viele Kollegen treffen Sie hier jeden Tag?
7) Wer kann mir helfen – und wann kann er mir helfen?

Exercise G.

Write questions to find the missing information.
1) Some colleagues are going hiking. (Number of colleagues? Time?)

   How many colleagues are going hiking?
   _____?

2) This country is famous for this product. (Country? Product?)
   _____?
   _____?

3) Many of these animals populate the lush pastures of this country. (Animals? Country?)
   _____?
   _____?

4) They have to learn this subject. (Who? Subject?)
   _____?
   _____?

5) My brother is trying out the new software. (Whose brother? Software?)
   _____?
   _____?

Let's look at words

I hope you are looking up all new words in a dictionary, writing them down and learning them (z. B. during = während; although = obwohl; usw.)! Don't forget words often come in families. Wenn man ein Wort kann, ist es oft nicht schwierig, dieses Wort in anderen Wörtern wieder zu erkennen. Im Text über Wales (Into the English World, Kapitel 4) haben wir gelernt: Cardiff is known for its <u>tolerance</u>. Higher in numbers than the human <u>inhabitants</u> Wales is populated by sheep. One third of the Welsh <u>earn</u> their <u>living</u> from farming. The

Welsh are still <u>attached</u> to their Celtic <u>roots</u>, <u>including</u> their Celtic language. Welsh is a <u>compulsory</u> subject at school. Wenn Sie die Bedeutung der unterstrichenen Wörter oben kennen, können Sie die angegebenen Wörter in der nächsten Übung erraten.

Exercise H.

Can you translate the following sentences?
1) I'm sending the document by email. It's in the <u>attachment</u>.
2) This island is <u>uninhabitable</u>.
3) Peter <u>detached</u> the address from the (top of) the letter.
4) The storm <u>uprooted</u> many trees.
5) Jeremy is quite <u>intolerant</u> of other opinions.
6) Marshall's brothers aren't very nice. They <u>exclude</u> poor Marshall from their games.
7) Donald's father is stupid: He <u>compels</u> his son to learn seventy Latin words every day.
8) My <u>earnings</u> in this job are not very high.

WATCH OUT! (4)

Im Leben ist einiges einfach und anderes dagegen ziemlich schwer. Genauso verhält es sich mit Wörtern! Schauen wir z. B. Erics und Freds Gespräch in Kapitel 4, Into the English World an. Bei der Übersetzung von „besuchen" haben wir ein Problem. Eric sagt: *She **attends** the course every weekend.* Aber er schlägt auch vor: *Better yet, **visit** her after work.* Beide Wörter lassen sich mit „besuchen" übersetzen. Der Unterschied besteht darin: *To visit* bedeutet, dass man als Gast oder Tourist etc. einen Menschen oder Ort besucht. *To attend* bedeutet, dass man eine Einrichtung regelmäßig besucht (school, church, series of lectures, course).

In anderen Fällen verwechseln Lernende der englischen Sprache englische Wörter mit Wörtern aus der Muttersprache (*false friends*). Fred sagt nicht: *But I **mean** we could find some time to hang out.* Sondern: *I **think** (= meinen!) we could find some time to hang out.* Wir erfahren: *Eric is sitting in his office... **wondering** what he wants to do on the weekend.* In der englischen Sprache bedeutet dies nicht, dass Eric sich wundert, sondern dass er sich fragt, was er am Wochenende tun will.

Here are some such "problem words". Read them and I'm sure that you can do exercise I. without too much difficulty.

German	English		
besuchen	a) to visit a place or person	b) to attend a school, course, etc.	
fahren	a) to drive	b) to go by bus, train, etc.	c) to ride a bike, moped, etc.
schwer	a) difficult (problem, exam, etc.)	b) heavy (weight)	
stark	a) strong (kräftig)	b) heavy (schwer, heftig)	

German	English	German	English
meinen	to think	bedeuten	to mean
Ich werde stricken	I will knit	Ich will stricken	I want to knit
sich wundern	to be surprised	sich fragen	to wonder
die Meinung	opinion	die Bedeutung	meaning
sparen	to save	übrig haben	to spare
sympathisch	pleasant, nice	mitfühlend	sympathetic
die Rente	pension	die Miete	rent

EXERCISE I.

Use the right pairs of words from the lists above:

1) In my __opinion__ the best way to find out the __meaning__ of a word is to use an online dictionary.

2) Many old people in the centres of our towns cannot pay the high _____ for flats because their _____ are so low.

3) I _____ that my little son doesn't know what the word "quiet" _____!

4) I can _____ money this month but unfortunately I can't _____ the time to go to the bank today.

5) Darling – you weigh more than 95 kilograms. You're too _____ for me to carry! And I feel so tired after my maths exam. It was so _____.

6) This is really _____ rain and the wind is so _____, but I can't run home faster. I'm a _____ smoker!

7) I can't find my glasses so I can't _____ my car or even _____ my motorbike. But I can always _____ by bus.

8) Tony _____ an English course at an evening institute. After the course he always _____ his uncle.

9) What a _____ sister you have! She is always so _____ when I tell her about my problems.

10) I'm _____ Tony isn't here. I _____ where he is.

DO YOU STILL REMEMBER?

Erinnern Sie sich noch an das, was wir in den ersten drei Sendungen und Kapiteln behandelt haben? Das können Sie gleich in diesen vier Übungen testen:

EXERCISE J.

Translate these sentences into English:
1) Michael ist Vegetarier.
2) Zur Abwechslung können wir zu Hause bleiben.
3) Herr Stanley muss heute nicht arbeiten.
4) Helen ist immer in Eile.
5) Oft trinke ich nach der Arbeit eine Tasse Tee im Garten.
6) Heute können wir die Möbel nicht kaufen – es ist Sonntag!
7) Susan, du darfst nicht zu spät nach Hause kommen!

EXERCISE K.

Make sentences with these words:

1) go / tomorrow / we / to the cinema / can't

   We can't go to the cinema tomorrow.

2) so late / mustn't /always / go / you / to school

3) learn / you / before work? / English words / often / do

4) onto his computer / Simon / the report / needn't / download

5) the printed version / can / next week / give / him / we

6) leaves / occasionally / Mr Hindly / before 3 pm on Friday / his firm

EXERCISE L.

What are the *plurals* of these words?

1) this child   2) that hobby   3) person

    these children   _____   _____

4) profit   5) potato   6) woman

_____   _____   _____

EXERCISE M.

Write the *questions* to find the missing information:

1) Julia is attending a knitting course.

    Is Julia attending a knitting course _____ **on Saturday and Sunday**?

2) Fred eats sauerkraut.

    _____ **for breakfast**?

3) Shirley attends a course every Tuesday.

    _____ **English course** _____?

4) Claudia is visiting someone this weekend.

    _____ **her parents**?

5) Mr Matthews can finish the work.

    Yes, but _____ **before 8 o'clock**?

6) Mary and her husband work in Bristol.

    Really? _____ **in the same company**?

7) This ring belongs to Salina.

    Oh, and _____ **this earring** _____, **too**?

8) Joan watched a film on TV last night.

    _____ **"Titanic"** _____?

9) My children aren't allowed to go to the disco during the school week.

    But, _____ **the weekend**?

That is enough for one chapter. The next topics – short answers and question tags – are not so long!

Chapter 5: question tags and short answers

Chapter five – that's a third of the book, **isn't it? Yes it is.**
We are making progress (wir machen Fortschritte), **aren't we? Yes, we certainly are.**
Question forms are useful, **aren't they? Yes, they are.**
But we mustn't forget the answers, **must we? No, we mustn't.**

In diesem Kapitel behandeln wir die „Frageanhängsel" und Kurzantworten. Am Ende des Kapitels betrachten wir – wie üblich – einige interessante Wörter und es gibt die Gelegenheit, noch einmal Wichtiges aus früheren Sendungen bzw. Kapiteln zu wiederholen.

Question Tags (Frageanhängsel)

In den meisten Sprachen gibt es irgendeine Floskel – „nicht wahr?", „oder?", „gell?", „vero?", „n'est ce pas?" usw. –, die man an das Ende eines Satzes anhängen kann, um vom Gesprächspartner eine Bestätigung zu bekommen. Im englischsprachigen Raum kommen sehr häufig die sogenannten *question tags* dafür zum Einsatz.

This **isn't** the new city hall, **is it**?
The tourist **talks** too much, **doesn't he**?

Wenn der Satz eine negative Aussage beinhaltet, dann nehmen wir im *question tag* die positive Form des Verbs.

This **isn't** the new city hall, **is it**?
–   +

Bei positiven Aussagen steht das Verb im *question tag* in der negativen Form.

The tourist **talks** too much, **doesn't he**?
+   –

Wie Sie sehen, wiederholen wir bei *to be* nur das Verb im *question tag*. Dies gilt auch für *can, could, must, should, has/have* (und *would, will, was, were* und *had*) – also für die sogenannten Hilfsverben (*auxiliaries*).

Mr and Mrs Henry **should** buy a new car, **shouldn't they**?
He **can't** speak Russian, **can he**?

Bei den Vollverben im *present simple* (und im *past simple*, wie Sie im nächsten Kapitel sehen werden) nehmen wir das Hilfsverb *do* (*did*):

Mary **eats** seven tons of crisps every week, **doesn't she**?
+   –

But she **doesn't get** fat, **does she**?
–   +

WATCH OUT! (1)
Keine Regel ohne Ausnahme!
a) Statt ~~amn't I~~, das für alle sensiblen Ohren ziemlich unangenehm klingt, sagen wir im Englischen: **aren't I?**
b) Bei höflichen Aufforderungen und Vorschlägen nehmen wir die positive Form des Verbs in beiden Teilen des Satzes:
   Let's go to the cinema, **shall we**? Take some milk from the fridge, **will you**?

Now it's time for you to try to form *question tags*!

EXERCISE A.

Add a *question tag* to complete the question:

1) John, you are very tired, _aren't you_?
2) Gillian's boyfriend can cook very well, _____?
3) Her children shouldn't eat so much, _____?
4) Malcolm doesn't answer many e-mails, _____?
5) That information is very useful, _____?
6) Ronald has got three children, _____?
7) Your wife works in our firm, _____?
8) There are lots of tourists in Munich, _____?
9) Tania's brother could help us to move the piano, _____?
10) I mean, he's got strong muscles, _____?
11) You don't live near us, _____?
12) Rebecca and Simon know a lot about Scottish history, _____?
13) The weather is so nice. Let's have a picnic, _____?
14) I'm not too late, _____?
15) Christine, please answer the phone, _____?
16) I'm too early, _____?

Tipp: Falls Sie die *question tags* selbst verwenden, werden Sie sicherlich einen großen Eindruck bei Ihrem englischen Gesprächspartner hinterlassen. Falls Sie sie aber im Moment nicht einwandfrei beherrschen, reicht es aus, wenn Sie sie verstehen und hören. Es gibt nämlich eine Alternative.
Obwohl es nicht so häufig angewandt wird wie „oder?", „nicht wahr?" oder „gell?", verwenden Muttersprachler gelegentlich das Wort *right?* (stimmt) am Ende des Satzes.

This is the way to the station, right?
You know George quite well, right?
Your brother hasn't had much luck recently, right?

Ihr Gesprächspartner wird sich kaum Gedanken machen, wenn Sie statt eines Frageanhängsels einfach dieses Wort am Satzende anbringen, *right?*

SHORT ANSWERS (KURZANTWORTEN)

And now we come to something very important. You can see how important the <u>right</u> short answers are in English in this short dialogue:

The beginning and end of a romance:
Janet: "Do you like England?"
Sepp: "Yes."
Janet: "Have you got friends in England?"
Sepp: "No."
Janet: "Do you like me?"
Sepp: "Yes."

Für das englische Ohr wirken diese Antworten ziemlich schroff und unhöflich, als ob der Gesprächspartner wenig Wert auf eine Fortführung des Gesprächs lege. Es ist eher unwahrscheinlich, dass sich eine romantische Beziehung aus so einem Gespräch entwickeln kann. Damit Sepp mehr Chancen bei Janet hat, muss er seine Antworten anders gestalten:

Janet: "Do you like England?"
Sepp: "Yes, I do."
Janet: "Have you got friends in England?"
Sepp: "No, I haven't."
Janet: "Do you like me?"
Sepp: "Yes, I do."

Noch besser:

Janet: "Do you like England?"
Sepp: "Yes, I certainly do."
Janet: "Have you got friends in England?"
Sepp: "No, unfortunately I haven't."
Janet: "Do you like me?"
Sepp: "Yes, I really do."

Wie Sie in der fünften Sendung gehört haben, werden die Kurzantworten auf ähnliche Weise wie die *question tags* gebildet: Die Verben *can*, *could*, *must*, *should*, *has/have* (und *would*, *will*, *was*, *were* und *had*), also die sogenannten Hilfsverben (*auxiliaries*), werden in die Kurzantwort aufgenommen.

Nur bei Fragen mit Vollverben im *present simple* und *past simple* wird *do/does/did* bzw. *don't/doesn't/didn't* eingesetzt, wie Cyril uns zeigt:

Cyril is in the restaurant with his new girlfriend.
"**Are** you hard working?" she asks him.
"Oh yes, I certainly **am**," he answers.
"And **do** you smoke?" she continues.
"No, I **don't**," he answers.
"And **do** you drink beer?"
"No, I certainly **don't**."
"**Do** you have any faults (Fehler)?" she asks him.
"Yes, I **do**," he says. "I don't always tell the truth."

Now it's your turn! (Jetzt sind Sie an der Reihe!)

Exercise B.

Write down the *short answers*:

1) "Can your sister play the piano?" "_Yes, she can_____. She even plays in concerts."
2) "Does Tom use the latest version of the BR–10–12 TK software?" "_____. It's too expensive."
3) "Must you go now?" "_____.We must be at the office at 2 pm."
4) "Have you got a brother?" "_____. In fact I've got a sister, too."
5) "Do you speak French?" "_____. But only a little."
6) "Are Harry and Maude interested in swimming?" "_____. Harold and Maude hate all sports!"
7) "Is Stephanie a good cook?" "_____. She eats in a restaurant every day!"
8) "Are the prices rising?" "_____. Everything is so expensive."
9) "Is English food wonderful?" "_____! Especially the fish and chips – I could eat that every day!"

LET'S LOOK AT WORDS

Look through chapter five of "Into the English World" and you can see the words: *groceries, belong, promoting, divided, founded, annoyed, surrounded, inspirationally, appearance* usw. As you remember from the last chapter words often come in families.

EXERCISE C.

Can you guess the missing words? What do they mean? The words in brackets can help you. (Tip: The endings *-ing, -ings, -ion* are useful.)

1) I am (inspirational) __inspired__ by the natural beauty of Ireland's landscape.

2) Most people do not go to a (groceries) _____ to buy their groceries – they go to a supermarket.

3) In 2011 there is the 80th anniversary of the (founded) _____ of the Republic of Ireland.

4) John has a really (annoyed) _____ habit. He's always late.

5) The (surrounded) _____ of Dublin are really spectacular.

6) Are these your (belong) _____, Christina?

7) Your husband (appearance) _____ to be a little overworked.

8) Despite (trotz) the (divided) _____ of Ireland into two parts it is now easy to travel from the Republic of Ireland to Northern Ireland.

> ### WATCH OUT! (2)
> In diesem Kapitel haben wir wieder einige Wörter, die Englisch Lernenden mit Deutsch als Muttersprache Probleme bereiten können.
> Eric and his group are in "Mary's Square" (Marienplatz) not "Mary's ~~Place~~" (chapter 5 A).
> Please compare these sentences:
>
> | | | |
> |---|---|---|
> | Bitte nehmen Sie **Platz**. | → | Please take a **seat**. |
> | Es gibt nicht genügend **Platz** hier. | → | There isn't enough **room** here. |
> | Dies ist ein netter **Ort**. | → | This is a nice **place**. |
> | Ich bin am Sportplatz. | → | I'm at the sports **field**. |
>
> The sightseer says: "... America is **actually** two continents."
> The meaning (Remember: Bedeutung!) of *actually* here is "tatsächlich". "Aktuell" means *current, topical, of great importance nowadays*.
>
> Eric says: "I only **wear** them (the 'Lederhosen') at the Oktoberfest."
> Many pupils make mistakes here, because in English there are two different words for the one German word "tragen". Please remember:
> "I **wear** special clothes when I have to **carry** dirty things."

Now try this short exercise:

Exercise D.

Put in the right translations for "tragen", "Platz", "Ort", "aktuell", and "tatsächlich".

1) This town is an interesting _place_ but there isn't much _room_ for so many cars.

2) "You're English, but you don't seem to be interested in the _____ situation in English politics." "Well, _____ I'm not English, I'm Irish."

3) "Helmut, why are you _____ ten pairs of 'Lederhosen'?"

   "Well, my friends from America and I want to _____ them at the Oktoberfest."

Another two exercises on vocabulary from past chapters.

Exercise E.

Which of these words does not fit and why?

1) delicious ◆ chips ◆ barbecue ◆ ~~telephone~~
2) Don't mention it. ◆ You're welcome. ◆ It's chilly. ◆ It's my pleasure.
3) fortresses ◆ mountains ◆ pastures ◆ hills
4) government ◆ parliament ◆ House of Commons ◆ capital
5) inhabitants ◆ landscape ◆ people ◆ population
6) deposit ◆ rent ◆ heating ◆ ceiling
7) boarding school ◆ farmstead ◆ uniform ◆ secondary level
8) internet access ◆ disconnect ◆ curriculum ◆ download
9) hiking ◆ opportunity ◆ knitting ◆ open air sports
10) fridge ◆ backyard ◆ wardrobe ◆ walk-in closet

EXERCISE F.

A small crossword puzzle. All the words come from units 1–5 of the book "Into the English World".

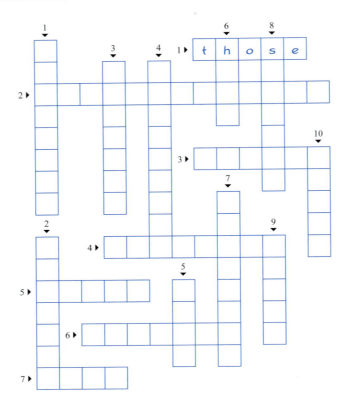

Across:
1) This book here is mine, but __those__ books are yours.
2) This is another word for "roughly".
3) This is like the word "choose".
4) Great Britain ____ of three different countries.
5) This cross is a ____ of Ireland's past.
6) You can't ____ for long without water.
7) I'm getting fat! I must go on a ____.

Down:
1) In contrast to state schools, a ____ school is not cheap.
2) I'm looking ____ to my next holiday in New Zealand.
3) Very young pupils go to the ____ school.
4) At the moment we are on an ____ to the geysers.
5) My sister wants to ____ me a woollen pullover.
6) Germany has a president as ____ of state.
7) You can usually find cows or sheep on these.
8) Sue is quite ____ because she doesn't eat much.
9) This tastes delicious on a steak.
10) This word means a subject to talk about.

Well, now for some light entertainment! In this joke you can find examples of *short answers* and *question tags*.

Exercise G.

Are the underlined words new for you? If so, try to guess their meanings from the context.

A man is driving a sports car. His girlfriend is sitting next to him. He sees another man on a moped ahead of him and wants to overtake him. So he accelerates from 60 km/h to 80 km/h. But the moped driver is still driving alongside him.
"He's really fast, **isn't he**?" the man in the sports car says to his girlfriend.
"Yes," she says, "**He is**. But you can drive much faster in your car, **can't you**?"
"Of course **I can**," he replies and soon he is driving at 120 km/h. The man on the moped, however, is still driving alongside him. "That's really amazing, **isn't it**?" says his girlfriend.
Then the driver of the sports car shouts out through the window to the man on the moped:
"You've got a tiger in your tank, **haven't you**?"
"**No, I haven't**," says the man on the moped.
"My jacket is caught in your door!"

underlined = unterstrichen

Do you still remember?

Try this little test on some of the structures and vocabulary from the last four programmes (OK – for our American friends: programs!) and chapters. Don't cheat! (Nicht mogeln!) Do the exercises first and then look at the solutions!

Exercise H.

Put in the pronouns (*I, my, me, mine,* etc.):

1) "Hey Fred – this book is __yours__, not mine."

2) "Bill, is this _____ sandwich?" "No, it isn't _____. I don't like cheese sandwiches, but one moment – there's Rose. Perhaps it's _____."

3) "Look – three bottles of lovely English wine. Would you like one of _____ Pat?" "No thanks. I've got enough bottles of _____ own."

4) "Bertha and I like Julia. _____'s a good friend of _____."

5) "Where are Sue and her brother? Can you see _____?" "No, I can't. But I can see _____ dog, so _____ can't be far away."

6) "Mr McCullough, I think this report is _____ and that is _____ diary, too." "Oh, thanks. Can you give _____ to _____, please." "There's the report." "Oh, put _____ over there on the table."

Exercise I.

Put these sentences into the negative:

1) Ray is always in the office before 7 am.

   Ray isn't always in the office before 7 am.

2) We can come to the office early tomorrow.

3) Mr Collins uses the latest software.

4) We need to install the new firmware.

5) Ms Kerry is finishing the report now.

6) Our customers are waiting for the new catalogue.

7) This firm in America wants to work with us.

Exercise J.

Put these words and expressions in the right order to make sentences:

1) you / do / every day / John / phone ?

   Do you phone John every day?

2) doesn't / Julia / before breakfast / usually / drink / vodka

3) in Rome / we're / your brother / tomorrow / seeing /

4) wants / next year / Samantha / a new job / in the neighbourhood / to find

5) reads / often / Philip / before work in the morning / the sales reports / at home

6) you / from home / phoning / now / are ?

_____

Exercise K.

An urgent call from the InterCity! Can you fill in the gaps?

"Hello John, this is Harry. Can you _hear_ (hear) me? Good. At the moment I _____ (sit) in the InterCity to Birmingham. I _____ (not / usually / phone) from trains, but this problem is urgent. I _____ (go) to my girl-friend's party in Birmingham this evening, but I _____ (not / have) a present for her. I _____ ("mustn't come" or "needn't come?") without a present. I would like to buy some flowers for her, but the shops _____ (shut) at seven o'clock and it's 6.40 pm now. Could you _____ (buy) some flowers for me to give her? You _____ ("mustn't buy" or "needn't buy?") an expensive bunch of flowers. £2 are enough. Oh – and please _____ (not / buy) tulips. She only _____ (like) roses – she _____ (not / like) tulips or other flowers. Oh, one moment – the train _____ (just / come) into Birmingham and it's only 6.45 now. Maybe I have the time to buy the roses myself!"

Well, once again we are at the end of a chapter. Please do the exercises conscientiously (gewissenhaft) and learn all new words. Then your English can get better and better.

Chapter 6: The Past Simple and Past Continuous

The Past Simple (Die einfache Form der Vergangenheit)

A scene from an unhappy marriage:
Mr Robins **finished** the soup. He **was** very happy. He **licked** his lips and **said** to his wife: "That soup **tasted** fantastic. **Did** you get the recipe (Kochrezept) from a cookery book?"
"No, I **didn't get** it from a cookery book," Mrs Robins said. "I **got** it from a thriller (Krimi). I **bought** it at the bookshop yesterday."

Hoffen wir, dass das Gift nicht gewirkt hat und dass Herr Robins immer noch unter uns weilt, während seine Frau ihre gerechte Strafe absitzt! Aber wenden wir uns nun dem ersten Hauptthema der sechsten Sendung zu: dem *past simple*. Diese Zeitform wird angewandt, wenn man über einen Vorgang in der Vergangenheit spricht, der schon abgeschlossen ist. Signalwörter wie *3 years **ago**, last week, in 1996, yesterday, in the twentieth century, in the Middle Ages* sagen uns, dass das *past simple* in der Regel nötig ist.
Bei den regelmäßigen Verben bilden wir positive Aussagesätze im *past simple*, indem wir ein *-ed* an den Infinitiv anhängen: *finish**ed**, lick**ed**, tast**ed***. Leider gibt es wie im Deutschen eine ganze Reihe von Verben, die eine unregelmäßige Form in der Vergangenheit haben. In unserem Witz: *was (were), said, got*.
Die Formen der unregelmäßigen Verben muss man einfach auswendig lernen. Die gute Nachricht ist, dass wir – im Gegensatz zum Deutschen – nur eine Form für positive Aussagen in der Vergangenheit lernen müssen: *I, you, he, she, it, we, you (plural), they **came***. Der arme Engländer, der Deutsch lernt, hat es wesentlich schwerer: Ich kam, du kamst, er kam, wir kamen, ihr kamt, sie kamen. Hier sind einige der wichtigsten unregelmäßigen Verben:

infinitive	past simple	deutsche Übersetzung	infinitive	past simple	deutsche Übersetzung
be	was/were	sein	grow	grew	wachsen, anpflanzen
become	became	werden	have	had	haben
begin	began	beginnen	hear	heard	hören
break	broke	(zer-)brechen	hurt	hurt	wehtun, verletzen
bring	brought	(mit-/her-)bringen	keep	kept	behalten
build	built	bauen	know	knew	wissen, kennen
buy	bought	kaufen	leave	left	verlassen, weggehen
choose	chose	(aus-)wählen	lose	lost	verlieren
come	came	kommen	meet	met	(sich) treffen, kennenlernen
cost	cost	kosten			
cut	cut	schneiden	make	made	machen
drink	drank	trinken	put	put	setzen, stellen
eat	ate	essen	read	read (red)	lesen
fall	fell	fallen	rise	rose	(an-)steigen
forget	forgot	vergessen	see	saw	sehen
get	got	bekommen	sleep	slept	schlafen
give	gave	geben	take	took	(mit-)nehmen
go	went	gehen, fahren	tell	told	sagen, erzählen

Wie Sie sehen, gehört das Verb *to be* zu den unregelmäßigen Verben (unregelmäßiger geht's nicht)!

past simple of *to be*	
I **was(n't)**	we **were(n't)**
you **were(n't)**	you **were(n't)**
he, she, it **was(n't)**	they **were(n't)**

Prägen Sie sich diese Verben gut ein. In den nächsten Kapiteln werden Sie weitere wichtige unregelmäßige Verben kennenlernen. Sie kommen immer wieder vor.

Tony **went** fishing and he **took** his little sister Liz with him. When he **came** back, he **told** his mum: "That **was** the last time that I go fishing with Liz. She **ate** all my worms."

Exercise A.

Put these sentences into the *past simple*:

1) Mary __watched__ (watch) TV all day yesterday.
2) I _____ (wait) for you for two hours yesterday.
3) We _____ (want) to go to the cinema on Saturday.
4) We _____ (go) to Italy last year.
5) Billy _____ (leave) the house at 6 am.
6) Mrs Simmonds _____ (arrive) at the airport very early.
7) Two years ago I _____ (be) in Buenos Aires and my sisters _____ (be) in New York.
8) On Monday I _____ (drive) to work, but yesterday I _____ (walk) there because I _____ (have) more time.
9) Gordon _____ (drink) three litres of coke at Joe's 100th birthday party three days ago.
10) Peter and Mary _____ (finish) work early on Friday.

WATCH OUT ! (1)
Viele Englisch Lernende mit Deutsch als Muttersprache übersetzen irrtümlicherweise „vor zwei Jahren", „vor drei Tagen" u.s.w. mit *for (before) two years*, *for (before) three days*, etc.
    vor zwei Tagen = two days **ago**

Um Fragen und verneinte Sätze im *past simple* zu bilden, verwenden wir – wie beim *present simple* – das Verb *to do*: also *did* bzw. *didn't*.

Where **did** she **go** yesterday? How long **did** he **work** last night? Why **did** Tom **work** so late?
Did Ms Salmon **contact** the client?
No, Ms Salmon **didn't contact** him. (**No, she didn't**) – I did.

Und auch für die Kurzantworten und *question tags* in der Vergangenheit benutzen wir im Englischen *did* bzw. *didn't*.

> ### WATCH OUT! (2)
> Es ist sehr wichtig,
> a) die sogenannte Umschreibung mit *did* bzw. *didn't* in Fragen und negativen Aussagesätzen einzusetzen.
> b) das Hauptverb im Infinitiv zu verwenden. Sätze wie ~~He came not here yesterday., Came he here yesterday?, They didn't watched TV last night.~~ sind falsch und für die Ohren eines Engländers ein Gräuel!
> Richtig heißen diese:
> *He didn't come here yesterday. Did he come here yesterday? They didn't watch TV last night.*

Now it's time to practise these forms.

Exercise B.

Put the verbs into the right form – positive or negative.

1) I **bought** a coke in the bar, but my sister *didn't buy* a coke. (She **drank** a coffee.)

2) They **gave** me a job, but unfortunately they _____ my friend one.

3) I **didn't take** the bus to work yesterday. I _____ the train.

4) My daughter **broke** three glasses this morning. Thank Goodness, she _____ my expensive ones.

5) We **met** Mr Symonds last week, but unfortunately we _____ his colleagues.

6) The software **didn't cost** much, but the T-box _____ a lot.

7) I **didn't know** his exact address, but I _____ the name of the street.

8) The profits of the firm **rose** last year, but they _____ the year before.

9) Our sales **didn't grow** much last year, but in the first three months of this year they _____ very fast.

10) Fred **came** to the conference yesterday, but his boss _____ .

Exercise C.

Finish the questions. Add question words *how*, *when*, *why*, *what*, *how long*, *where* if necessary.

1) (you/go) _When did you go_ on holiday? We went in August.
2) (you/spend) _____ your holiday? In Norway.
3) (you/go) _____ there alone? No, we didn't. We went with our kids.
4) (they/like) _____ Norway? Oh, very much.
5) (you/stay) _____ in Norway? Oh, for three weeks.
6) (you/choose) _____ to go there? Because we wanted to see the beautiful landscape there.
7) (you/see) _____ the fjords? Of course we did. They came so close to the car that we could feed them!

Wie im *present simple* werden Fragen und Negativaussagen im *past simple* beim Verb *to be* und bei den Hilfsverben (z. B. *could*) nicht mit *to do* umschrieben:

"How **was** the exam?"
"The first three questions **weren't** difficult, but the other questions **were** very difficult."
"What **were** the first three questions?"
"Name, age and address."

> ### WATCH OUT! (3)
> Die einfache Vergangenheit von *I must go* ist *I **had to** go*.
> Die einfache Vergangenheit von *I needn't go* or *I don't have to go* ist *I **didn't need to** go* bzw. *I **didn't have to** go*.

I don't think that you will find the next exercise difficult:

Exercise D.

Put the verbs in brackets into their correct forms:

1) Yesterday I _couldn't come_ (not/can/come) to school because I (not feel) _didn't feel_ well.

2) Ms Dubovie _____ (not/send) me the report last week because she (not/can find) _____ it.

3) I _____ (not/read) your e-mail yesterday because I _____ (not/ be) in the office.

4) We _____ (must/work) hard yesterday because the computer _____ (be) broken and nobody _____ (can/repair) it.

5) _____ (George/leave) his laptop on the train when he _____ (come) home from work yesterday? Yes, he _____ (be) so tired and when he _____ (get) off the train he _____ (leave) the laptop on the seat. He _____ (forget) about it until he _____ (arrive) home. When he _____ (go) back to the train station it _____ (not be) there any more.

6) _____ (can/repair/the electrician) the new DVD player before the football match _____ (start)? No, he _____ . He _____ (not have) all the necessary components.

THE PAST CONTINUOUS (DIE VERLAUFSFORM DER VERGANGENHEIT)

The patient **was** very angry when he **woke up** from the anaesthetic and **saw** the two scars (Narben) on his stomach (Bauch). When the surgeon (Chirurg) **came** he **shouted** at him:
"Dr Smith, why have I got two scars on my stomach? You **operated** on my leg, not on my stomach!"
"I am so sorry," the surgeon replied, "but I **sneezed** (nieste) twice while I **was operating**."

Der arme Patient! An seiner Stelle würde ich einen Prozess gegen Dr. Smith anstrengen. Was uns aber hier interessiert, sind die Zeiten. Wenn ein Zustand oder eine Handlung in der Vergangenheit abgeschlossen ist, benutzen wir die einfache Form der Vergangenheit: The patient **was** angry when he **woke up** and **saw** the two scars. Einige Handlungen oder Zustände jedoch sind zu einem bestimmten Zeitpunkt noch nicht abgeschlossen – sie sind immer noch im Gange. In unserem Fall mit dem unseligen Dr. Smith: *I sneezed twice while I was operating*. Zwar hat er zweimal geniest, aber er hatte zu diesem Zeitpunkt die Operation nicht abgeschlossen. Das *past continuous* ist das Pendant zum *present continuous* in der Vergangenheit:

Das *present continuous* wird verwendet, um Vorgänge zu beschreiben, die in der Gegenwart gerade vor sich gehen und nicht abgeschlossen sind. Das *past continuous* hat dieselbe Funktion für Vorgänge und Zustände in der Vergangenheit. Das *past continuous* kommt auch zum Einsatz, wenn wir betonen wollen, dass ein Vorgang in der Vergangenheit eine längere Zeit angedauert hat. Nehmen wir Erics Beispiel: *Apple* **was selling** computers which cost over $10,000 dollars until co-founder Steve Jobs and his design team **created** the MAC. Wie Sie sehen, bilden wir diese Zeitform mit **was/were** + **Verb** + **-ing**.
That's enough explanation. Now it's your turn!

EXERCISE E.

Put the verbs in brackets into their correct forms – *past simple* or *past continuous*:

1) While I _was sleeping_ (sleep) last night, the telephone _rang._ (ring).
2) Yesterday _____ (be) a hard day. I _____ (work) in the office the whole day.
3) Mary _____ (just/leave) the house when her mother _____ (ask) her to do the washing up.
4) They _____ (work) on the computer when suddenly there _____ (be) a power cut (Stromausfall).
5) Terry _____ (eat) his hamburger during the film when his dog _____ (take) it out of his hand and _____ (eat) it in three seconds!
6) "What _____ (you/do) when I _____ (see) you in the street yesterday?" "Oh, I _____ (just/look) at shop windows."
7) Now I'm working in the office, but this time last week I _____ (lie) on the beach at Brighton.
8) I _____ (not get) a telephone call from the client while I _____ (work) in the office yesterday.
9) Last night we _____ (watch) a horror film on TV from beginning to end.
10) Mrs Thompson _____ (write) an e-mail to the client when her boss _____ (tell) her it _____ (not be) necessary. The client _____ (be) already in his office.

> ### WATCH OUT! (4)
> In der englischen Sprache gibt es zwei mögliche Übersetzungen für das deutsche Wort „während". *While* wird bei Verben benutzt:
> *while* they were working; *while* Rebecca was watching TV
> *During* wird benutzt, um einen bestimmten Zeitraum zu bezeichnen:
> *during* the week; *during* the lesson; *during* our holidays

Phew! That **was** a lot, **wasn't** it? Don't worry if you have difficulties with the *past continuous*. At the moment it is only important to recognise (erkennen) it when you see or hear it. However, the *past simple* is very, very important. Think of what you did or didn't do yesterday (I ate a small breakfast yesterday; I went to work early; I didn't watch TV yesterday, etc.)!

LET'S LOOK AT WORDS

> ### WATCH OUT! (5)
> Im Buch „Into the English World" 6D erfahren wir, dass *they're (the English) are addicted to tea.*
> „Süchtig nach"/„abhängig von" wird mit *addicted to* übersetzt. Sonst übersetzt man „abhängig sein von" mit *to be dependent on*:
> *James is dependent on his parents for financial help.*

In supermarkets in England you can often see the sign: "Buy one and get one free!" or "Two for the price of one". With words we could say: "Learn one and get five or six free!" Wir haben bereits gelernt, dass Wörter in „Familien" vorkommen. Auch wenn wir sie nie vorher gesehen haben, können wir häufig die Bedeutung unbekannter Wörter aus derselben Familie erraten. Zum Beispiel haben wir im Buch „Into the English World" 6A das Wort *employee* (Angestellte/r) gelernt. Können Sie die unterstrichenen Wörter in den folgenden Sätzen übersetzen?

Tom Bradly was an employee in the Science Museum of Malford but he became unemployed a few weeks ago. His employer Mr David Grant says that unfortunately he cannot employ more than three employees because the museum does not have enough visitors. Mr Bradly hopes to find employment in another museum in the town.

Nicht zu schwierig, oder? Die unterstrichenen Wörter bedeuten: arbeitslos (unemployed); Arbeitgeber (employer); beschäftigen/einstellen (employ); Beschäftigung (employment).

Now it's your turn! Let's take the following words from the sixth programme (6A, 6D): collection (Sammlung); taste (Geschmack); dedicated (gewidmet); suggest (vorschlagen); impressive (beeindruckend) separate (trennen); conqueror (Eroberer); probably (wahrscheinlich); diverse (vielfältig); doubt (Zweifel); enjoy (genießen). You can easily guess the underlined words in the next exercise:

EXERCISE F.

Translate these sentences into German:

1) Graham is a keen stamp collector.

   Graham ist ein eifriger Briefmarkensammler.

2) London made a huge impression on Tony.
3) The Norman conquest of England in 1066 is an important date in English history.
4) Bill suffered very much from his parents' separation.
5) Norma's suggestion was accepted by everyone.
6) Is John at work now? That's very improbable – it's only six o'clock in the morning!
7) It's doubtful that he has so much dedication to his work!
8) We had an enjoyable time at the party, but I must say Derek's behaviour was rather tasteless.
9) The diversity of architectural styles in these houses is very impressive.

Words like *on, up, in, without, to, across* (prepositions) are important in all languages. In English they often change the meaning of a verb. Save yourself time: Learn the verb or expression together with the preposition! Don't learn the verb *to separate*, learn the expression *to separate... from*.

EXERCISE G.

Complete the following sentences with the right expressions from the column in the middle.

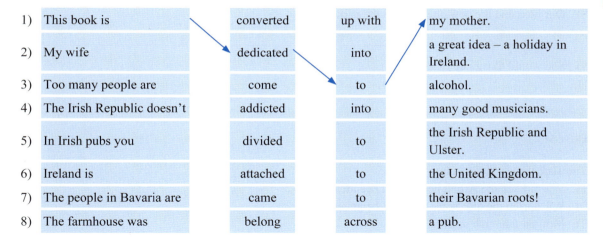

1)	This book is	converted	up with	my mother.
2)	My wife	dedicated	into	a great idea – a holiday in Ireland.
3)	Too many people are	come	to	alcohol.
4)	The Irish Republic doesn't	addicted	into	many good musicians.
5)	In Irish pubs you	divided	to	the Irish Republic and Ulster.
6)	Ireland is	attached	to	the United Kingdom.
7)	The people in Bavaria are	came	to	their Bavarian roots!
8)	The farmhouse was	belong	across	a pub.

DO YOU STILL REMEMBER?

And now, as usual a few exercises to help you remember some of the grammar from the chapters before!

EXERCISE H.

Write down questions from these sentences:

1) Mary is doing her homework.

   Is Mary doing her homework?

2) John helps his mother every day.
   _____

3) Mr Feldman can install the new program tomorrow.
   _____

4) The two firms work together on this project.
   _____

5) They could use a different software.
   _____

6) The new colleague is connecting the computer to the power supply.
   _____

7) Mr Bentley and the new secretary eat in the canteen together.
   _____

8) Our boss and the new client are in the park.
   _____

9) She would like a cup of tea.
   _____

EXERCISE I.

Translate these sentences into English:
1) Wir müssen die Arbeit heute nicht beenden.
2) Wir dürfen die alte Software nicht benutzen.
3) Morgen fahre ich nach Bristol.
4) Gewöhnlich isst er in einem teuren Restaurant, aber jetzt sitzt er in einem billigen Fast-Food-Restaurant, obwohl er Fast Food eigentlich (actually) nicht mag.
5) In London haben viele Leute ein eigenes Auto.

EXERCISE J.

Put the words in the right order to make sentences:

1) live / Mr and Mrs Simons / nice / do / neighbourhood / a / in / ?

   Do Mr and Mrs Simons live in a nice neighbourhood?

2) never / home / Peter / before / in the evening / seven o'clock / comes
   _____

3) you / new / this / could / program / help / please / me / with / ?

   _____

4) always / toast / in the morning / our colleague / for breakfast / eats

   _____

5) are / to London / we / next week / flying

   _____

6) sells / in the Antarctic / this firm / in winter / many sandals / seldom

   _____

7) usually / many people / during the week / go / the museum / do / to / ?

   _____

8) doesn't / the manager / the sales reports / check / before Friday / often

   _____

Chapter 7: The Future Tenses

In this chapter **we are going to look** at the *future tenses* in English, but before we do that here are a few more irregular verbs to learn!

infinitive	past simple	deutsche Übersetzung	infinitive	past simple	deutsche Übersetzung
bite	**bit**	beißen	lead	**led**	führen, leiten
catch	**caught**	fangen, erwischen	lie	**lay**	liegen
burst	**burst**	platzen	pay	**paid**	(be-)zahlen
deal	**dealt**	handeln (von), sich beschäftigen (mit)	run	**ran**	rennen; leiten
			say	**said**	sagen
feed	**fed**	füttern	sell	**sold**	verkaufen
feel	**felt**	fühlen	spend	**spent**	(Geld) ausgeben; (Zeit) verbringen
fly	**flew**	fliegen			
freeze	**froze**	(ge-)frieren	steal	**stole**	stehlen
hide	**hid**	(sich) verstecken	teach	**taught**	unterrichten, lehren
hit	**hit**	schlagen, treffen	throw	**threw**	werfen
			write	**wrote**	schreiben

The Future Tenses (Die Zukunftsformen)

In der englischen Sprache stehen uns verschiedene Möglichkeiten zur Verfügung, die Zukunft auszudrücken.

a) The Present Continuous

Diese Form wird häufig benutzt, um Zukünftiges auszudrücken (besonders wenn etwas fest abgemacht bzw. vereinbart wird).

 I**'m starting** work early tomorrow.

> **WATCH OUT! (1)**
> Im Gegensatz zum Deutschen wird das *present continuous* angewandt, um zukünftige Handlungen oder Ereignisse auszudrücken. Wir können den Satz „Morgen sehen wir ihn." normalerweise nicht mit ~~We see him tomorrow.~~ übersetzen. Richtig heißt es:
> We**'re seeing** him tomorrow.

b) The Future Simple (Will Future)

Diese Zukunftsform wird verwendet
a) für spontane Entscheidungen, Angebote, Zusagen, Bitten oder Versprechen.
  It's OK, we**'ll do** (we **will do**) the shopping today.
  I promise that I**'ll come** (**will come**) early next time.

Sidney is at the theatre. "How much are the tickets?" he asks.

"£30 for a seat in the first three rows, £20 for a seat in the next ten rows, £10 for a seat in the back row and the programme costs £2," says the man who is selling the tickets.

"Good," says Sidney, "then I won't sit on a seat. I'll sit on a programme."

b) Weiterhin gebraucht man diese Zukunftsform, um sachlich und neutral über zukünftige Ereignisse zu sprechen:

The flight **will cost** me 1144 Euros.

"What's the time?" little Fred wants to know.
"In ten minutes it**'ll be** (it **will be**) 11 o'clock," his mother says.
"Yes, in ten minutes. But what's the time, now?" Fred asks again.

Wie wir gesehen haben, verkürzt man meistens *will* zu *'ll*. Und *will not* wird zu *won't*.

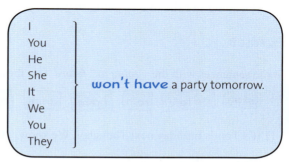

WATCH OUT! (2)

Germans sometimes confuse (verwechseln, durcheinanderbringen) *will* and *want*.

| I **want to** go to the cinema this evening | = | Ich **will** heute Abend ins Kino gehen. |
| I **will** go to the cinema this evening | = | Ich **werde** heute Abend ins Kino gehen. |

EXERCISE A.

Translate these sentences. Use a form of the *future simple*:
1) Einen Moment, bitte. Ich schließe das Fenster.
2) Diese Taschen sind zu schwer. Wir helfen Ihnen.
3) Es ist dein Geburtstag – ich zahle für die Getränke.
4) (Was magst Du – den italienischen Grappa oder den französischen Wein?) Ich nehme den französischen Wein, bitte.
5) Ich rufe dich morgen an.
6) Nächste Woche werde ich 94 Jahre alt.
7) Malst du ein Bild für mich?

c) THE "GOING TO" FUTURE

Das *"going to" future* wird verwendet, um feste Absichten oder Pläne für die Zukunft auszudrücken.

"Fred, **are** you **going to play** football on Sunday?"
"No, I'm not. On Sunday, I**'m going to help** Dad with my homework."

Diese Zukunftsform wird mit dem *"going to" future* von *be* (häufig die Kurzform) + *going to* + Infinitiv des Hauptverbs gebildet:

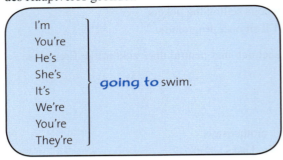 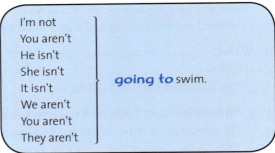

Das *"going to" future* wird auch verwendet, um Vorhersagen auszudrücken.
It's going to rain. We're going to get very wet.

Exercise B.

Write sentences with the *"going to" future*. Use these words:

stay | be late | rain | have | drink | cycle | write | send | leave | wait | open

1) It's Tom's birthday next Thursday. We know. **We're going to send** him a birthday card.
2) There are three flies in Tom's beer. I'm sure _____ it. (s. Watch out! (3))
3) It's 10 o'clock and the bus isn't here. I _____ any longer.
4) Do they have a train ticket to Brighton? No, they don't. _____ there.
5) At present there aren't any shops here, but next year they _____ a supermarket in the town centre.
6) Look at all that work on Helen's desk. I don't think _____ early this evening!
7) It's 10 o'clock and the bus isn't here. We _____ .
8) Oh dear. Look at those black clouds. I think _____ .
9) My phone isn't working so _____ Bob an e-mail.
10) Our daughter is ill so _____ at home today.
11) I know you're late for work, but _____ breakfast before you go?

In der Sendung wurden zwei weitere Zukunftsformen behandelt:

d) The present simple

Diese Zukunftsform wird gebraucht, um feste Termine (Fahrpläne, Programme etc.) auszudrücken.
The train **arrives** at 7.50 am. The President **begins** his official visit on Tuesday.

Darüber hinaus wird diese Form in Nebensätzen verwendet (z. B. nach *when*, *if*, *before*, *until*):
   We'll wait here until John **comes**.

e)   THE FUTURE CONTINUOUS

Diese Zukunftsform wird gebraucht (vgl. *present continuous* oder *past continuous*), um Handlungen oder Vorgänge zu beschreiben, die zu einem bestimmten Zeitpunkt in der Zukunft nicht abgeschlossen sein werden.
   At 10 pm I'm going to sleep and at 10.15 **I'll be sleeping** in my warm bed.
Diese Form wird mit dem *future simple* von *to be* (häufig in der Kurzform) + Verb + *-ing* gebildet:

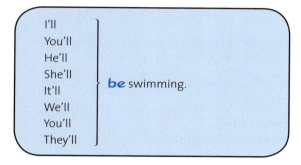
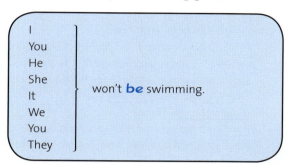

WATCH OUT! (3)
Es ist ein grober Fehler, den Ausdruck „es gibt" mit ~~it gives~~ zu übersetzen!
   Es gibt (Es sind) drei Fliegen in Toms Bier.   =   **There are** three flies in Tom's beer.
   Es gibt einen interessanten Film im Kino   =   **There is (There's)** an interesting film in the cinema.

EXERCISE C.

Decide which *future tense* (*present simple*, *"going to" future*, *future continuous*) is the best in these sentences:

1) Our plane __departs__ (depart) at 4.30 pm. At 4.35 we _____ (sit) in our seats and I _____ (drink) a cup of coffee.

2) Just think! This time next month we _____ (lie) on the beach in the Bahamas.

3) I'm sorry, but I _____ definitely (ganz gewiss) _____ (not do) your homework for you. You must do it without my help.

4) Before we _____ (go) out, we must do the washing up.

5) I usually start my breakfast at 7 am, so if you phone me a little after 7 am, I _____ (eat) my toast!

6) The new shopping centre _____ (open) at 8 o'clock tomorrow morning. Believe me – a few minutes after the opening, thousands of shoppers _____ (search) for good bargains.

7) Look at Tony. He's walking on the wall, but I'm absolutely sure he _____ (fall) off it in a moment.

8) When you _____ (get) off the bus, you'll see the Houses of Parliament in front of you.

LET'S LOOK AT WORDS

> **WATCH OUT! (4)**
> Es gibt einige Ausdrücke im Buch „Into the English World" 7A, die Lernenden mit Deutsch als Muttersprache Schwierigkeiten bereiten können:
> a) Das Substantiv zu *to fly* ist *flight*. Ein Engländer würden sehr lachen, wenn Sie sagen würden: "Please can you tell me when the next fly to London is." Übersetzt heißt das nämlich: „Bitte können Sie mir sagen, wann die nächste Fliege nach London ist!"
> b) That was fun. = Das machte Spaß.
> c) mobile phone = Handy
> handy = praktisch, nützlich, geschickt, leicht erreichbar, zur Hand
> Have you got a hammer handy? A mobile phone is a very handy thing to have.
> d) Check your pockets and luggage again = Überprüfen Sie bitte Ihre Taschen und Ihr Gepäck noch einmal.
> to control = beherrschen. The rebel troops controlled most of the country.
> e) Eric behauptet: I save five hours.
> to save = (sich) sparen
> to spare = (sich) erübrigen, verschonen

I'm sure that you can spare a few minutes to learn these words. Please check that you know them – they will be very handy in conversations with speakers of English next time you are on a flight to London. I will spare (schonen) you in this chapter, but there will be an exercise on these expressions in the next chapter!

EXERCISE D.

Write in the missing words. The first two letters of one word in the sentence are the last two letters of the other word! You'll find the words in the book "Into the English World". (The numbers in brackets are the units).

1) The travel agent can _provide_ (7D) you with information about the arrivals and _departures_ (7A) of all flights.

2) Many people decide to _____ le (7D) in London because of all the le_____ (2D) possibilities in this great city.

3) I can _____ re (7D) you that it is not always a good idea to go to a re_____ _____ (2A) to find a flat.

4) An _____**or** (7D) of my wife's made this **or**_____ (5D) wrought iron (Schmiedeeisen) gate.

5) There was an **up**_____ (6A) when Kate spilled the _____**up** (1A) all over Clive's new jacket.

6) The **ve**_____ (5A) always _____**ve** (7A) very early to sell their goods.

7) Paul had to fill in a _____**re** (3A) about the **re**_____ (7D) from his new business.

George had to paint a flagpole (Fahnenstange), but he didn't know how much **paint** he needed. His friend said to him:
"My **suggestion** is to lay the flagpole down, measure the **length** and **width** and write the **measurements** down. Then you'll know how much to buy."
"That's no good," George said, "I need to know the **height** not the **length** of the flagpole."
There are some really silly people around, aren't there?
Wie Sie sehen, unterscheiden sich Substantive im Englischen häufig sehr von den Verben und Adjektiven, mit denen sie verwandt sind:

| to suggest ⇨ suggestion | to measure ⇨ measurement | to paint ⇨ paint |
| long ⇨ length | wide ⇨ width | high ⇨ height |

Am besten lernt man die Substantive im Zusammenhang mit den Verben. In der folgenden Übung geht es um Substantive, die Sie in der siebten Sendung, aber auch in früheren Sendungen kennengelernt haben.

Exercise E.

Write down the right nouns from the words in brackets:

1) Bob's (appear) _appearance_ changed a lot – after two wild parties and two sleepless nights!

2) The Maoris are now a (minor) _____ group in New Zealand society.

3) One of the (employ) _____ who works for the company showed us the way to the (produce) _____ line.

4) Can you tell me the (depart) _____ times of the (fly) _____ to London Heathrow, please?

5) My (advise) _____ to you is not to rent a flat in the (surround) _____ of Heathrow Airport!

6) Mr Grove's (collect) _____ of water colour paintings is on (display) _____ at the Sheffield Art Gallery.

7) People say that Peter is a hard-working colleague, but I have my (doubt) _____.

Do you still remember?

Do you still remember what we talked about in the last programmes and chapters? Do the exercises below and you can see how much you remember. If you have difficulties, please read the previous (vorhergehenden) chapters.

Exercise F.

Write in the *short answers*:

1) Were you at home yesterday? No, _I wasn't (we weren't)_____.

2) Did you spend a lot of money at the market yesterday? Yes, _____.

3) Could you help me, please? Yes, of course, _____.

4) Does your son have difficulties at school? Thank Goodness, _____.

5) Can you speak Russian? Unfortunately _____.

6) Are you tired? No, _____. Are you?

7) Did they leave work early yesterday? _____. They left at midday.

8) Was your son at school yesterday? _____. He was ill.

9) Are you and Jenny coming to our party tomorrow? _____. When does it start?

10) Were your brothers watching TV when I phoned yesterday? I'm afraid _____.

Exercise G.

Write in the *question tags*:

1) You weren't here yesterday, _were you_____?

2) Sally doesn't work here, _____?

3) Your sister speaks English fluently, _____?

4) Your husband didn't feel well yesterday, _____?

5) You're flying to America next Monday, _____?

6) We can go now, _____?

7) Please put the bags down here, _____?

8) Ben and Julia sold the car, _____?

Exercise H.

Put the verbs in brackets into their correct forms:

Mrs Douglas _doesn't like_ (not like) opera, but she _____ (love) pop songs. Every day she _____ (sit) in the bath and _____ (sing) old songs by the Beatles and Rolling Stones. In fact, right now I can _____ (hear) her. She _____ (sing) "I Can't Get No Satisfaction". So, her neighbours _____ (not need/buy) a CD player to listen to the songs! The problem is that they _____ (not like) her singing so much.

One evening last January something terrible _____ (happen). Mr Douglas _____ (watch) "Who Wants to be a Millionaire" on TV in the living room, when his wife _____ (rush) into the room. She _____ (not show) any interest in Mr Douglas's programme.

"George," she _____ (shout). "Our neighbour Mr Henry _____ (throw) a stone through the window while I _____ (sing) 'She Loves You Yeah, Yeah, Yeah'."

"What an idiot," George _____ (say). "Now he can _____ (hear) you even better."

Exercise I.

Put the verbs into the *past simple*:

1) The thief didn't steal my car. He _stole_ my neighbour's car.
2) Mary didn't drink any alcohol at the party. She _____ orange juice.
3) I didn't sleep the day before yesterday, but I _____ a lot last night.
4) We didn't sell much last Saturday, but we _____ a lot at the market yesterday.
5) Mr and Mrs Cheeseman didn't choose a holiday in Spain, they _____ a holiday in Scotland.
6) I didn't catch the mouse. Our cat _____ it.
7) Stella didn't pay for the drinks. Who _____ for them, then?
8) They didn't build the house in the centre of the town. They _____ it outside the town.

9) What a stupid thief! He didn't hide the money in the wood. He _____ it in the bank!

10) What did Mr Stanley bring with him yesterday? He _____ a memory stick.

Well, that was hard work, wasn't it? Please don't worry if the different future forms are a little difficult for you. If you recognise them when you hear or read them, that is usually enough. If you use the *future simple*, speakers of English will understand you!
And now for some light entertainment here are some of the structures from this chapter and the past ones (*"going to" future; present simple; past simple; present continuous; past continuous; short forms; question tags*).
There are two expressions which might be new: *fishmonger* and *rub out*, but I'm sure you can guess them from the context.

A man **was walking** along a street when suddenly he **saw** a fishmonger. The fishmonger **was writing** a sentence on his shop window in paint: WE **SELL** FRESH FISH HE … The fishmonger **finished** the sign: WE SELL FRESH FISH HERE TODAY. One moment, **said** the man in the street. "Why **did** you **write** 'TODAY'. You **aren't going to sell** the fish tomorrow, **are you**?". That's right, said the fishmonger and he
5 **started to rub** out the word "TODAY".
"One moment," the other man said. "Why **are** you only **rubbing** out the word 'TODAY'? You **don't need** the word 'HERE'," said the man in the street. "You **aren't going to sell** the fish in the next street or in Buckingham Palace, **are you**?"
"That's also true," the fishmonger said and he **rubbed** out the word "HERE". His sentence now **was** shorter:
10 WE SELL FRESH FISH.
"One moment," **said** the man in the street. "You **don't need** the words 'WE SELL'. You **aren't going to give** away your fish free, **are you**?"
"You're right," the fishmonger **said** and he **rubbed** out the words "WE SELL".
His sentence **was** now very short. In fact it **wasn't** a sentence! FRESH FISH.
15 "That's OK," the man in the street said. "But, why **don't** you **rub** out the word 'FRESH'. You **aren't going to sell** fish that **isn't** fresh, fish that is bad, **are you**?"
"No, I'm not," the fishmonger said and **rubbed** out the word 'FRESH'. Now **there** was only one word on his window: FISH.
"And you **don't need** the word 'FISH', the other man said. "I **could smell** your fish while I **was walking**
20 down this street!"

fishmonger = Fischhändler   rub out = wegwischen, ausradieren

Chapter 8: The Present Perfect Simple and Present Perfect Continuous

How are you getting on (zurechtkommen) with the irregular verbs? In my sixth and seventh chapter I gave you a number of them to learn. I hope you are learning a few irregular verbs each day! Here are some more irregular verbs for you to learn.

infinitive	past simple	deutsche Übersetzung	infinitive	past simple	deutsche Übersetzung
bend	bent	(sich) biegen, (sich) beugen	hold	held	(fest-)halten
			let	let	(zu-)lassen
bet	bet	wetten	mean	meant	bedeuten
bleed	bled	bluten	ride	rode	reiten; (Rad) fahren
broadcast	broadcast	senden, übertragen	shake	shook	schütteln
drive	drove	(Auto) fahren, antreiben	shut	shut	schließen, zumachen
			spread	spread	(sich) verbreiten; aufstreichen
fight	fought	kämpfen			
find	found	finden	stand	stood	stehen
forecast	forecast	vorhersagen	understand	understood	verstehen
win	won	gewinnen	wake	woke	aufwachen, wecken

The Present Perfect Simple (Die einfache Form des Perfekts)

Nun wenden wir uns dem Thema der achten Folge zu: dem *present perfect*. Welchen von diesen beiden Sätzen würden Sie sagen?
a) „Gestern habe ich Günther gesehen."
b) Oder: „Gestern sah ich Günther."

Wahrscheinlich würden Sie Satz b) vorziehen, wenn Sie aus dem norddeutschen Raum kommen, und Satz a), wenn Sie in Süddeutschland leben. In der englischen Sprache gibt es jedoch einen großen Unterschied zwischen *I **have seen** Günther.* und *I **saw** Günther.* Betrachten wir einige Sätze:

I **arrived** yesterday.	I **have** just **arrived**.
He **made** a reservation last week.	He **has** already **made** a reservation.
We **didn't go** to the cinema on Saturday.	We **haven't been** to the cinema since Saturday.
Three weeks ago I **rented** a car./ I rented a car three weeks ago.	Up to now I**'ve rented** a car many times.
She **was** ill for two weeks in March.	She**'s been** ill for a month.
She **wasn't** at school in March.	She **hasn't been** at school since March.

Bei den Sätzen auf der linken Seite wird Ihnen auffallen, dass sie sich auf einen Zeitpunkt beziehen, der in der Vergangenheit abgeschlossen wurde (*yesterday*, *last week*, *three weeks ago*, *for two weeks in March*). Die Aussagen auf der rechten Seite beziehen sich auf Zeiträume, die zwar in der Vergangenheit anfingen, aber jetzt noch andauern (*already*), oder die gerade abgeschlossen wurden (*just*).
Wie Carolin erklärt hat, stellt das *present perfect simple* eine Brücke zwischen Vergangenheit und Gegenwart dar.

Falls all dies zu theoretisch klingt, kann man sich das Leben leichter machen: man merkt sich die Signalwörter, die häufig im Zusammenhang mit dem *present perfect simple* verwendet werden. Dabei hat uns Carolin mit ihrem Merkwort JEANNY sehr geholfen: *just* (gerade), *ever* (jemals), *already* (schon), *never* (nie), *not yet* (noch nicht) und *yet* (bis jetzt – in verneinten Sätzen und Fragen). Die Anfangsbuchstaben der Signalwörter ergeben das Merkwort.

Weitere wichtige Signalwörter sind: *up to now* (bis jetzt), *so far* (bis jetzt) und vor allem *for* (seit) und *since* (seit). Beide Wörter geben einen Zeitraum an, der in der Vergangenheit anfing und bis jetzt andauert. If you remember the word FUSS (unnötige Aufregung) it might help you here, too. You might think that this is all a lot of FUSS about nothing (viel Lärm um nichts), but it is quite important!

> **J**ust   **F**or
> **E**ver   **U**p to now
> **A**lready   + **S**ince
> **N**ever   **S**o far
> **N**ot yet
> **Y**et

WATCH OUT! (1)
Die zwei Wörter *since* und *for* sind für Deutsche eine Fehlerquelle, da es in ihrer Sprache nur ein Wort, nämlich „seit", gibt. Der Unterschied zwischen den beiden Signalwörtern liegt darin, dass sich **since** auf einen **Zeitpunkt** und *for* auf einen **Zeitraum** bezieht. Bezogen auf einen Zeitraum in der Vergangenheit wird *for* anders übersetzt:
a) I **haven't seen** him **for three days**.
    Ich **habe** ihn **seit** drei Tagen nicht **gesehen**.
b) I **didn't see** him for **three days last week**.
    Ich **habe** ihn letzte Woche drei Tage **lang** nicht **gesehen**.
Die Zeitform im Deutschen bleibt dieselbe.

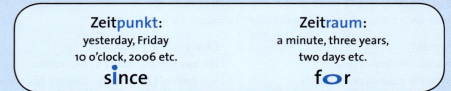

Well, that's enough theory! After the next few exercises everything will be clearer.

Exercise A.

Put in *since* or *for*:

1) _since_ last Tuesday   2) _____ my birthday   3) _____ the fourth of June
4) _____ three months   5) _____ 3 o'clock   6) _____ September
7) _____ a few seconds   8) _____ five weeks   9) _____ Christmas
10) _____ 200 years   11) _____ a century   12) _____ I last saw you

Exercise B.

Choose the right alternatives.

1) I haven't played table tennis **a) for the last two years.** b) two years ago.
2) We haven't watched television a) Sunday evening. b) since Sunday.
3) Peter a) has come b) came here last week.
4) My mother-in-law didn't visit us a) at Easter. b) so far.
5) Have you finished the work a) last week? b) yet?
6) a) Did your husband make b) Has your husband made the reservation in February?
7) Mr Peters hasn't painted the living room a) for b) since many years.
8) When a) did you build b) have you built that beautiful house?
9) Rachel and I got married a) since 1999. b) in 1999.

Im *present perfect simple* werden die Formen von *have* auch gerne abgekürzt:

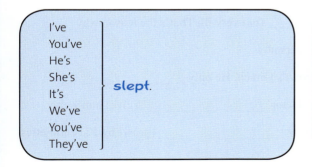 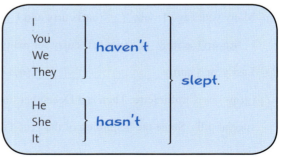

Bei den unregelmäßigen Verben ist die dritte Form, das *past participle,* oft anders als das *past simple* (aber glücklicherweise nicht immer!). Bei den regelmäßigen Verben haben wir – Gott sei Dank! – keine Probleme:
  I played the piano yesterday. I have played the piano since yesterday.

Allerdings gilt dies auch für Verben in der deutschen Sprache: gehen, ging, gegangen; sprechen, sprach, gesprochen; usw. Warum sollen es Deutsche, die Englisch lernen, besser haben als Engländer, die Deutsch lernen? Am besten lernen Sie die unregelmäßigen Verbformen einfach auswendig.

infinitive	past simple	past participle		infinitive	past simple	past participle	
be	was/were		been	grow	grew		grown
become	became		become	have	had		had
begin	began		begun	hear	heard		heard
break	broke		broken	hurt	hurt		hurt
bring	brought	I, you, we, they have	brought	keep	kept	I, you, we, they have	kept
build	built		built	know	knew		known
buy	bought		bought	leave	left		left
choose	chose		chosen	lose	lost		lost
come	came		come	meet	met		met
cost	cost		cost	make	made		made
cut	cut		cut	put	put		put
drink	drank	he, she, it has	drunk	read	read (red)	he, she, it has	read
eat	ate		eaten	rise	rose		risen
fall	fell		fallen	see	saw		seen
forget	forgot		forgotten	sleep	slept		slept
get	got		got	take	took		taken
give	gave		given	tell	told		told
go	went		gone				

Diese Übung wird Ihnen helfen, das *present perfect simple* zu verstehen.

EXERCISE C.

Put the verbs in brackets into their correct forms:

1) Many years ago I __ate__ (eat) curry and I __was__ (be) very ill. That's the reason why I __haven't eaten__ (not eat) curry for many years now.

2) Last year Timmy _____ (not grow) so much. He only _____ (grow) by 1 millimetre. Then last December, the doctor _____ (give) him some special pills. Since the beginning of the year Timmy _____ (grow) by 12 centimetres and he _____ (not stop) growing yet.

3) Prices _____ (rise) enormously since January. Before that they _____ (not rise) much at all (überhaupt nicht), although last September they _____ (rise) by 3 % because of the increase in the price of oil.

4) "Mary, somebody has _____ (take) the car!" "It's OK, our son _____ (take) it to the disco a few hours ago. He'll be back before midnight."

5) "That's the fourth glass that you _____ (break) since the beginning of the week!" "That's not true. I _____ (not break) any glasses on Tuesday. I only _____ (break) nineteen glasses on Wednesday and Thursday and in the last two days I _____ (not break) any at all."

6) Mandy _____ (hurt) her boyfriend after the party on Saturday. She _____ (not take) the cigarette out of her mouth when she _____ (kiss) him and it _____ (burn) a hole in his lips. Poor Bill _____ (be) in hospital for the last three days and he _____ (not drink) or _____ (eat) anything up to now.

EXERCISE D.

Translate these sentences into English:
1) Im Sommer 2008 sind wir nach Italien gefahren, aber seitdem sind wir dort nicht mehr gewesen.
2) Vor drei Jahren haben wir Harry gesehen, aber seitdem haben wir nichts von ihm gehört.
3) Hast du Jacob gestern getroffen?

WATCH OUT! (2)
Im Deutschen gibt es Verben, deren Perfektform mit „haben" gebildet wird (schlafen, lesen, essen usw.), und auch Verben, deren Perfektform mit „sein" gebildet wird (einschlafen, fahren, fallen, gehen, sein, werden usw.) Im Englischen nehmen wir *to have* bei allen Verben im *present perfect simple*:
  Tom **has** just fallen off his bike.
  Mary **has** never been ill in her whole life.
  I **have** driven to Manchester three times since Monday.

WATCH OUT! (3)
  Ich kenne ihn auch.   =   I know him, **too**.
  Ich kenne ihn auch nicht. =   I don't know him, **either**.

THE PRESENT PERFECT CONTINUOUS (DIE VERLAUFSFORM DES PERFEKTS)

In der englischen Sprache gibt es auch eine zweite Variation dieser Zeitform: the *present perfect continuous*. Nehmen wir Carolins Beispiel aus der Sendung:

I **have been renting** cars from your agency for a long time now.

Eric mietet schon lange bei dieser Firma Autos. <u>Und er tut es immer noch</u>. Deshalb verwenden wir die Verlaufsform des Perfekts. Falls das zu kompliziert klingt, wie wäre es mit einem Witz:

The man in the bus is very angry:
"Young people today are terrible. No one stands up to give his seat to an old man or woman."
"But you've got a seat!" another passenger says.
"Yes," says the man, "I've got a seat. But my poor 88-year-old mother hasn't got a seat. She**'s been standing** for the last half an hour."

What a heartless son! In diesem Zusammenhang würde man im Deutschen die Gegenwartsform verwenden: Meine arme 88-jährige Mutter **steht** seit einer halben Stunde.
Bei *to be* und *to have* (im Sinne von „besitzen") wird die Verlaufsform nicht benutzt:

Ich bin hier seit drei Stunden   =   I've been here for three hours.
Seit Januar haben wir ein Auto   =   Since January we've had a car.

Now it's your turn!

EXERCISE E.

Put the verbs in the *present perfect continuous form*. Use the short forms when possible.

1) It **'s been snowing** _____ (snow) the whole week.

2) I _____ (lie) in bed with the flu since Monday.

3) He _____ (practise) the piano for thirty-eight hours now.

4) My wife _____ (work) in a youth club since 1950.

5) Graham _____ (learn) to cook for many years now.

6) Up to now they _____ (play) the piano all the time.

7) Since the beginning of 1997 my brother and I _____ (live) in New York.

Let's look at words

> **WATCH OUT! (4)**
> Wieder einmal gibt es einige Ausdrücke, die Schwierigkeiten bereiten können:
> a) Der Angestellte fragt Eric: "Have you ever <u>rented</u> a car before?"
>   Please remember: to rent = mieten; the rent = die Miete; die Rente = pension; rentabel = profitable
> b) Der Angestellte sagt auch: "You'll see the car parked <u>in front of</u> the building.
>   Remember: I am standing <u>in front of</u> Big Ben.
>   in front of = vor (örtlich)
>   "A" comes <u>before</u> "B" in the alphabet. We went home <u>before</u> he came.
>   before = vor (Reihenfolge, zeitlich)

Exercise F.

Here is an exercise to test some of the "problem words" we have had in the last few chapters. Translate these sentences:
1) Herr Martin wird seine Rente vor seiner Frau bekommen.
2) Ich muss die Abrechnung für mein Handy kontrollieren.
3) Es macht keinen Spaß, nach Alkohol süchtig zu sein.
4) Ich besuche einen Skikurs und habe keine Zeit, meine Tante zu besuchen.

Exercise G.

Too many words! Replace the words in brackets with a single word. The first letter of each word is given. Make any necessary changes.
1) I have __rented__ (paid the company money to use) the car.
2) The people in this part of Ottawa are **i**_____ (people who have come from other countries to live here).
3) We have checked all the **i**_____ (things on the list).
4) John is only fourteen and he drove his dad's car without a **d**_____ (document to show he has passed a driving test).
5) Many buildings in Canada are **r**_____ (make us think) of nineteenth century British architecture.
6) The Maoris were **a**_____ (promised that they would have) their civil rights. After all, they are the **i**_____ part of the population (who lived in New Zealand long before the other settlers came).

DO YOU STILL REMEMBER?

As usual, I am going to give you some exercises on some of the things that we learned in the chapters 1–7. Are you ready? Here we go.

EXERCISE H.

Correct these sentences:
1) ~~That's a colleague of us.~~   **That's a colleague of ours.**
2) ~~John smokes not usually in the living room.~~
3) ~~This newspaper is my. She is very interesting.~~
4) ~~Went you to the party yesterday?~~
5) ~~I am occasionally working in the office, but right now I work at home.~~
6) ~~We have an own car.~~
7) ~~Our colleague didn't got to work early yesterday.~~
8) ~~Gerry has two sister. I like her very much.~~
9) ~~It gives a interesting film in the cinema.~~
10) ~~Tom live near his work.~~
11) ~~It's too warm in here – I open the window.~~
12) ~~Our boss on Mondays in the firm meets often new clients.~~
13) ~~During I was working yesterday, the computer was breaking down three times.~~
14) ~~Before we will start our work we'll have a cup of coffee.~~

EXERCISE I.

Change these sentences into questions (?), positive sentences (+) or negative sentences (–).

1) You bet on that horse and won a lot of money. (?)
   Did you bet on that horse and win a lot of money?

2) Neville didn't meet us at the station on Wednesday. (?)

3) Jennifer doesn't often forget names. (+)

4) We understood everything the maths teacher taught us. (−)

5) Harry kept a cool head in the exam. (−)

6) Graham may come in now. (?)

7) Sue and Pat didn't buy a present for the host and didn't bring a bottle of wine to the party.
They didn't leave the party early and didn't catch the last bus home. (+)
_____
_____

8) You were watching me when Ron's dog bit me and hurt my leg. (?)
_____

9) Malcolm will be sleeping in his office when we come in! (?)
_____

10) Simon and his wife are going to emigrate to the USA next year. (?)
When _____

11) George had to write a hundred e-mails yesterday. (?)
How many _____

Exercise J.

Put the verbs in brackets into their correct forms:

It _____ (be) 4 pm in the afternoon of July the fifteenth, 2006. Mr and Mrs Rose and the other passengers in the aeroplane _____ (enjoy) their flight. Mr Rose _____ (drink) a small glass of champagne in only a few seconds. His wife _____ (not drink) champagne as she _____ (not like) alcohol, but she _____ (take) a cup of coffee from the stewardess. "Just think," Mrs Rose _____ (say) to her husband, "we _____ (land) at Los Angeles airport at 12.30. Before we _____ (get) out of the airport it will be 1.30 pm. But then – this time in ten hours – we _____ be _____ (lie) on the beach at San Barbara. Don't you _____ (feel) excited?!"
Suddenly, while they _____ (talk), the engines of the aeroplane _____ (stop). The passengers _____ (scream) when they _____ (see) the pilot of the aeroplane with a parachute (Fallschirm) on his back. "What _____ (he/do) here?" Mr Rose _____ (ask) his wife. He should be in the cockpit!" "Don't worry," the pilot _____ (shout), "everything is OK. I _____ _____ (jump) out of the aeroplane and get help."

Bei den Lösungen finden Sie einige zusätzliche Erklärungen zu dieser Übung, damit Sie sich Grundlegendes zu den englischen Zeitformen noch einmal ins Gedächtnis rufen können.

Well once again, that was a lot to learn. Don't worry if you still have difficulties with this tense. We have a lot of time in the preparatory course and in the main course. In my next two chapters I will give you more examples with this tense. If you use the *present perfect simple* instead of the *present perfect continuous*, that is usually not a big problem!
As a reward (Belohnung) for the hard work, here are two jokes: One with the *present perfect simple* and one with the *present perfect continuous*. I hope you enjoy them!

"**Did** you **pass** your driving test yesterday?"
"I don't know. The driving examiner **hasn't come** out of hospital yet."

The trumpet player says to his wife:
"**I've been playing** nursery rhymes (Kinderlieder) on my trumpet to our baby son for the last half an hour. I don't understand why he isn't sleeping."

Chapter 9: Adjectives and Adverbs, the Position of Adverbs and Comparisons

I hope that you're enjoying the preparatory course. I also hope that you are doing a little English every day. The English say "Rome wasn't built in a day" (Rom wurde nicht an einem Tag erbaut) and even if you just read a part of my chapter every day, do one or two exercises a day and often read through the last chapters, you will have a good basis for the Telekolleg course. In this letter we are going to look at two important aspects of English grammar which Carolin and Eric showed us in the ninth episode.

Adjectives and Adverbs (Adjektive und Adverbien)

Let's begin with a situation many mothers are familiar (vertraut) with:

Little four-year-old Tim is in bed and his mother is reading him a **nice** story. After half an hour he says to his mum: "Mummy – could you please read the story **quietly**. I'm **tired** and I want to sleep."

Vergessen wir für einen Moment die große Enttäuschung, die Tims Mama sicherlich spürt, und schauen wir uns die drei Wörter *nice*, *quietly* and *tired* an. Warum schreiben wir *quietly* und nicht *quiet*? Kurze Rede langer Sinn: Die Antwort auf diese Frage ist, dass im Gegensatz zu *nice* (bezieht sich auf *story*) oder *tired* (bezieht sich auf *I* = Tim) *quietly* das Verb *read* beschreibt. Es ist ein sogenanntes *adverb of manner* (Adverb der Art und Weise) und antwortet auf die Frage „Wie?" (Wie hat er es getan?). Dies ist ein Problem, aber nur ein kleines Problem für Deutsche, da es nur einen kleinen Unterschied zwischen den beiden Formen gibt: Herr Smith ist ein langsamer Fahrer (*Mr Smith is a **slow** driver*). Herr Smith fährt langsam (*Mr Smith drives **slowly***). Wie Carolin erklärt hat, gibt es gelegentlich kleine Änderungen in der Rechtschreibung, aber viel wichtiger ist es, sich einige unregelmäßige Formen zu merken:

adjective	adverb	adjective	adverb
loud	loud**ly**	late	late*
careful	careful**ly**	friendly	in a friendly way
simple	simp**ly**	lively	in a lively way
polite	polite**ly**	funny	in a funny way
happy	happ**ily**	hard	hard*
basic	basic**ally**	fast	fast
		high	high*

* lately = in letzter Zeit; hardly (ever) = kaum; highly = höchst (That is **highly** interesting.)

With this little exercise, everything should become clear:

EXERCISE A.

Put the word in brackets into the correct form:

1) Look at all the mistakes here! Your son doesn't do his homework __carefully__ (careful) enough. His brother is much more __careful__ (careful) when he does his work.

2) My mother is a very _____ (careful) driver.

3) I _____ (hard) know the boy, but he hit me so _____ (hard).

4) Jeremy is not very _____ (polite). He always interrupts his teacher _____ (impolite).

5) What a _____ (slow) car! Well, the car isn't _____ (slow). It's just that Mr Gilbert prefers to drive _____ (slow).

6) Oh Gladys, my darling. Your voice is so _____ (wonderful) and you sing so _____ (beautiful). I want to kiss you _____ (passionate = leidenschaftlich) on your _____ lips (lovely).

> **WATCH OUT! (1)**
> Bei Verben der Wahrnehmung (*it **feels** funny, it **sounds** strange*, etc.) und bei Verben des Scheinens und Werdens (*appear* = erscheinen, *seem* = scheinen, *become* = werden, *get* = werden, *grow* = im Sinne von „werden") steht ein Adjektiv beim Verb:
> I'm <u>getting</u> **ill** and <u>becoming</u> very **dizzy** (schwindelig). That medicine doesn't <u>seem</u> very **nice**. It <u>looks</u> **horrible**. It <u>smells</u> **awful** (scheußlich) and it <u>tastes</u> **nasty** (widerlich) – but I'll drink it.

> **WATCH OUT! (2)**
> Um ein Adjektiv (oder Adverb) näher zu beschreiben, verwenden wir im Englischen das Adverb:
> Stuart is **really** kind. He is **extremely** nice to his great-grandmother and sings her old Rolling Stones songs (**exceptionally** well!) every Sunday.

EXERCISE B.

Which is correct?

1) Mr and Mrs Douglas are __late__ (late/lately) for the opera. The usherette (Platzanweiserin) says to them: "Please walk to your seats _____ (extreme/extremely) _____ (quietly/quiet). The opera is just beginning." "Why should we be so _____ (quietly/quiet)?" Mr Douglas asks. "Is everyone sleeping already?"

2) "Is this milk _____ (fresh/freshly)?" "Yes, madam. Two hours ago it was still grass."

3) "Waiter! The kitchen in this restaurant must be _____ (exceptional/exceptionally) _____ (clean/cleanly)." "Thank you, sir. That's _____ (really/real) kind of you to say that. But how do you know how _____ (cleanly/clean) our kitchen is?" "Well, the soup tastes very _____ (strange/strangely) – it tastes of soap!"

4) Mark asks his girlfriend: "Am I your first boyfriend?" She replies: "Maybe. You look _____ (familiarly/familiar = vertraut)."

5) My husband is so _____ (helpful/helpfully). He knows that I have many jobs to do in the garden and in the house and he knows that I forget important things very _____ (easy/easily). So yesterday, before the football match on TV, he spent ten minutes for me. I was _____ (complete/completely) surprised this morning when I saw a long list on the table. It was a _____ (useful/usefully) list of all the things I had to do. What a _____ (thoughtful/thoughtfully = rücksichtsvoll, aufmerksam) husband! And he never gets _____ (angry/angrily) with me when I clear up (aufräumen) the living room while he's watching a football match on TV.

(In the meantime, I'm pleased to say that she has at last woken up and has got a divorce (Scheidung)!)

THE POSITION OF ADVERBS (DIE WORTSTELLUNG DER ADVERBIEN)

In der dritten Sendung und im dritten Kapitel haben wir uns mit der Wortstellung im Englischen beschäftigt. Wohin kommen die Adverbien der Art und Weise? Schauen wir uns diesen Satz an:

Bertha	always	plays	the electric guitar	very loudly	in the bath	at midnight.
⇩	⇩	⇩	⇩	⇩	⇩	⇩
Subjekt	**Adverb der Häufigkeit (Wie oft?)**	**Verb**	**Objekt**	**Adverb der Art und Weise**	**Ort**	**Zeit**

I am happy that Bertha isn't my neighbour, although her life expectancy (Lebenserwartung) is probably quite low (it is quite dangerous to play the electric guitar in the bath). However the important thing here is the position of the *adverb of manner*.

Obwohl die Regeln des englischen Satzbaus nicht immer einfach sind, können Sie sich viel Mühe sparen – nicht wenn Sie Berthas Verhalten nachahmen, sondern wenn Sie den obigen Satz auswendig lernen, weil er uns zwei wichtige Dinge zeigt:
1) Im Englischen dürfen wir nie das Adverb der Art und Weise zwischen das Verb (hier *plays*) und das Objekt stellen.
2) Die normale Reihenfolge für den Satz ist: Adverb der Art und Weise – Ort – Zeit, wobei wir wissen, dass wir die Zeit an den Anfang des Satzes stellen können. Auch wenn andere Möglichkeiten bestehen: „simplify your life" (wie der Bestseller heißt) und beherzigen Sie diese Regel.

That's too much theory, isn't it? Once again, everything will become much clearer after this exercise:

Exercise C.

Put these words and expressions in the right order to make correct sentences:

1) his / Cedric / quickly / in the morning / breakfast / eats / always

   Cedric always eats his breakfast quickly in the morning.

2) worked / hard / yesterday / in his firm / my husband / very

3) come / meetings / usually / late / Brian / to / doesn't / important

4) hardly ever / Sue / hard / during the week / works

5) to the clients / before he leaves the office / He / urgent emails / often / extremely / sends

Comparisons (Steigerung/Vergleiche)

It is always important to choose your friends careful**ly** – especial**ly** if you go on holiday with them, as you can see from the following story:

Two friends, Mr Watson and Mr Jones were on a safari in the African jungle. One day while they were coming out of their tent they saw a lion. The lion came nearer and nearer. It looked very hungry. Mr Watson put on his sneakers (Turnschuhe).
"Don't be silly," Mr Jones said. "You can't run fast**er than** the lion. You can't even run **as** fast **as** the lion. That lion has much **more powerful** muscles on its feet **than** you have."
"That's right," Mr Watson said, "I can't run fast**er than** the lion. But I don't need to run fast**er than** the lion. I only need to run fast**er than** you!"

Well, Mr Watson is a really horrible friend, isn't he? In fact he's **the worst** friend I can imagine. Anyway, my friends are all nic**er than** he is.
Ich glaube, Sie haben es erraten: Heute wollen wir über die Steigerung von Adjektiven und Adverbien sowie über Vergleiche im Englischen reden. Im Leben gibt es oft unterschiedliche Stufen z. B. bei Arbeitskollegen:

Rose is a **good/nice** colleague.
John is **better/nicer** than Rose, but Steve is **the best/nicest** colleague.

Es gibt zwei verschiedene Steigerungen im Englischen: Eine Steigerung für Wörter mit einer Silbe und eine Steigerung für Wörter mit zwei oder mehr Silben. Ein Beispiel für die zweite Stufe der Steigerung:

Gerald: "There are some dogs that are nic**er** and **more intelligent than** their owners: Their owners aren't **as** nice or **as** intelligent **as** their dogs."
David: "Yes, that's right. I've got a dog like that."

Ausnahmen gibt es natürlich immer – Gott sei Dank nur bei zweisilbigen Adjektiven.

> ### WATCH OUT! (3)
> Wir können in negativen Aussagesätzen auch das Wort **so** verwenden:
> *Their owners aren't **so/as** nice or **so/as** intelligent **as** their dogs.*
> Jedoch ist dies nur in negativen Aussagesätzen möglich, nicht in positiven Sätzen. Warum das Leben komplizierter machen, als es schon ist? (*Why make life **more** complicated **than** it already is?*) Lernen wir nur eine Form *as … as* – das lässt sich sowohl in negativen als auch in positiven Aussagesätzen anwenden.

> ### WATCH OUT! (4)
> Bitte verwechseln Sie nicht die Wörter *like, as* und *than*!
> a) That tower looks **like** the Eiffel Tower (sieht aus wie).
> b) But it isn't **as** high **as** the Eiffel Tower.
> c) That's true. The Eiffel Tower is much higher **than** this tower.
> Häufig verwechseln Lernende der englischen Sprache auch *than* (als) und *then* (dann):
> *Jane bought a big ice-cream, but I bought a bigger ice-cream **than** her and **then** I ate it.*

Auch bei der dritten Stufe der Steigerung, dem sogenannten *superlative*, gibt es einen ähnlichen Unterschied zwischen einsilbigen und mehrsilbigen Adjektiven:
 "Brunhilde, my darling. You've got the small**est** but **most** beautiful nose in the world!"
Mit diesen Merksätzen können Sie sich die Regel leicht merken:

> That computer is cheap and efficient.
> This computer is cheap**er** and **more** efficient **than** that one.
> However, John's computer is **the** cheap**est** and **most** efficient one.

Mit einer nützlichen Eselsbrücke von Carolin können Sie sich auch die wenigen Ausnahmen bei der Steigerung der zweisilbigen Adjektive merken:
 „Auf der **Er le** sitzt ein **Y**, **o**h w**e**h."
Dieser Satz gibt die Endungen von denjenigen – wenigen – zweisilbigen Adjektiven an, die mit *-er* und *-est* gesteigert werden, z. B:

clev**er**	clev**er**er	clev**er**est
simp**le**	simp**l**er	simp**l**est
eas**y**	eas**i**er	eas**i**est
narr**ow**	narr**ow**er	narr**ow**est

The teacher asks Paul:
"One plus two is three. What is two plus two?"
"That's typical," says Paul. "You answer the eas**iest** question yourself and ask me the **most** difficult one."

Übrigens auch Adverbien, die mit *-ly* enden, werden mit *more* gesteigert:
   Thomas drives **more** careful**ly than** his brother does.

Es gibt – wie könnte es anders sein – zusätzlich zu *much/many – more – the most* einige unregelmäßige Formen. *Simplify your life* – lernen Sie diese einfach auswendig.

good	**better** (than)	the **best**
well	**better** (than)	the **best**
bad	**worse** (than)	the **worst**
badly	**worse** (than)	the **worst**
far	**further** (than)	the **furthest**
little	**less** (than)	the **least**
much/many	**more** (than)	the **most**

WATCH OUT! (5)
Die Wörter *little* und *much/many* sind häufig Fehlerquellen für Lernende der englischen Sprache. Wie Carolin in der neunten Sendung erklärt hat, verwenden wir sowohl die Formen *few – fewer (than) – the fewest* als auch die Formen *many – more (than) – (the) most* bei Substantiven, die wir zählen können (z.B. *books, toys, houses, unemployed people, children, coins*). Wenn wir dagegen Substantive nicht zählen können (z.B. *air, sugar, alcohol, sadness, unemployment*) nehmen wir sowohl die Formen *little – less (than) – (the) least* als auch *much – more (than) – (the) most.* („Zwei Lüfte", „vier Arbeitslosigkeiten", „sechs Alkohole" gibt es auch im Deutschen nicht!)

Die folgenden Merksätze können Ihnen helfen, die Unterschiede zu sehen:

   too **much** alcohol   =   too **many** problems   /   **little** alcohol   =   **few** problems
       more alcohol   =   **more** problems   /   **less** alcohol   =   **fewer** problems

          much = viel, many = viel<u>e</u>; little = wenig, few = wenig<u>e</u>

WATCH OUT! (6)
Zwei nützliche Konstruktionen im Zusammenhang mit der Steigerung:
   It is getting cold**er** and cold**er**. = Es wird immer kälter.
   The more expensive the train tickets are **the fewer** people travel by train. =
   Je teurer die Fahrkarten sind, **desto weniger** Menschen fahren mit dem Zug.

Now it's your turn. After these exercises, comparisons in English will be much clear**er**!
You will find the comparisons in English **less** difficult **than** you do now!

EXERCISE D.

Put in *little*, *less*, *the least*, *many*, *much*, *more*, *the most*, *few*, *fewer* where necessary:

1) I really have very __little__ time – I have to finish this report before 12.00 o'clock and it's already 11.50!

2) I've got even _____ time than you. I have to finish two reports before midday.

3) Travelling by train is _____ expensive than going by taxi. But the _____ expensive way to travel is to walk.

4) So _____ people came to the party, but so _____ stayed after the party to clean up. That's why it looks a big mess!

5) _____ people live in Ireland than in Germany.

6) The _____ people live in China.

7) There are too _____ cars on the street and they cause too _____ pollution.

EXERCISE E.

Make sentences with *as ... as*, *-er than* (e.g. bigger than) or *more ... than* (e.g. more beautiful than).

| popular | old | expensive | bad | good | ~~cold~~ | successful | young | successful |

1) It was twenty degrees centigrade yesterday, but today it's five degrees centigrade.

   It's colder today than (it was) yesterday.

2) This old car here costs £3000, but the Cabriolet costs £30,000.

   The Cabriolet _____.

3) You put too much salt on the meat, but the vegetables are OK.

   The vegetables taste much _____.

4) Jane passed all her exams and Philip passed all his exams too.

   Philip _____.

5) Not many people saw the film "Clean Dancing", but millions of people saw the film "Dirty Dancing."

   The film "Dirty Dancing" _____.

6) My sister is twelve years old and my brother is also twelve years old.

   My sister _____.

7) Terry passed four exams and Camilla passed three exams.

   Terry _____.

8) My mother is 38 years old and my father is 43 years old.

   My mother _____.

9) Both Mrs Collins and Mrs Blake can drive. However, Mrs Collins has had three accidents since this morning. Mrs Blake hasn't had any accidents since 1950.

   Mrs Collins is a _____ driver _____.

EXERCISE F.

Put the *adjectives* or *adverbs* in brackets into the correct form and add words where necessary:

1) For me it is much _easier_ (easy) to learn Italian than it is to learn Japanese.

2) I have a big problem: I have the _____ (beautiful) wife in the world. And I buy her the _____ (fine) jewellery that I can find.

3) We live in the _____ (expensive) house in a suburb of Bristol. My six children go to the _____ (good) boarding schools (Internate) in Switzerland. My problem is that I earn only 500 euros a month which is not _____ much _____ I need to pay for all this!

4) I speak English quite well – _____ well _____ my brother. My wife, however, worked in New Zealand for three years so she speaks (good) _____ English _____ I do. However, she thinks that people from Oxford speak _____ (good) English of all.

5) This pencil costs fifty cents. That pencil is a little _____ (expensive) – it costs eighty cents. The gold plated pencil over there is _____ (expensive) of all: It costs eight hundred euros.

6) Man in a restaurant: "Waiter, this coffee is _____ _____ (bad) the one you gave me yesterday. In fact it is the _____ (bad) cup of coffee that I have ever drunk. I don't think you've used _____ much coffee _____ usual.

   Waiter: "That's not true, sir. I've used more water _____ I did yesterday."

7) _____ (safe) way to use a hammer is to ask another person to hold the nails!

8) I play chess quite well, but my wife plays much _____ (well) than me and our five-year-old son, however is _____ (good/well) than his brothers, sister, dad or mum. He plays _____ of all of us – a new Bobby Fisher.

Exercise G.

Translate these sentences:
1) Diese Schule ist eine der modernsten in der Stadt.
2) Das Kino ist näher als die Schule.
3) Ist dieses Auto billiger oder teuerer als dein altes Auto?
4) Die Milch schmeckt schlechter als die Limonade.
5) Er fährt weniger vorsichtig als seine Frau.
6) Ein Harry Potter-Buch ist für viele Kinder genauso interessant wie eine Fernsehsendung.

Let's look at words

> **WATCH OUT! (7)**
> a) Wenn Eric in Kapitel 9 „Into the English World" *pretty good* oder *pretty tasty* sagt ist das Wort *pretty* ein Synonym für *rather* oder *quite* (ziemlich).
> b) Der Verkäufer sagt: *So it (the weather) will be pretty nice, let's hope so.* Deutsche verwechseln häufig die Wörter *leave* und *let*. Die folgenden Beispiele werden Ihnen die Unterschiede zeigen:
>   a) Please don't leave all your clothes on the floor.
>   b) Oh dear – I've left my book in the train.
>   c) Mary, please let me do the washing up for you!
>   d) It's sunny – let's go outside.

Exercise H.

Write in the right words in these sentences (Deutsch: lassen):

1) After he had caught the fish he __let__ it go.
2) I don't really want to drive today. _____ go by train.
3) Have you seen my mobile phone? I'm sure I _____ it in this room.
4) The teacher _____ the pupils hand in their homework a day later.

EXERCISE I.

Add two letters and you will get a proper word! You'll find the words in "Into the English World", chapter 9.

1) I mustn't eat any more _pastry_ (atry, 9A). I'll get too fat!

2) Arsenic is a dangerous _____ (oiso, 9C).

3) It is not important for John where he lives. He can _____ (adp, 9D) to all situations.

4) _____ (lthouh, 9C) Raimund speaks good English he is too shy to speak it.

5) Oh no! Mary is wearing one of her _____ (wed, 9A) hats again. It looks so silly.

6) We must remember that many countries do not have such _____ (abndan, 9D) supplies of water as we do.

7) The weather looks _____ (rett, 9A) bad today.

8) _____ (ntiues, 9A) at a flea market are generally less expensive than in a shop.

EXERCISE J.

Choose the right words:

1) The conditions in this part of Canada are quite **a) harsh b) spectacular c) relaxing**. It's not easy to survive when it is so very cold.
2) Some animals can **a) adapt b) captivate c) reach** to any conditions.
3) Canada is a country with **a) harsh b) abundant c) nature** supplies of water.
4) I didn't leave the party until three o'clock in the morning **a) also b) although c) because** I was tired.
5) **a) Eventually b) Eventual c) Perhaps** he will come to the party tomorrow but I'm not sure.
6) **a) Please b) Pardon c) Certainly** – I can't hear you very well – there's too much noise here!
7) The private car seems to be the most popular **a) way b) means c) chance** of transport in our country.
8) **a) Because of b) Although c) Despite** the bad weather we decided to go out for a walk.

DO YOU STILL REMEMBER?

EXERCISE K.

I hope that you haven't forgotten the *pronouns* from the first programme. Do this exercise to see!

1) Mary fell down yesterday and hurt __herself__.

2) My girlfriend and I love _____ _____. She phones _____ twenty times a day and I phone _____ thirty times a day.

3) "Why are you looking at _____ in such a funny way?" "I like the hat you are wearing. The Queen wears rather strange hats and your hat looks just like one of _____."

4) Mary and Robert live here and Henrietta – a friend of _____ – lives in the flat above them. They have known _____ _____ for many years now.

Es kann wirklich sehr störend sein, wenn jemand mitten in einer wichtigen Besprechung plötzlich einen Hustenanfall erleidet, besonders wenn er dabei ist, wichtige Informationen mitzuteilen!

EXERCISE L.

Make *questions* to find the missing information.

1) … COUGH … installed the software last COUGH.

   __Who installed the software? When did he install the software?__

2) Last COUGH this firm made a profit of $3.

   When _____?

3) Mr Smedley is going to contact our customer, Ms…COUGH, … next Monday.

   Who(m) _____?

4) … COUGH …'s personal assistant will be accompanying him to the meeting next week.

   Whose _____?

5) Mrs Simon works in the ... COUGH ... department of the firm.

   _____?

6) A hundr …COUGH and COUGH firms have opened in this region since last year.

   _____?

7) Mrs … COUGH … attends a management course every Monday evening.

_____?

8) Terence was … COUGH …ing in his office when the sales manager telephoned.

_____?

Dieser Liebesbrief wirkt nicht sehr überzeugend! Zumindest hätte Martin die gravierenden Zeiten-Fehler in diesem Brief an seine Verflossene in Manchester vermeiden können, wenn er die letzten Kapitel dieses Buchs gelesen hätte. Ich bin mir jedoch nicht sicher, ob seine Chancen bei Sally wesentlich gestiegen wären!

EXERCISE M.

Please correct the grammar mistakes.

Darling Sally,

We last ~~have seen~~ saw each other two years ago. Since then I am so unhappy and I now am knowing that you are the only woman I can love. Remember you that day when I first kissed you? You smoked your pipe when I was taking it out of your mouth and was giving you a big kiss. I have been so silly two years ago. When I left you I really knew not how much I loved you. For the last two years I thought about you. Right now – at this very moment I look at your picture and tears are in my eyes. Why I was so stupid to leave you? Please come back to me. Next weekend I drive to Manchester and I hope we can meet.

   Lots of love,
   Martin

P.S. I have watched you on television yesterday and saw you in "Who Wants to be a Millionaire". I was so happy when you were answering the million pound question correctly. Congratulations!

Chapter 10: The Past Perfect Simple, the Past Perfect Continuous and the Future Perfect

The Boss of Police Constable Dobbin **is** angry with him.
"Why **didn't** you **stop** the thief?" he **asks** angrily.
"I'm very sorry," **replies** the policeman, "but after he **had seen** me he **ran** into a cinema."
"And why **didn't** you **run** into the cinema after him?"
"Because I **had** already **seen** the film."

The Past Perfect Simple (Die einfache Form der Vorvergangenheit)

I'm really happy that Police Constable Dobbin is an exception and that most policemen and -women have a much high**er** sense of responsibility (Verantwortungsgefühl) **than** him. Uns jedoch interessiert die neue Zeitform: das *past perfect simple*. Die deutsche Bezeichnung „Vorvergangenheit" ist eigentlich hilfreicher, da sie uns klarmacht, worum es geht: Eine Handlung ist vor einer anderen Handlung in der Vergangenheit abgeschlossen. Zuerst hat der Dieb den Polisten gesehen und erst dann rannte er ins Kino. Der Polizist ist ihm nicht ins Kino gefolgt, weil er den Film schon **gesehen hatte**. Eigentlich keine zu schwierige Struktur, da man im Deutschen eine ähnliche Zeitform hat.

past perfect (Vorvergangenheit)	past simple	present
He **had seen** me.	He **ran**.	The police sergeant **is** angry.

Die Vorvergangenheit wird sehr häufig mit bestimmten Signalwörtern angedeutet. Schwierig zu bilden ist diese Form nicht. Wir nehmen einfach *had + past participle* des Hauptverbs. Sie werden oft die Abkürzungen *'d* oder (in negativen Sätzen) *hadn't* hören.

Signalwörter	Kurzform		past participle
after	I'd	(I hadn't)	swum
already	you'd	(you hadn't)	eaten
because	he'd/she'd	(he/she hadn't)	walked
before	we'd	(we hadn't)	worked
when	you'd	(you hadn't)	gone
as soon as	they'd	(they hadn't)	painted

I'm sure you won't have too many difficulties with the next exercise! However, before you do it, please look at the other *past participle*s of common verbs in the list below. Some of them might help you. As you can see the *past participle* is in over fifty per cent of the cases the same as the *past simple*.

infinitive	past simple	past participle	infinitive	past simple	past participle
bite	bit	bitten	lie	lay	lain
catch	caught	caught	pay	paid	paid
burst	burst	burst	run	ran	run
deal	dealt	dealt	say	said	said
feed	fed	fed	sell	sold	sold
feel	felt	felt	sind	sang	sung
fly	flew	flown	spend	spent	spent
freeze	froze	frozen	steal	stole	stolen
hide	hid	hidden	teach	taught	taught
hit	hit	hit	throw	threw	thrown
lead	led	led	write	wrote	written

EXERCISE A.

Put the verbs in brackets into the past simple or the past perfect simple as required:

1) I _had to go_ (must go) to the doctor's yesterday because a snake _had bitten_ (bite) me.

2) Mr and Mrs Simmonds _____ (be) very happy in life – and then they _____ (meet).

3) Agatha _____ (give) her boyfriend a big kiss, but he _____ (not find) it very romantic because, unfortunately, Agatha _____ (eat) half a kilogram of garlic (Knoblauch) a few hours before.

4) My girlfriend _____ (not phone me or write) to me for twenty-five years, so I _____ (take) the decision to get in touch with her again.

5) When I _____ (get) to my car yesterday, I _____ (realize) that I _____ (leave) my car keys at home.

6) The thief _____ (forget) where he _____ (hide) the money which he _____ (steal) from the bank.

7) I _____ (suffer = leiden) from terrible jet lag after we _____ (fly) from Munich to San Francisco.

8) We _____ (manage) to get the train but we _____ (must run) two kilometres to get to the station.

9) As soon as we _____ (water) the flowers it (start) _____ to rain.

THE PAST PERFECT CONTINUOUS (DIE VERLAUFSFORM DER VORVERGANGENHEIT)

Wir haben die Bekanntschaft mit vier *continuous*-Formen schon gemacht: *present continuous, past continuous, present perfect continuous* und *future continuous*. Deshalb werden Sie keine allzu großen Probleme mit dem *past perfect continuous* haben. Diese Form wird verwendet bei Handlungen bzw. Vorgängen, die bis zu einem bestimmten Zeitpunkt in der Vergangenheit nicht abgeschlossen waren, d. h., sie waren immer noch im Gange. Nehmen wir das Beispiel eines außergewöhnlich unbegabten Sängerduos:

1. Fred and Julia **had sung** only two Mongolian folk songs when the audience **started** throwing rotten eggs (faule Eier) and tomatoes at them.
2. Fred and Julia **had been singing** Mongolian folk songs for only seven minutes when the audience **started** throwing rotten eggs and tomatoes at them.

In beiden Sätzen geht es um eine Handlung, die vor dem Wutausbruch des Publikums stattfand. Im ersten Satz jedoch ist die Handlung abgeschlossen: Sie schafften es gerade zwei Lieder von sich zu geben, bevor sie das Weite suchen mussten. Im zweiten Satz geht es darum, dass die Handlung (das Singen) im Gange, also nicht abgeschlossen war. You'll find more examples in this exercise:

EXERCISE B.

Choose the best options:

1) After Sam _had been studying_ (studied/had been studying) archaeology and Chinese for twenty-two semesters, he _decided_ (decided/had decided) that it _was_ (was/had been) time to leave the university and look for a job. Before he _____ (left/'d been leaving) the university he _____ (took/'d taken) only one exam: the test for his driver's licence.

2) On Saturday evening I _____ (visited/had visited) my girlfriend Myrtle. She _____ (looked/had been looking) tired because she _____ (had worked/had been working) in the kitchen for two hours. She _____ (made/had made) us a huge meal. First we _____ (started/had been starting) with the salad. I _____ (ate/had been eating) for only about two minutes when I suddenly I _____ (felt/'d felt) sick. I _____ (looked/had looked) at the salad and I _____ (saw/had seen) three snails (Schnecken). Myrtle _____ (had forgotten/had been forgetting) to wash the lettuce (Kopfsalat) before she _____ (gave/had given) it to me and I _____ (ate/'d eaten) one of the snails.

3) We _____ ('d run/'d been running) to the station for about an hour when I _____ (felt/'d felt) out of breath (atemlos). We _____ ('d run/'d been running) about six kilometres and we still _____ (had/had been having) about another three kilometres to run.

4) George suddenly _____ (got/had been getting) up from his armchair and _____ (switched/had been switching) off the television. He was very angry because he _____ ('d watched/'d been watching) television for five hours and none of the programmes _____ (were/had been) really good.

Wie Carolin in der zehnten Sendung erklärt hat, wird das *past perfect continuous* nicht so häufig verwendet. Es reicht aus, wenn Sie die Form in Texten oder Gesprächen erkennen können, ohne dass Sie die Form selbst einsetzen. Dasselbe gilt für die nächste Zeitform:

ANOTHER FUTURE FORM: THE FUTURE PERFECT
(EINE WEITERE ZUKUNFTSFORM: THE FUTURE PERFECT)

Johnny's grandfather had a glass of beer on the table in front of him. Johnny was only nine years old, but he wanted to drink some of his grandfather's beer.
"I'm sorry," said his grandfather, "but **you'll have to wait** until you're 18 years old before you can drink my beer."
"But, that's silly," Johny said. "You**'ll have drunk** the beer **by then**!"

Johny meint nicht, dass sein Opa das Bier unbedingt heute, morgen, nächstes Jahr oder in fünf Jahren austrinken wird. Bis zu seinem 18. Geburtstag jedoch **wird** er das Bier **ausgetrunken haben.** Wie Sie sehen, gibt es in der deutschen Sprache dieselbe Form.

Bitte wenden Sie in der nächsten Übung die verschiedenen Zukunftsformen an.

EXERCISE C.

Choose the best option:

1) Maybe we _won't finish_ (don't finish/won't finish) the work on Wednesday or even on Thursday, but _we'll have finished_ (we'll be finishing/we'll have finished) it by the end of the week.

2) Go to the library in Katharine Street at 10. 15 am. _____ (I'll have waited/I'll be waiting) for you there.

3) Before you _____ (kiss/you'll kiss) me _____ (you're having/you'll have) to take the chewing gum out of your mouth.

4) Else and I have decided something important: _____ (We'll emigrate/We're going to emigrate) to Australia.

5) I think _____ (I'll be/I am) home tomorrow at five thirty or six, or maybe even six thirty. So, if _____ (you phone/you'll be phoning) at seven o'clock, _____ (I'll be arriving/I'll have arrived) home.

6) Bob tells me that _____ (he'll have installed/he'll be installing) the new software by Saturday at the latest, unless he _____ (will have/has) to fly to America this week.

7) _____ (We're seeing/We see) our American cousin Christine tomorrow. Her flight _____ (leaves/will have left) Miami at 4.15 am, so at 4.20 she'll be in her seat and _____ (she'll be watching/she watches) movies. Before _____ (she lands/she's going to land) in Frankfurt she _____ (is watching/will have watched) at least three movies.

Let's look at words

Before we deal with some of the vocabulary from the tenth programme, please relax with this crossword puzzle on some of the words we've had in the past chapters:

Exercise D.

Crossword puzzle:

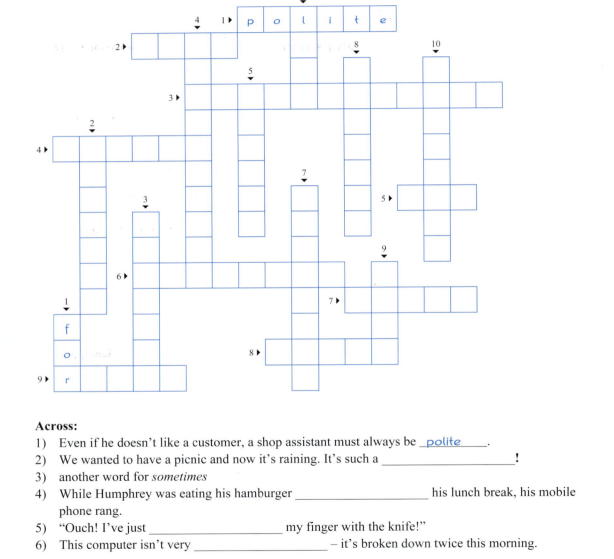

Across:
1) Even if he doesn't like a customer, a shop assistant must always be __polite__.
2) We wanted to have a picnic and now it's raining. It's such a _____!
3) another word for *sometimes*
4) While Humphrey was eating his hamburger _____ his lunch break, his mobile phone rang.
5) "Ouch! I've just _____ my finger with the knife!"
6) This computer isn't very _____ – it's broken down twice this morning.
7) "Tom, please wash your dirty hands before you play the piano!" "That's not necessary, Mum. Today I'm only _____ to play on the black keys."(Tasten)

102 | Chapter 10: the past perfect simple, the past perfect continuous and the future perfect

8) Anabella doesn't do more than she has to. She's the _____ ambitious person I've ever met.
9) The price of petrol didn't rise much before May, but since May it has _____ enormously.

Down:
1) "Let's go to the theatre instead of the cinema _for_ a change."
2) The rent for the flat is quite reasonable, but the _____ costs for electricity etc. are quite high.
3) The medical _____ in many countries is not as good as it is here in Europe.
4) "It was very _____ (rücksichtsvoll) of you to offer to help me."
5) We _____ the bus yesterday just at the last minute. We'll have to leave the house earlier tomorrow!
6) Many people drink _____ water than they should.
7) a rather irregular plural
8) Please don't _____ (verwechseln, durcheinanderbringen) the words *since* and *for*.
9) "These shoes don't cost much, do they?" "No, they don't, but last month they _____ $3 more."
10) _____ it was raining heavily we still decided to go out and play tennis.

Exercise E.

Can you find the words in the book "Into the English World" chapter 10 that these words refer to (sich beziehen auf)?
1) No part of the political governmental system can rule without the control of other parts of the system.
2) There is a big ceremony before a person becomes president of the USA.
3) You can say that Big Ben, the Niagara Falls and the Statue are all examples of these.
4) This expression means that members of a parliament, senate, etc. come together to decide on laws.
5) This amazing gadget can help you if you lose your way.
6) This means that the people of a country come together to think about a special event (Ereignis) in their history.

1) _checks and balances_   4) _____
2) _____   5) _____
3) _____   6) _____

DO YOU STILL REMEMBER?

We begin this revision part with a few exercises to help you remember the grammar that we've talked about in the last nine chapters. To start with two funny stories. I hope you like them:

EXERCISE F.

In a raffle (Tombola, Verlosung) you can sometimes get good prizes! Entscheiden Sie sich, welche der jeweils zwei Möglichkeiten in der folgenden Geschichte richtig sind.

Brian Davis was very __tired__ (tired/tiredly) and __while__ (while/during) he __was sleeping__ (slept/was sleeping) __peacefully__ (peacefully/peaceful) in his office, Mr Parks, his boss came in.

"Good morning, Mr Davis, I can see you __aren't working__ (don't work/aren't working) very __hard__ (hardly/hard) at the moment," he said. "And I'm afraid I must complain: You __have come__ (came/have come) late to work four times since the beginning of the week. If I remember __correctly__ (correctly/correct) your working day begins at nine o'clock, not ten o'clock. Why don't you come early for a change?"

"I'm __extremely__ (extreme/extremely) sorry, sir," Mr Davis said, "but since Monday I __have had to make__ (must make/have had to make) arrangements for my holiday in Miami next week."

"Holiday! What holiday?" Mr Parks shouted.

"Oh, I am spending five weeks in Florida in the biggest and most expensive hotel in Miami. My plane __leaves__ (leaves/leave) London Heathrow airport at 7 pm tonight. This time next week, I __will be lying__ (will be lying/lie) on the beach."

"But I don't understand," Mr Parks said. "How can you afford such a holiday. And another thing: That car of __yours__ (you/yours) – it's much bigger and more expensive __than__ (as/than) mine. You __have only been working__ (have only been working/were working) with us __for__ (for/since) three months and you only earn $500 a month. That isn't as much __as__ (as/than) you need for such a holiday and such a car!"

"Well," Brian said, "I'll tell you the secret. There are 800 employees in your firm, Mr Parks, and at the end of each month I sell a raffle ticket to each employee for $5. The winner __gets__ (gets/becomes) my salary of $500."

EXERCISE G.

Put the words in brackets into their correct forms:

Last year Mr Brady, a manager of an American oil firm, and his wife __flew__ (fly) to Europe to spend their holiday. They __had already seen__ (already/see) Rome, Madrid and Munich and now they wanted to see the capital of France.

On the second day of their stay in Paris, they __were walking__ (walk) along the River Seine when Mr Brady __said__ (say) to his wife: "We __have been walking__ (walk) along the Seine for the last ten minutes and we __haven't seen__ (not see) anything interesting yet."

"What __do you mean__ (you/mean)?" his wife __said__ (say).

"We __are walking__ (walk) along one of the __most interesting__ (interesting) rivers in Europe now! And you …" Suddenly, while Mrs Brady __was speaking__ (speak), they __saw__ (see) a big tower. "Look," Mrs Brady __shouted__ (shout) __excitedly__ (excited). "That tower looks __funny__ (funny) – it's made of iron! It's __higher__ (high) and __more interesting__ (interesting) than any tower that I know."

"Huh!," her husband __replied__ (reply) __impatiently__ (impatient). "That's the Eiffel Tower. The French are __really__ (real) __slow__ (slow). They __built__ (build) that derrick (Bohrturm) over a hundred years ago but so far, not a drop of oil __has come__ (come) out of it."

EXERCISE H.

In comparisons we can say *He's taller than I am.* or *He's taller than me*.
Instead of *That's as good as my car.* we can say *That's as good as mine*. Change these sentences:

1) Mr Frewer's wife is taller than Mary.

   Mr Frewer's wife is taller than **her**.

2) Ms Finch's office isn't as large as my one is.

   _____

3) James's car is more expensive than our car is.

   _____

4) My sister-in-law is older than her husband.

   _____

5) Our house is nearer the town centre than their house is.

6) I've got much less time than they have.

7) His computer is more reliable than Marshall's computer is.

8) I really think that your wife works more than you do.

9) She can play the piano better than her brother.

10) Our car breaks down as often as your car does.

11) Geraldine doesn't live in the same house as her sister does.

12) Raphael speaks as many languages as we do.

13) John's job isn't as exhausting (anstrengend) as Martina's is.

Exercise I.

Translate these sentences:
1) Während wir gestern im Garten schliefen, fing es an zu regnen.
2) Ich habe gestern auch nicht gearbeitet.
3) Seit drei Stunden spielt sie mit ihrem Sohn Fußball.
4) Warum benutzt er weniger Wasser für seinen Garten als wir?
5) Seine Stimme hörte sich sonderbar an und ich konnte ihn nicht so gut hören.
6) Immer weniger Leute fahren in London (mit dem Auto). Je weniger Leute mit dem Auto fahren, desto besser ist die Luft (desto weniger Luftverschmutzung° gibt es).

° Luftverschmutzung = air pollution

CHAPTER 11: THE PASSIVE, RELATIVE PRONOUNS AND CLAUSES

In diesem Kapitel haben wir vieles zu diskutieren: die Passivkonstruktion und die Relativsätze. Meine Empfehlung ist wie immer: dose it! Wenn Ihnen wenig Zeit zur Verfügung steht, dann machen Sie am Tag wenigstens eine oder zwei Übungen. Wir werden auf die beiden Konstruktionen in den folgenden Kapiteln und im Verlauf des Telekolleg-Hauptkurses zurückkommen. Deshalb brauchen Sie sich überhaupt keine Sorgen zu machen, falls Sie nicht alles sofort verstehen und verdauen können. Remember: Rome wasn't built in a day!

THE PASSIVE (DAS PASSIV)

Question: Where **are** elephants **found**?
Answer: Elephants are so big that they **are** hardly ever **lost**!

Wie im Deutschen können wir im Englischen unsere Sätze so umstellen, dass wir das, was wir als wichtig erachten, mehr betonen: Das Wichtige wird zum neuen Subjekt.
Statt *Where **do** people **find** elephants?* können wir sagen: *Where **are** elephants **found**?*
Statt *People hardly ever **lose** elephants.* können wir sagen: *Elephants **are** hardly ever **lost**.*
Das Passiv wird dabei genauso wie im Deutschen gebildet, außer dass man eine entsprechende Form des Verbs *to be* statt des Verbs *werden* verwendet. Betrachten wir die zwei Beispiele aus der Sendung sowie zwei zusätzliche Beispiele und das Vorgehen wird Ihnen klar sein:

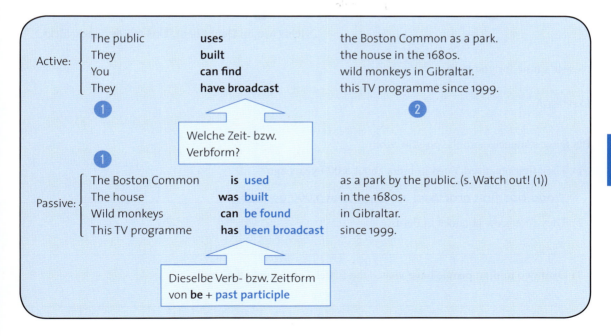

> **WATCH OUT! (1)**
> Für die Präposition „von" gibt es im Englischen drei Übersetzungen:
> 1. St Paul's Cathedral was designed **by** Sir Christopher Wren. (Passivsätze)
> 2. This is one **of** my books. (Genitiv)
> 3. I drove **from** London to Cambridge.
>   His dad took the cigarette **from** him.
>   We work **from** 9 am to 5 pm. I come **from** Germany.
>   (= Änderung des Orts, Angabe eines Zeitraumes, Herkunft)

Die alten Objekte *the Boston Commons*, *the house*, *wild monkeys*, *TV programmes* werden in den Passivsätzen zu den Subjekten der Sätze.

In der aktiven Form haben wir das *present simple* (*uses*), das *past simple* (*built*), *can + infinitive* (*can find*) und das *present perfect* (*have broadcast*). Im Passiv nehmen wir jeweils genau dieselben Formen von *to be* (*is*, *was*, *can be*, *have been*) + die *past participles* der Hauptverben (*used*, *built*, *found*, *broadcast*). Wie Sie sehen, müssen wir bei unserem letzten Beispiel statt *have been boadcast has been broadcast* nehmen, da unser neues Subjekt jetzt in der Einzahl steht (TV programme).

Häufig hat man die Wahl zwischen zwei möglichen Subjekten eines Passivsatzes:

Activ: They sent **us the new catalogue**.
Passive: **The new catalogue** was sent to us.   Oder: **We** were sent the new catalogue.

Nicht (wie im Deutschen): **Uns** wurde ... geschickt.

Now it's time for you to try.

EXERCISE A.

Put these sentences into the *passive form*:

1) They first practised Yoga in India about 5,000 years ago.

   Yoga was first practised in India about 5,000 years ago.

2) They first grew potatoes in Peru.

3) Over two million people have visited the Eiffel Tower since they built it.

4) The people in Afghanistan usually celebrate the birth of a child six days after its birth.

5) On this day they give the baby a name.

6) In Algeria people consider (betrachten, dafür halten) it impolite to point at people or objects.

7) They actually built the Statue of Liberty in France and then they transported it to America as a present.

8) They speak eight hundred different languages in Papua New Guinea.

9) When a child loses a tooth in Malaysia they must bury it. The Malaysians think that they should give the tooth back to the Earth, because it is a part of the human body.

10) In future they won't build new nuclear power stations (Kernkraftwerke) in Germany.

11) The firm has offered each of the employees a new job.

Exercise B.

Put the verb in the right form:

1) Many cars were __sold__ (sell) last year.
2) A big shopping centre _____ (build) in the town next year.
3) This house _____ (not paint) since we bought it.
4) This computer _____ (cannot repair) so easily.
5) At present, the engines of our cars _____ (manufacture = herstellen) in our factory in Belgium.
6) I _____ (tell) the good news last week.

RELATIVE PRONOUNS AND CLAUSES (RELATIVPRONOMEN UND -SÄTZE)

Circus owner: "Do you know that you left the lion's cage open last night?"
Employee: "Don't worry. I don't know anyone **who** would want to steal a lion."

Der zweite Schwerpunkt des elften Kapitels sind die Relativsätze. Erfreulich ist, dass sich der Satzbau im Relativsatz nicht ändert.

He would steal a lion.   ⇨   I don't know anyone **who** would steal a lion.

Auch in Nebensätzen anderer Art (z. B. in einem dass-Satz) bleibt der Satzbau gleich:

You left the lion's cage open last night.   ⇨   Do you know **that** you left the lion's cage open last night?

Wie in allen Sprachen klingt es (und liest es sich) besser, wenn mehrere Informationen (aber nicht zu viele!) in einem Satz und nicht in mehreren Sätzen untergebracht werden. Sie erinnern sich sicherlich an Carolins Beispiel:

Paul Revere is a national hero. He died in Boston.
Diese zwei Sätze werden zu:
Paul Revere, who is a national hero, died in Boston.

Um Relativsätze zu bilden, brauchen wir meistens Relativpronomen. Diese Übersicht kann uns dabei helfen:

who	wer
whose	wessen
to/for whom	an/für wen
whom	wen, wem
= persons	
which	der, die, das
= things or animals	

Häufig kann man auch *that* statt *who*, *which* und *whom* verwenden.

Die folgende Übung wird Ihnen helfen, die richtigen *relative pronouns* anzuwenden:

EXERCISE C.

Put in the right *relative pronouns*:

1) The man ___whose___ bike you're using is my brother.

2) Wendy is the attractive woman _____ wants to marry my brother.

3) BMW is the name of the car _____ is easiest to spell.

4) This swimming pool is the one _____ only good swimmers can use.

5) And the empty swimming pool is for people _____ can't swim.

6) The students for _____ this course is aimed at can already speak some English.

7) Dr Smith, _____ patient was sitting nervously in front of him, was very happy: "I've got some good news for you, Mr Davis," he said. "It wasn't your pulse _____ stopped. It was your watch!"

8) "Darling, you're the only woman _____ I love. Will you always remember me?" "Of course, I will. You're the man _____ name I always forget."

Now try to make *relative clauses*.

EXERCISE D.

Make one sentence instead of two. Use *relative pronouns*.

1) John lives near us. He works in my firm.
   John, who works in my firm, lives near us. / John, who lives near us, works in our firm.

2) Mary Collins works hard for her family. You know her husband.
   _____

3) This book is very interesting. I borrowed it from the library.
   _____

4) "I can do something. The other children in my class can't do it," says Sally proudly. "I can read my handwriting."
   _____
   _____

5) This book is about doing repairs in the house. I bought it for my husband.
   _____

6) Fred jumped into the river and saved the little girl's life. He deserves a medal.
   _____
   _____

7) Cedric wrote a letter to his grandmother. It was very long.

_____

8) This car would be best for our needs. It is unfortunately too expensive.

_____

9) We have informed the employees. Some of them live far from the factory. (whom!)

_____

10) This horse is really beautiful. It belongs to Humphrey.

_____

11) You saw a woman yesterday. She is my English teacher in Telekolleg.

_____

12) My neighbour is an aggressive man. His dog is looking at you very strangely.

_____

> **WATCH OUT! (2)**
> Es gibt drei Fehlerquellen, die im gesprochenen oder geschriebenen Englisch die Kommunikation erschweren können:
> a) Verwechseln Sie bitte nicht *who* (nur bei Menschen zu verwenden) und *which* (nur bei Dingen und Tieren). Wie Sie in Übung D. sehen, kann man dem Problem oft aus dem Weg gehen, indem man das Relativpronomen *that* benutzt.
> b) Verwechseln Sie bitte nicht *what* und *which*. *Which* bezieht sich auf etwas, das vorher im Satz erwähnt wird. *What* bezieht sich auf etwas, das nachher im Satz erwähnt wird.
> c) Verwechseln Sie bitte nicht *who's* (= *who is*) und *whose* (dessen, wessen).

> Joe has got his first book and, **what** is more, he has already read two pages of it.
>
> The book, **which (that)** he is reading, is called: "Men can cook, too!"
>
> Joe is not really someone **who's** interested in such books. **(who's = who is)**
> But I know **who's** given him the book. **(who's = who has)**
> The person **whose** idea it was to give him the book was his wife.

EXERCISE E.

Choose the right alternative:
1) I'll never forget __what__ (what/~~which/whose/who's~~) we've seen on our holiday together.
2) The professor said many things _____ (what/which/whose/who's) I didn't understand.
3) I'm sorry, I didn't hear _____ (what/which/whose/who's) you just said.
4) The beautiful little girl _____ (what/which/whose/who's) standing there is my daughter.
5) The things _____ (what/which/whose/who's) come your way in life are not always _____ (what/which/whose/who's) you are expecting …
6) Children _____ (what/which/whose/who's) parents speak different languages often learn foreign languages more quickly.
7) I don't know _____ (what/which/whose/who's) making so much noise in the street.
8) Do you know _____ (what/which/whose/who's) car this is? George's or Miriam's?

Es ist möglich – und im informellen Englisch sehr gebräuchlich –, die Relativpronomen *who*, *which* und *that* in Relativsätzen auszulassen, wenn sie Objekt eines Verbs (oder einer Präposition) sind:

After he has driven in the town for an hour, the tourist finally finds a free parking lot.
"Great," he says. "I've found a parking lot. Now all **I have to do** is find out the name of the town **I'm in**."
Unser unterhaltsamer Tourist sagt: *all I have to do* statt *all **that** I have to do*.
Und weiter: *the name of the town I'm in* statt *the name of the town **which/that** I'm in*.

You'll get the idea when you do the next exercise.

EXERCISE F.

Make eight sensible sentences (siehe auch Watch out! (4)):

1)	Somebody has found	we're waiting for	his friends give him.
2)	The exhibition	you're reading	is an expert on Paul Revere.
3)	The woman	one of the restaurants	was once a Roman road.
4)	Glenda has already read about	the money	has works by local painters.
5)	We went to	we were walking on	we saw at the cinema.
6)	That newspaper	you planted last autumn	you lost at the shop.
7)	Tim didn't know that the road	you talked to yesterday	my wife likes so much.
8)	Those seeds	the film	is going to be late.
9)	I'm sure that the bus	we went to	isn't very objective.
10)	He never listens to	the advice	have become beautiful flowers.

Tipp 1: Wieder haben wir eine Konstruktion, die Sie in gesprochenen oder geschriebenen Aussagen erkennen sollen. Ich empfehle Ihnen aber, auf Nummer sicher zu gehen: Wenn Sie sich nicht ganz klar darüber sind, ob Sie *who*, *which* oder *that* auslassen können, verwenden Sie immer ein Relativpronomen. Die Sätze *Somebody found the money* **which** *you lost at the shop.* und *Now all* **that** *I have to do is find out the name of the town* **which/that** *I'm in.* sind vollkommen in Ordnung.

Tipp 2: In der elften Sendung hat Carolin den Unterschied zwischen dem *defining* und dem *non-defining relative clause* erklärt. Der einzige Unterschied besteht darin, dass bei „notwendigen Relativsätzen" Kommas gesetzt werden. Wir werden im Hauptkurs darauf zurückkommen. Aber ob Sie ein Komma zu viel oder zu wenig setzen, ist nicht so wichtig. Carolin hat auch erklärt und Sie haben es ebenso in den Übungen festgestellt, dass man häufig *that* statt *who* oder *which* verwenden kann. Dies gilt aber nicht bei Ausdrücken wie *none of which* (keiner von denen), *a few of which* und so weiter.

LET'S LOOK AT WORDS

WATCH OUT! (3)

Es gibt eine Reihe von englischen Wörtern, die deutschen Wörtern erstaunlich ähnlich sind. Vorsicht! Diese sind sogenannte *false friends* – sie haben im Englischen eine ganz andere Bedeutung.
Here are some of the *false friends* that you have had so far:

English	German
rent	Miete
pension	Rente
country	Land
land	Boden
actually	tatsächlich
topical/of importance nowadays	aktuell
room	Platz, Zimmer
place	Ort, Stelle
sensible	vernünftig
sensitive	sensibel
to visit	besuchen
to attend	regelmäßig besuchen (Schule usw.)

EXERCISE G.

Write in words from the list above to complete the sentences:

1) I'm sorry, but I can't _visit_ Reinhard tonight – every Thursday evening I _attend_ my English course in the VHS.

2) It's not a _____ thing to argue with John – he's too _____!

3) _____, I don't think this problem is _____ nowadays.

4) He can't afford to pay the _____ for his flat because his _____ is too low.

5) This town is a nice _____, but unfortunately, there's not much _____ to build new houses in it.

6) Marjorie bought some _____ in a far-away _____.

WATCH OUT! (4)

Josh sagt in „Into the English World", 11A: *There used to be a third floor up on top.* (Früher gab es eine dritte Etage ganz oben). Bitte verwechseln Sie diese Form nicht mit *to be used + ...ing*.
He is used to speaking English = Er ist daran gewohnt, Englisch zu sprechen.
He used to speak English. = Früher hat er Englisch gesprochen (aber er spricht nicht mehr Englisch).

EXERCISE H.

There are fourteen words – or variations of words – from the book "Into the English World" 11A and 11D here. Can you find the other twelve?

a	l	s	u	f	f	e	r	n	i	o
p	s	e	p	a	r	a	t	e	g	u
r	c	d	e	p	e	n	d	e	n	t
o	a	b	o	m	x	o	p	d	a	s
t	m	d	g	u	i	d	e	s	s	k
e	n	u	o	k	e	i	u	t	n	i
c	e	m	e	t	e	r	y	o	y	r
t	e	p	a	n	f	i	j	r	e	t
e	v	o	l	u	n	t	e	e	r	s
u	l	s	r	o	s	h	a	r	e	s
f	k	t	u	i	r	e	l	x	h	a
b	c	o	r	n	e	r	e	l	i	b

EXERCISE I.

Use some of the words from exercise H. to complete these sentences:

1) Raymond didn't swim in the Dead Sea – he just _floated_ on the surface (Oberfläche) of the water.

2) European countries are _____ on other countries for the import of raw materials.

3) The secretary of this environmental organisation gets a regular salary but the others who work here are unpaid _____.

4) Miriam has a _____ bedroom in the flat, but she _____ the bathroom and kitchen with two other students who live in the flat.

5) The rent is quite low but unfortunately the flat is on the _____ of two busy roads.

6) It's really terrible! Some people _____ their old furniture in this wood. They must think this beautiful wood is their own rubbish _____!

7) In some countries people have to pay a lot of _____ from their salaries.

8) People who live on the _____ of big cities often need a very long time to get to their work in the centre.

Chapter 11: the passive, relative pronouns and clauses

Do you still remember?

As usual, here are a few exercises to test what we have looked at in the last few programmes and chapters.

Exercise J.

Translate the words in brackets:

1) In Monaco nearly 33,000 people live in (weniger als) __less than__ two square kilometres. That means 16,500 people per square kilometre. England is not as densely (dicht) populated (wie) _____ Monaco. There are only 246 people per square kilometre in England. So Monaco is one of the (bevölkerungsreichsten) _____ countries in the world.

2) There are (mehr Kängurus als) _____ people in Australia.

3) There are six times (so viele) _____ sheep in the United Kingdom (wie) _____ there are in the USA.

4) Canada has the (höchste) _____ proportion of left-handed people.

5) The United Kingdom is (teurer) _____ to live in (als) _____ Germany. Japan is perhaps one of the (teuersten) _____ countries in the world.

6) Vatican City is 0.44 square kilometres – Hyde Park is (dreimal so groß) _____ _____. Only 800 people live in Vatican City so it is the (am wenigsten bevölkerte) _____ country on earth.

7) The (kleinste) _____ and (am wenigsten bequeme) _____ church in the world is in Kentucky, USA. In this church there is (viel weniger Platz als) _____ in any other church. Actually there is room for only three people inside the church!

Exercise K.

Put the words and expressions in the right places!

1) Mabel doesn't sing Mongolian folk songs. (on Sundays, often, in the bath)

   __Mabel doesn't often sing Mongolian folk songs in the bath on Sundays.__

2) On the one hand the cost of living high in England. (is, extremely) However, on the other hand, a lot of interesting things to see in the English countryside. (always, are, there)

_____
_____
_____

3) We stayed in a small hut in the Alps. (a few years ago)

_____

4) Georgette and Raymond Rowley played Hector Millstein's concerto for mouth organ and bagpipes at the concert on Sunday. (beautifully)

_____
_____

5) I've had to travel abroad in these last few years. (seldom)

_____

Exercise L.

Translate these sentences:
1) Sie arbeiten in dieser Firma seit vielen Jahren, nicht wahr?
2) Obwohl Alexander normalerweise Hollywood-Filme nicht mag, schaut er im Moment einen James-Bond-Film an.
3) Vor siebzig Jahren habe ich meine Frau zum ersten Mal geküsst.
4) George wurde ungeduldig, weil er vier Stunden auf den Zug warten musste.

Phew! That was a lot for one chapter, wasn't it! Never mind: "Nothing is achieved without effort." – as the English say (ohne Fleiß, kein Preis). As you have worked so hard, here are two last jokes with five *passives* and a *relative clause*!

A driver of a sports car is stopped by the police.
"You were driving too fast and you've been photographed."
"Great!" says the driver. "After the photos have been developed (entwickeln) could you send me three copies, please?"

John Smith has been arrested (verhaften) because he sold a **medicine he promised** would give eternal life (ewiges Leben). He was arrested for the same crime in 1567, 1778 and 1856.

Remember? We can say: *which he promised* or we can leave out the word *which*.

Chapter 12: indirect speech

In this chapter we're going to look at a structure that you will often see in texts in English: *indirect speech*. I will be giving you a few exercises to support Carolin's explanations in the twelfth programme of the preparatory course. At the end, as usual, there are a few exercises to help you to remember some of the structures we have discussed in the past eleven programmes and chapters.

Indirect Speech I: Statements (Indirekte Rede I: Aussagesätze)

Sehr oft müssen wir wiedergeben, was ein anderer sagt, schreibt oder denkt bzw. gesagt, geschrieben oder gedacht hat:

Africans say: "Until the lions have their own historians, stories of hunting will always glorify the hunter and not the lion."

Africans **say that** until lions **have** their own historians, stories of hunting **will** always glorify the hunter and not the lion.

Wie Sie sehen, brauchen wir das Gesagte kaum oder überhaupt nicht zu ändern, wenn das Verb des Sagens oder Meinens in der Gegenwart steht.
Etwas schwieriger wird es, wenn das *reporting verb* in der Vergangenheit steht:

The Italian writer Italo Svevo said over eighty years ago: "There are three things I always forget. Names, faces – the third one I can't remember."

The Italian writer Italo Svevo said over eighty years ago that there **were** three things **he** always **forgot**. He mentioned names and faces but **couldn't** remember the third one.

Man ändert also in der englischen Sprache einfach die Zeitform des Verbs, statt wie im Deutschen eine zusätzliche Form, nämlich den Konjunktiv, zu verwenden (gäbe, vergesse, könne). In unserem Beispiel nimmt man statt des *present simple* das *past simple*.
Das Verfahren nennt sich **backshift** oder noch besser **tense shift** – Zurückverschieben: *present simple* wird zu *past simple*; *past simple* wird zu *past perfect*; *will* wird zu *would*. Eine ganze Reihe von Formen ändern sich nicht. Falls Ihnen dies alles kompliziert erscheint, dürfte diese Übersicht für Klarheit sorgen. Andere Formen können Sie leicht selbst ableiten (z. B. *I'm going to work hard = She said she <u>was</u> going to work hard.*)

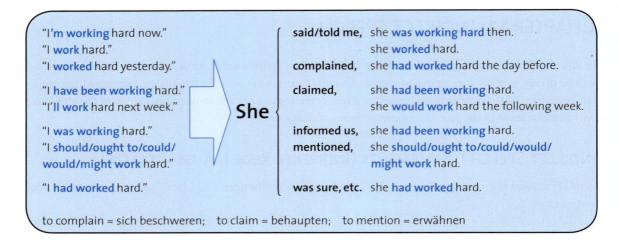

In der Tabelle können Sie sehen, dass man häufig einige kleine Änderungen bei den Zeitangaben, Pronomen und anderen Wörtern vornehmen muss:

Zeitangaben:
yesterday ⇨ the day before/the previous day
tomorrow ⇨ the following day/the next day
the next month ⇨ the following month
last night ⇨ the night before
now (mit Bedeutung „sofort") ⇨ then/at that time/at once/right away/immediately/usw.
Manchmal kann man *now* einfach weglassen.

Pronomen (abhängig von Sprechsituation):
I ⇨ he, she
we ⇨ they
us ⇨ them
etc.

Andere Wörter, z. B.:
this, that ⇨ the, that
here ⇨ there

Die folgende Übung wird Ihnen helfen, das Prinzip zu begreifen:

Exercise A.

What did they say?

1) "We'll be quite busy tomorrow."

   The secretary said they would be quite busy the following/next day.

2) "Dr Gray is away on business."

   Dr Gray's personal assistant told us (that) _____.

3) "They haven't found the client's new address."

   The manager was sorry that _____.

4) "We should hold the meeting here in our office."

   My colleague thought _____.

5) "We cannot supply the goods before the end of next month."

   I was told that _____.

6) "The nurse gave me my sleeping pill at 4 o'clock in the morning after she had woken me up to do it!"

   The patient complained that _____.

7) "Although my computer beats me at chess it doesn't beat me at kick boxing."

   Our son claimed that although _____.

8) "My dad has just got a new car and last night he painted it and changed the number plates."

   Little Sue told us that _____.

9) "This week we're working on your new order."

   The production manager assured us _____.

10) "While the thief was driving away in my car, I noted down the number of the car."

    The silly man told the police _____.

> **WATCH OUT! (1)**
> **tell/say**
> *Tell* verlangt normalerweise ein indirektes Objekt:
> He told **me (you/her/us/them/the postman/George)** that he was tired.
> ~~He told that he was tired.~~
> (Ausnahmen: to tell a joke; to tell a story; to tell a lie; to tell the truth)
> Bei *say* bitte aufpassen:
> Statt: He said ~~me~~ that he was tired. He said he was tired. Oder: he said <u>to me</u> that he was tired.

INDIRECT SPEECH II: QUESTIONS (INDIREKTE REDE II: FRAGEN)

Seven-year old Marian was puzzled and asked her mum what **sheep counted when they couldn't get to sleep.**
You can imagine what Marian actually said: "Mummy", she asked, "what do sheep count when they can't get to sleep?"

The boy asked his teacher **if/whether** he knew the name for an Arab milkman.
Again in *direct speech*:
The boy asked his teacher: "Do you know the name for an Arab milkman?"
(The teacher didn't know, but the answer is, of course: a milk sheikh.)

Sie sehen, dass bei Fragen in der indirekten Rede die Umschreibung mit *do* nicht verwendet wird. Wenn ein Fragewort, wie z. B. *when, why, who, how many, whose* etc. fehlt, nehmen wir *if* oder *whether* (ob).

EXERCISE B.

Put these questions into *indirect speech*:

1) "Do you know your client's phone number?"

   Michael asked Tania _if she knew her client's phone number._

2) "Can you install the computer today?"

   The sales manager asked us _____.

3) "Where did you buy that mobile phone?"

   Mr Dykes asked his colleague _____.

4) "Are you the person responsible for security in our firm, Mr Clark?"

   George enquired (a synonym for *to ask*) _____
   _____.

5) "When are you going on holiday?"

   Our neighbour asked Mr and Mrs Skiffle _____.

6) "Is there a synonym for the word *synonym*?"

   Chaim asked his teacher _____.

7) "Why haven't you informed your passengers that there will be a delay?"

   The angry passenger asked the train driver _____

   _____.

8) "Will there be many guests at your party tomorrow, Rose?"

   Peter asked _____

   _____.

9) "What time did you get home last night?"

   Mrs Samuels asked her teenage daughter _____

   _____.

10) "Must we really leave the party now?"

    Mrs Roe was a bit disappointed and asked her grandson _____

    _____.

INDIRECT SPEECH III: REQUESTS AND COMMANDS (INDIREKTE REDE III: BITTEN UND AUFFORDERUNGEN)

"Tom! Take your goldfish out of the bath immediately!"	⇨	She told Tom *to take* his goldfish out of the bath immediately!
"Tom, please don't put your finger in my soup."	⇨	Tom's mother asked him *not to put* his finger in her soup."

I'm glad that not all children are as badly behaved (benehmen sich schlecht) as Tom. His poor mum must have a difficult time. However, the two sentences show us how we can express requests and commands in *indirect speech*:

In der indirekten Rede werden Aufforderungen und Bitten normalerweise mit *ask/tell* + *to* + Infinitiv oder in der Verneinung mit *ask/tell* + *not* + *to* + Infinitiv ausgedrückt.

Now it's your turn!

Exercise C.

Put these sentences into *indirect speech*:

1) "Don't smoke here, in our house."

   Bertha's mother told her not to smoke (there) in their house.

2) "Waiter! Take these three snails out of my salad right now!"

   The customer _____.

3) "Please wait for me in my office, Ms O'Connell."

   The boss _____.

4) "Darling, please don't play the saxophone in bed."

   Mrs Smith _____.

5) "Sheila! Remove the paper before you eat the chocolate."

   Sheila's mum _____.

6) "Please don't eat so much, Terry."

   Terry's dad _____.

Exercise D.

Translate these sentences. Use the structure: ask/tell + (not) to + infinitive.

1) Sie sagten mir, ich solle nicht zu spät kommen.
2) Unser Chef bat uns darum, den Kunden einen Katalog zu schicken.
3) Alan bat sie darum, den Brief schnell zu schreiben.
4) Miranda bat uns darum, ihr Handy zu reparieren.
5) Der Lehrer sagte zu Philip, er solle von anderen Schülern nicht abschreiben.

> **WATCH OUT! (2)**
> Two more examples of *false friends*:
> **German: Chef = English:** boss, employer   **English: chef = German:** Hauptkoch

Well, that was a lot for today. If you still wish to see examples of *indirect speech*, please look at the mini-dialogues in exercise E. Can you find the mistakes?

EXERCISE E.

In each text on the right, there are two mistakes. Please find them.

Dentist: "I will have to take out one of your teeth, but it will only take me a minute." Patient: "How much will it cost?" Doctor: "It will only cost you one hundred pounds. Patient: "One hundred pounds is very expensive for something that only takes a minute!" Dentist: "Well, I could take your tooth out more slowly if you wish."	The dentist told his patient that he ~~will~~ **would have** to take out one of the patient's teeth. But he added (said) that it would only take him a minute. The patient asked him how much it would cost and the dentist answered that it would only cost him one hundred pounds. The patient thought that one hundred pounds was very expensive for something that only took a minute. The dentist then said (replied) that he could take his tooth out more slowly if he wishes.
Girl: "Do you think that I'm vain (eitel)?" Boyfriend: "No, I don't. Why do you ask?" Girl: "Because girls who are as beautiful as me are usually vain."	The girl asked her boyfriend he thought she was vain. (The girl wanted to know her boyfriend thought she was vain.) Her boyfriend told her that he didn't think that and wanted to know why she had asked. His girlfriend replied that girls who were as beautiful as she was are usually vain.
Teacher: "Billy, this letter from your father looks as if it was written by you!" Tommy: "That's because he borrowed my pen to write it."	The teacher thought that the letter from Terry's father looked as if it had been written from Terry himself. Terry replied that was because his father borrowed his pen.
Teacher: "Can anyone tell me what happens to a car when it gets old and starts to rust?" Terry: "My dad buys it."	The teacher wanted to know if anybody could say her what happened to a car when it got old and started to rust. Terry told that then his dad bought it.

You might like to try this exercise, too:

EXERCISE F.

What did they actually say?

1) The young woman said to her boyfriend that she would like to buy him a book for his birthday. He thanked her but told her that he already had one.

   Young woman: "I would like to buy you a book for your birthday."

   Boyfriend: "Oh thank you, but I've already got one."

2) A man ordered a pizza at an Italian restaurant and the waiter asked him if he should cut the pizza into six pieces or into twelve. The customer asked him to cut it into six because, he said, he could never eat twelve.

_____
_____
_____.

3) The man asked the doctor if he could cure his sleepwalking. The doctor handed him a packet and told him to take it. The man enquired whether there were sleeping pills in the packet.
The doctor told him that there weren't and that they were drawing pins (Reißnägel). He told him to put them on the floor near his bed every night.

_____
_____
_____
_____.

LET'S LOOK AT WORDS

EXERCISE G.

Write in synonyms or synonymous expressions for the underlined words. They all come from the book "Into the English World" text 12A. These words may help you (but don't forget to change them where necessary)!

> destination | passer-by | to overlook | intersection | keep in touch
> to have no clue | a local | consider

It was my first day in London. This great city is often thought _considered_ to be one of the most confusing cities in the world and now I understand why!

I hadn't stayed in contact _____ with my friend Tim and now that I was in London I had arranged to meet him under Big Ben, the famous clock near the Houses of Parliament. Anyway, I had probably not noticed _____ a sign or notice and taken the wrong road because I was completely lost!

I was standing at a busy place where a number of streets came together _____ and I really didn't know _____ how to get to Big Ben. Then I saw a man who was walking along the road _____ and I hoped that he lived in the area _____ and could help me.

I went up to him and asked him how I could get to (the place I wanted to go to)_____.

"Oh, it's easy," he said: "Just go down this road, turn left at the traffic lights and walk down the road to the end. Then you'll see Big Ben in front of you. You can't miss it – it's opposite the fast food restaurant on the corner of the street."

EXERCISE H.

The writers of these sentences have made some big spelling mistakes. Find them and correct them.
1) We have to ~~repair~~ *prepare* the fish before we put it in the oven.
2) This room is in a big mass. My son hasn't cleared it up for months!
3) Those lobsters don't look so fresh and frankly, I don't think that they are worse so much money.
4) This is a last area! There is room to build lots of houses here.
5) This hotel doesn't off a good service.
6) The stall in the hotel were not very helpful. We had to carry our luggage into our rooms by ourselves.
7) Mr Soames is a multi-millionaire and is always on Forbe's list of the healthiest people in the world.

2) _____   5) _____
3) _____   6) _____
4) _____   7) _____

DO YOU STILL REMEMBER?

EXERCISE I.

Choose the right alternative:

1) Mr and Mrs Collins __have been living__ (have been living/are living) in New England _____ (since/for) many years.

2) _____ (While/During) her daughter _____ (read/was reading) "Alice in Wonderland" in bed at midnight, Mrs Simmonds _____ (has come/came) into the room.

3) The _____ (rent/pension) for this flat is very _____ (high/highly).

4) Many lobsters _____ (caught/were caught) _____ (from/by) the fishermen.

5) I don't know _____ (what/which) I can do to help him.

6) Lewis Carroll is the author _____ (of/from) "Alice in Wonderland".

7) We aren't very _____ (happy/happily) with our new neighbour. She sings much too _____ (loud/loudly) in the bath at one o'clock in the morning.

8) Many people drink too _____ (less/little) water _____ (during/while) the day.

9) Prices are in general higher in Japan _____ (as/than) in many European countries.

10) Although the title of the book "Bees in your garden" doesn't _____ (sound/sounds) very _____ (interestingly/interesting) it is actually _____ (extreme/extremely) fascinating.

11) _____ (I/Me) was given twenty-four hours to decide whether (ob) I wanted to accept the job.

12) _____ (We're visiting/We visit) our grandmother tomorrow.

EXERCISE J.

Translate into German (for a change!):
1) They were informed about the new contract.
2) The book you gave me is quite boring.
3) We have been trying to find the solution to this problem for three hours so far.
4) Normally he doesn't get up so early. But today he is getting up at six o'clock because he has an important appointment (Termin).

EXERCISE K.

Correct the sentences where necessary.

1) Can you tell me ~~whose~~ taken the car? _Can you tell me who's (=who has) taken the car?_

2) I went to bed early because I was so tired.   ✓

3) I got up late, what meant that I missed the train.   _____

4) The music I like isn't played very often on the radio.   _____

5) The secretary usually arranges the appointments is ill today.   _____

6) They told me about their financial problems, something what I already knew.   _____

7) Henrietta didn't know which she could do.   _____

8) Do you know whose car this is?   _____

9) I didn't know that you many years ago in Italy lived.   _____

10) The clients which came to the presentation were very impressed (beeindruckt).   _____

11) All those customers who have used our software are very satisfied (zufrieden). _____

12) The students, all of who live in the suburbs, have a long way to the university. _____

Exercise L.

A or *an*?

1) _a_ unique experience   2) _____ interesting book   3) _____ nice aunt   4) _____ uncle

5) _____ cake   6) _____ appointment   7) _____ explanation   8) _____ solution

That's all for now. In the next chapter we will discuss the secrets of *infinitives* and *gerunds* in English.

Chapter 13: Infinitives and Gerunds

In this chapter we have a lot to discuss. Mit den *infinitives* and *gerunds* in diesem Kapitel wird es Ihnen gelingen, sehr vieles über sich und Ihr Leben (und das Leben nahestehender Menschen) auszudrücken. Fangen wir an mit einem etwas sonderbaren Fluggast:

In the aeroplane:
"Do you **want to sit** here or **would** you **like to sit** next to the window?"
"Oh, I'**d rather sit** next to the window, please. I really **enjoy breathing** in fresh air."

What a strange passenger! I'm sure that pilot and stewardesses **aren't used to having** such idiots on board. **Let** us **hope** the passenger doesn't insist **on** (darauf bestehen) **opening** the window of the aeroplane when the aeroplane is half-way over the Atlantic Ocean!

Wir wollen uns hier aber nicht mit diesem problematischen Fluggast weiter beschäftigen, sondern mit Infinitiv und Gerundium. Wie Sie sehen, verwenden wir – je nach Verb oder Präposition – einen Infinitiv mit *to*, z. B. *(Do you want/would you like) to sit*, einen Infinitiv ohne *to*, z. B. *(I'd rather) sit, (Let us) hope,* oder ein Gerundium (= Verb + ing), z. B. *(I enjoy) breathing, (... insist on) opening*. Es kann sogar vorkommen, dass wir vor das Gerundium ein *to* setzen: *(... aren't used to having) to having*. Aber keine Bange: Mithilfe einiger Witze und Übungen werden Sie diese Konstruktionen sehr schnell begreifen und beherrschen.

Infinitives (Infinitiv)

In der Sendung haben wir viele Infinitivsätze gehört:

Is there a guide **to show** me around?
We were the first **to enter** and the last **to go**.
I don't know how **to use** this tool.
Boston is so old and fascinating (that) I wondered what **to visit** first.
She's happy **to earn** her own money.
Was it her decision **to marry** him?
Etc.

In etlichen Fällen haben die deutsche und englische Grammatik dieselbe Form (außer des Satzbaus natürlich).

Mary helped us to repair our car. ⇨ Mary half uns, das Auto zu reparieren.
There's a lot to do. ⇨ Es gibt viel zu tun.

Um Absichten auszudrücken, nimmt man im Deutschen das Wort „um":

Do you want to stop here to watch the game?

Wollen Sie hier haltmachen, um das Spiel anzuschauen?

Die Übersicht A zeigt bestimmte Fälle, in denen der Infinitiv + *to* verwendet wird.

Übersicht A

1.	Nach **the first, the last** etc.	3.	Andere Beispiele für den Gebrauch von *to* +Infinitiv statt eines Nebensatzes:
Jack was the	the first (one) the second mechanic the last (one) the best man — to apply the worst one — for the job. the only one the most competent man		Is there a bus **to take** me to the city? I bought a map **to find** my way to the town hall. Here is a taxi **to take** us to the ice hockey match. (Gibt es einen Bus, der in die Stadtmitte fährt? Ich kaufte mir einen Stadtplan, damit ich den Weg zum Rathaus finden kann/konnte. Hier ist ein Taxi, das uns zum Eishockeyspiel fahren kann.)
2.	Nach Fragewörtern	4.	Nach den Verben:
I don't know	when where how — to repair how often — the car. whether etc.		to can afford (sich leisten können) — to offer (anbieten) to agree — to plan to arrange — to promise to attempt/try — to refuse (sich weigern) to choose/decide — to seem to expect — to want to fail (es nicht schaffen) — would like to forget — to love to hope — to learn to manage (es schaffen)

> **WATCH OUT! (1)**
> Do you know what a frequent mistake is that many speakers of German make in English? They **forget to use** *to* after **want** and **would like**. In English we say:
>   I **want to** learn these important verbs; I **would like to drink** a milk shake.
> Do you **promise not to make** the mistake?

Auch die wichtigsten Verben, die einen Infinitiv + *to* benötigen, sind in der Übersicht A angegeben, und sicherlich werden Sie diese im Verlauf der nächsten Wochen lernen! I'm sure you won't **refuse to learn** them and you'll **manage to find** a few minutes every day **to learn** one or two of the words. Please don't **forget to do** this – it's very important! And now it's your turn!

EXERCISE A.

Say the same thing with an *infinitive*:

1) Joe was the last person who left the office.

   He was the last person to leave the office.

2) We have dozens of things that we must talk about.

   _____ .

3) Don't worry, if you come a little late – I've got a letter that I have to write.

_____.

4) We really need something which we can open this bottle with.

_____.

5) Tony is the most intelligent man who has tried to solve the problem.

_____.

6) Can you tell me how often I should give the cat its food?

_____.

7) He gave me a book, which I could read on the long train journey.

_____.

8) Sally was the only one in the school who was accepted for a place at Oxford University. (Careful: *infinitive + passive!*)

_____
_____.

Tipp:
Wenn Sie solche Infinitivstrukturen verwenden, werden Sie Ihren Gesprächspartner sicherlich beeindrucken. Ein normaler Relativsatz ist meistens jedoch nicht falsch. Sie sollen die Infinitivstrukturen verstehen, müssen diese aber nicht unbedingt selbst anwenden – wie bei einigen anderen Strukturen, die wir besprochen haben. Sehr wichtig dagegen sind die Verben in Übersicht A, Punkt 4. auf der vorherigen Seite und die nächsten zwei Konstruktionen (Übersicht B und C):

Übersicht B   Übersicht C

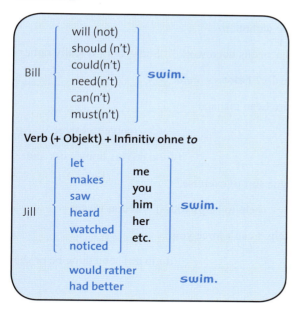

to allow = erlauben
to persuade = überreden
to invite = einladen
to advise = den Rat geben
to enable = befähigen/ermöglichen;

to encourage = ermutigen
to forbid = verbieten
to force = zwingen
to get (hier!) = veranlassen
to remind = daran erinnern

Bei einigen Verben werden im Englischen die nachfolgenden Infinitive ohne *to* gebildet. Selbstverständlich gehören dazu die sogenannten Modalverben *should, must, can* und *could*. Vier andere Verben, die Sie in diesem Zusammenhang lernen sollten, sind: *let* (erlauben); *make* (veranlassen, zwingen); *would rather* (Abkürzung: *'d rather* = etwas lieber tun); *had better* (Abkürzung: *'d better* = es wäre besser).

Six-year-old Tim is angry after his first day at school: "I don't **want to go** back to school tomorrow. I **can't read**, I **can't write**, they **make** me **sit** on a chair and they won't **let** me **speak**. You**'d better phone** the teacher and tell her that I**'d rather stay** at home."

Auch bei Verben der Wahrnehmung kann die Infinitivkonstruktion ohne *to* vorkommen, wenn man einen ganzen Vorgang gesehen, gehört, beobachtet usw. hat:

Angry mother: "I **heard** you **use** a horrible word today!"
Sandra: "But even Shakespeare used it."
Angry mother: "Then you mustn't play with Shakespeare again."

And now you**'d better do** this exercise. I'm sure you'll manage **to do** it without any difficulty!

Exercise B.

Decide whether to use an *infinitive* with *to* or an *infinitive* without *to*.

1) "Let me _help_ (help/to help) you with your maths homework." "Sorry, but I'd really rather _____ (do/to do) it alone." "Really? I always prefer _____ (do/to do) my homework with friends." "Oh, I'm sure I can manage _____ (finish/to finish) the homework alone. I know how _____ (solve/to solve) quadratic equations. I watched my brother _____ (do/to do) his homework and he had _____ (do/to do) the same sort of exercise."

2) "Well, all I can do is offer _____ (help/to help) you. If you don't want _____ (accept/to accept) my help, I can't force you _____ (take/to take) it! Nobody can make anyone _____ (do/to do) something he or she doesn't want to."

3) "Don't get me wrong, Clive, I don't usually refuse _____ (accept/to accept) your help, but today I'd like _____ (try/to try) _____ (solve/to solve) the problems by myself. Next week, there's a maths exam and I can't afford _____ (fail/to fail) for the second time. In the exam I won't have an expert like you _____ (help/to help) me! Anyway, please excuse me, but I really should _____ (concentrate/to concentrate) on my homework now, because I want _____ (watch/to watch) the football match at 6 o'clock." "OK, I get the message! I'd better _____ (leave/to leave) you alone then!"

And now we come to something very, very important. Es gibt, wie Sie in der Übersicht C sehen können, viele Verben, die nach der Formel Verb + Objekt + *to* + Infinitiv gebildet werden. Viele dieser Verben verlangen eine ähnliche Struktur im Deutschen: Jill überredete ihn, die Hausaufgaben zu machen. Jill riet ihm, die Hausaufgaben zu machen.

> **WATCH OUT! (2)**
> Im Deutschen werden Nebensätze bei den Verben „wollen", „möchten", „warten" mit „dass" gebildet. Dies verleitet zu Fehlern.
> Nicht: ~~I want that he comes.~~   Sondern: I want him to come.
> Nicht: ~~We would like that they go.~~   Sondern: We would like them to go.
> Nicht: ~~He's waiting that I phone.~~   Sondern: He's waiting for me to phone.

Sabrina has just finished her first day at school. Her mum and dad **are waiting** excitedly **for her to tell** them about her first day. "Sabrina," her mum says, "I **would like you to tell** me about your first day at school. Did you learn a lot?" "No, mummy, I didn't," says Sabrina sadly. "The teacher **wants me to come** back again tomorrow."

Well, I **want you to do** this next exercise on this important structure. **I'd like** (= I **would like**) **you to look** at the table (Übersicht) C again. This will **enable you to do** the exercise with little difficulty.

Exercise C.

Write down sentences as in the example.

1) "Oh dear, Mr Thompson hasn't come yet.   (wait)

    _We're waiting for him to come_____."

2) "Barbara doesn't want to do her homework.   (persuade)

    You should _____."

3) "Harry, the window is open and it's cold in here.   (would like/close)

    I _____."

4) "Oh no, Terry and Helen you're making too much noise!   (want)

    Your dad and I _____."

5) "We can't repair this computer by ourselves.   (help)

    John, please can _____?"

6) "Next Saturday Frank will be 94 years old and he's having a birthday party. (invite/come)

    I hope _____."

7) "Mrs Green doesn't know about the meeting next Thursday.   (would like/inform)

    Mrs Collins, I _____."

8) "Our clients haven't asked for an estimate (Kostenvoranschlag) yet.   (expect)

    We _____ soon."

9) "You're always in the office after 6 pm, George. You're working too hard.   (not want)

    We _____."

10) "Mr and Mrs Graham haven't sent us the contract yet. (wait)

    We _____."

11) "I haven't got the time to send Siemans the fax. Simon has more time than me.   (get)

    I'll _____."

12) Dr Miriam Hallamore is sitting outside my office. "I'm free now.   (ask)

   Miss Harper, please _____."

GERUNDS (GERUNDIEN)

a)   GERUNDS AFTER VERBS (GERUNDIEN NACH VERBEN)

Discuss**ing** grammar is not something everybody likes do**ing** and I know that not all of you are interested **in** read**ing** about such matters. Certainly few of us **enjoy** learn**ing** lists of verbs. I, myself, however, think that it is really worth you occupy**ing** yourselves with the gerund, because we can use it for say**ing** many things about our hobbies, interests and lives.

Wie Sie sehen, gebrauchen wir in der englischen Sprache das Verb sehr häufig nicht nur in der Form eines Infinitivs – mit oder ohne *to* –, sondern auch mit einem *-ing*: Das ist das sogenannte *gerund* (Gerundium). Eigentlich ist die ganze Sache nicht kompliziert: Wir müssen nur die Verben und Ausdrücke lernen, die ein *gerund* verlangen. In Übersicht D finden Sie einige der wichtigsten und gebräuchlichsten Verben:

Übersicht D

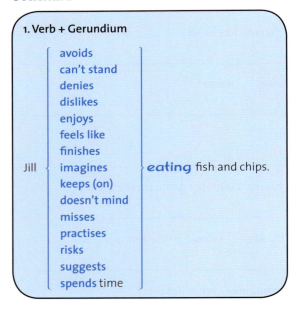

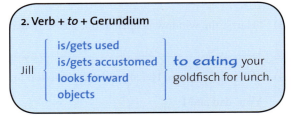

to avoid = vermeiden
to deny = leugnen, abstreiten
to dislike = nicht mögen
to enjoy = genießen
to feel like = es ist (mir, ihm etc.) danach
to imagine = sich vorstellen
to keep = weitermachen
to not mind = es macht (mir etc.) nichts aus

to miss = vermissen
to suggest = vorschlagen
to spend = verbringen
to be used/accustomed to = daran gewöhnt sein
to get used/accustomed to = sich daran gewöhnen
to look forward = sich darauf freuen
to object to = etwas dagegen haben

As you can see, there are some verbs which require (benötigen) *to + gerund*. You'll find the four most important ones in the table D. Well, that's all you need to know to do the next exercise.

Exercise D.

Write appropriate (passende) sentences with a *gerund*. The first letter of the verb will help you.

1) "You want me to wash the plates. How horrible! You know I d<u>islike washing plates</u>."

2) Every day Jennifer smokes 50 cigars. She's u_____.

3) "Quick, let's cross the road! There's my ex-boyfriend Eustace. I don't want to meet him."
   Last Saturday Amy a_____.

4) Let's go to the theatre for a change, instead of the cinema.
   Margaret s_____.

5) "I still can't play this Beethoven sonata on my mouth organ.
   I really must p_____ more."

6) "Well Dennis, guess what! You'll see your aunt Maude tomorrow."
   "Ugh! I'm not l_____. She k_____ me horrible, wet kisses."

7) "It's 7.30 and we're still waiting for Jim."
   "I _____ m_____. I'm sure he'll be here soon."

8) "It's so hot, I must drink something.
   I really f_____ a glass of lemonade."

9) "Look, there's an advertisement here in the newspaper for a job in Alaska. That could be a job for you!"
   "Oh I can't i_____. It's much too cold for me there."

10) "Yesterday somebody stole an elephant from the circus. We've found a suspect (eine Verdächtige) but she d_____."

11) "Another five cakes to bake for my son's birthday party tomorrow! I'm sure I won't f_____ before midnight!"

b) GERUNDS AFTER PREPOSITIONS (GERUNDIEN NACH PRÄPOSITIONEN)

Auch nach Präpositionen, wie z. B. *after*, *before*, *instead of*, *apart from* (außer), *by* (indem), *without*, *in*, *on* usw., wird meistens das Gerundium verwendet:

"I must apologize **for** runn**ing** over your cat," the motorist said, "of course, I'll replace it." "Thanks," said the farmer, "how good are you **at** catch**ing** mice?"

"My brother is bad **at** do**ing** sums. He can't count up to twenty **without** tak**ing** his shoes off!"

Es lohnt sich, bestimmte Verben, Adjektive und Substantive gleich mit den dazugehörenden Präpositionen zu lernen. Zu den wichtigsten zählen diese (siehe Übersicht E):

Übersicht E

Verb + Gerundium		Adjektiv + Gerundium		Substantiv + Gerundium		
apologize	for	afraid	of	advantage	of	
blame him, etc.	for	famous	for	chance	of	
complain	about	good	at	in danger	of	
dream	of	bad	at	difficulty	in	
insist	on	interested	in	interested	in	
prevent him, etc.	from	proud	of	hope	of	**verb + ing**
succeed	in	sorry	for/about	idea	of	
talk	about	sick	of	interest	in	
thank him, etc.	for	tired	of	possibility	of	
think	about	used	for	reason	for	
worry	about	worried	about	trouble	in	
believe	in	crazy	about			

Tipp: Sie müssen selbstverständlich nicht alle Wörter sofort lernen. You can **succeed in** learn**ing** these verbs, adjectives and nouns with their prepositions **by** dos**ing** your learning. Just three or four expressions every day and your chances **of** learn**ing** them all in a month are very good! You'll thank me **for** giv**ing** you this advice!

Well, it's time for another exercise. This one is about *infinitives* and *gerunds*.

EXERCISE E.

Put the verbs in their right forms. Add *prepositions* if necessary:

1) I have great difficulty *in getting* _____ (get) out of bed in the morning.

   I just can't get used _____ (wake) up before 7 o' clock but my wife wants

   me _____ (make) her breakfast so early.

2) "I really don't want you _____ (come) home so late, my son."

"But Dad you know how much I enjoy _____ (go) to the disco on Saturdays and I'm the only one among my friends _____ (leave) so early. I really am sick _____ (have) these silly discussions every weekend. After all, dad, I am forty-five years old."

3) At the library:

Customer: "Good morning madam, I would like you _____ (give) me ten thick books."

Librarian: "Ten thick books! I'd like you _____ (tell) me why you need <u>thick</u> books."

Customer: "Well, my son is very interested _____ (play) soccer and his teacher has encouraged him _____ (practise) football as much as he can. He thinks he'll succeed _____ (make) it to the top. And my wife, unfortunately lets him _____ (practise) _____ (play) soccer in the living room. Well, yesterday he kicked the ball at our television table and managed _____ (break) the table. I don't know what _____ (do). I don't mind _____ (miss) television dramas, but I'm really looking forward _____ (watch) the football match between Albania and Syria tonight. I need the thick books _____ (put) my TV on."

Librarian: "Well, I'm sorry but I'd better _____ (talk) to the director of the library before _____ (take) a decision on the matter. He's at lunch at the moment, so we'll have to wait _____ him _____ (come) back."

c) GERUNDS AS VERB NOUNS (GERUNDIEN ALS VERBALSUBSTANTIVE)

Das Gerundium kann man auch verwenden, um ein Verb in ein Substantiv umzuwandeln. Im Deutschen nimmt man dafür einen Infinitiv:

Living on the earth (Auf der Erde zu leben) may be expensive, but you get a free trip around the sun every year.
Stuart's hobby is **catching** spiders and **putting** them in his sister's bed.

d) GERUNDS AFTER SPECIAL EXPRESSIONS (GERUNDIEN NACH BESTIMMTEN AUSDRÜCKEN)

Es gibt (Gott sei Dank!) nur wenige Ausdrücke, die das Gerundium verlangen. Hier sind die wichtigsten:

It's worth + ...**ing**	Es lohnt sich ...
It's no use/good + ...**ing**	Es hat keinen Sinn ...
There's no point + ...**ing**	Es hat keinen Sinn ...
How about + ...**ing**/What about + ...**ing**	Wie wäre es mit ...

Terry comes home really dirty after a football match.
"Go into the bath," his mum tells him.
"**It's not worth having** a bath today," Terry replies.
"Next week, we're playing the return match."

e) GERUNDS AND TWO SUBJECTS (GERUNDIEN UND ZWEI SUBJEKTE)

Wie Carolin erwähnt hat, kann es vorkommen, dass das Gerundium und das Hauptverb verschiedene Subjekte haben. Zwei Beispielsätze:

I apologized for coming late.   I apologized for my brother coming late.
Im ersten Satz bin ich derjenige, der zu spät gekommen ist. Im zweiten Satz ist es mein Bruder.

A little exercise should make everything clearer.

EXERCISE F.

Change the sentences as in the example.

1) Bill always comes too late. I'm used _to him always coming late._

2) Can you finish the work soon?

    Is there a possibility _____.

3) Oh dear I think Bill and his wife might miss their flight.

    We're worried _____.

4) Sue should stay in an English family for six months. (Then she'll learn English well.)

    It's really worth _____.

5) You had to wait four hours for your flight.

    My parents are sorry _____.

6) It's OK. Thomas can listen to his radio programme while I'm typing this letter.

    I don't mind _____
    _____.

7) My boss doesn't think that Susanne and I will ever get married!

    My boss can't imagine _____.

INFINITIVE OR GERUND (INFINITIV ODER GERUNDIUM)?

Es gibt einige wenige Verben, bei denen, je nach Bedeutung der Aussage, ein *to-* Infinitiv oder ein Gerundium steht. Hier sind drei wichtige Verben dieser Art (Übersicht F):

Übersicht F

> I must **remember to post** the letter.
> Ich muss mich daran erinnern, den Brief abzuschicken.
>
> He **stopped** his work **to smoke**.
> Er unterbrach seine Arbeit, um zu rauchen.
>
> I **consider** him **to be** clever.
> Ich halte ihn für klug.
>
> I **used to get** up early.
> Früher bin ich früh aufgestanden.
>
> ⇔
>
> I **remember posting** the letter.
> Ich erinnere mich daran, den Brief abgeschickt zu haben.
>
> He **stopped smoking**.
> Er hörte mit dem Rauchen auf.
>
> I'm **considering going** to Rome at Easter.
> Ich ziehe es in Betracht, Ostern nach Rom zu fahren.
>
> I'm **used to getting** up early.
> Ich bin daran gewöhnt, früh aufzustehen.

LET'S LOOK AT WORDS

In diesem Kapitel haben wir viele Ausdrücke mit Präpositionen kennengelernt, mit deren Hilfe Sie eine Menge über Ihr Leben, Ihre Vorlieben und Abneigungen sagen können. Rufen wir uns diese Ausdrücke in Erinnerung. Zugleich werden Sie eine resolute, psychologisch geschulte Frau kennenlernen!

For many years, Mr O'Conner had **dreamed of** spending his retirement in the country. Finally when he was 65 years old, the day he had been **waiting for** came and he and his wife moved into a lovely house in a small, quiet village near Dublin. Mr and Mrs O'Conner had a hobby: ornithology. They **were interested in** studying everything about birds. They **were** especially **fond of** listening to all the beautiful birds in their garden
5 and really **looked forward to** going into their garden every morning to listen to them. "What a beautiful life," they thought, "the lovely quiet of the village and the beautiful bird song."
But that all stopped, on the tenth of September when the school year started. The same day, at 4 pm after school, a group of six schoolboys ran down their quiet street and beat all the metal trash cans outside the houses in the street. This **went on** every day at 4pm after school. Nobody **succeeded in** stopping them and
10 the noise almost **triggered off** a nervous breakdown in poor Mr Conner.
Finally, Mrs O'Conner **decided to** solve the problem. One afternoon, she went to the boys and said: "My husband and I **are** really **crazy about** drum music. We **used to go** to jazz concerts when we were young. You're all so **good at** making wonderful rhythms with your sticks on the trash bins. Please do that every day. I'll give you each one euro every week for it."
15 The kids **were**, of course, very **happy at** getting so much money for their "concerts" and they came every day and beat the trash cans. The next week, Mrs O'Conner went out to the boys and said sadly: "Thank you so much **for** making your beautiful music. I'm very sorry, but we're having **difficulty in** finding six euros for you every week. However, we can **afford to** give you fifty cents each."
The boys, of course, didn't like **the idea of** getting only fifty cents for their "hard work", but they continued
20 coming back to hit the trash cans every afternoon.

The next week, while they boys were hitting the trash cans with their sticks, Mrs O'Conner came out and said: "I'm sorry, but this week we can only **offer to** give you 20 cents each for your drum music."

The leader of the group became really angry and shouted at Mrs O'Conner: "I'm sorry, but in that case we **refuse to** play our music for you. **It's not worth** playing on your trash cans for only twenty cents each!"

25 And that was the last they saw of the "drummers". Mr and Mrs O'Conner have been enjoying the peace and quiet in their street for the last twenty years.

EXERCISE G.

Now it's your turn! Überlegen Sie sich drei Sätze über sich oder Ihre Familie, Ihre Kollegen und Ihre Freunde unter Verwendung dieser Ausdrücke. Hier ein paar Beispielsätze:

I'm good at table tennis. My brother is interested in collecting stones. Traudi is looking forward to going to England in summer. I'm looking forward to Christmas. My colleagues have difficulty in using the new software. Last year we decided to … It's worth … It isn't worth … My boyfriend is crazy about … etc.

Wir haben oft über die Notwendigkeit gesprochen, neue Wörter aus ihrem Zusammenhang zu verstehen oder neue Wörter von bekannten Wörtern abzuleiten. In der nächsten Übung finden Sie abgeleitete Wörter von Wörtern aus „Into the English World" 13 D. Können Sie sie erraten?

EXERCISE H.

Was bedeuten die unterstrichenen Wörter? Mit welchen Wörtern in „Into the English World" 13D sind sie verwandt?

1) The film Titanic, **starring** Di Caprio and Kate Winslet was very popular.

   starring = mit ... in den Hauptrollen   star = Stern

2) The **coverage** of the events in the Arab world by the BBC was very good.

   _____

3) Peter's knowledge of American history is quite **remarkable**.

   _____

4) The **globalization** of the economy does not only have advantages.

   _____

5) **Powerful** lobbies can often prevent important reforms.

   _____

6) The teacher gave the pupil **permission** to leave early.

   _____

7) Travelling to six countries in four days – what a **ridiculous** idea.
_____

8) His clothes were rather **ragged**.
_____

9) Students of English should **enlarge** the number of words they use actively.
_____

DO YOU STILL REMEMBER?

EXERCISE I.

Put the words in brackets into their correct forms or add words:

While the barber __was cutting__ (cut) his hair six months _____ , George _____ (tell) him about his plans for a holiday in England. "I _____ (always/want) to spend a holiday in England, ever since I was a child," George said. "Who knows? Maybe I _____ (see) the Queen when I _____ (be) in England in July."

"That's impossible," the barber said. "She only meets people who are _____ important _____ you – like other queens, kings or politicians."

Two months later George _____ (come) back to the barber's shop and asked the barber _____ he could remember what he _____ (say) two months previously. The barber said he _____ (can).

"Well," said George, "you're going to be _____ (extreme/surprise) to hear this. I _____ (walk) in the gardens of Buckingham Palace, when suddenly the Queen saw me, invited me for a cup of tea and asked me a question."

"Good Heavens!" the barber said _____ (excited). "What _____ _____ (she/ask) you?"

George replied: "She asked me who _____ (give) me my terrible hair cut."

Exercise J.

Put these sentences into *indirect speech*:

1) "Happiness is good health and a bad memory."

   The philosopher said that happiness was good health and a bad memory.

2) "My husband's really good at woodwork. He's just bought some shelves for our living room and now he's writing some books to put on them." (Don't forget: He's = he has or he is!) Mrs McDonald …

3) "Where is the wisdom that people have lost in knowledge? Where is the knowledge that people have lost in information?" The poet T. S. Eliot once …

4) "Do not believe what statistics say until you have carefully considered what they do not say." The statistician told the audience …

Exercise K.

Rearrange the words to make sensible sentences:

1) is / A hospital / at 5 am in the morning / a sleeping pill / a place / they wake you / where / to give / you

   A hospital is a place where they wake you at 5 am in the morning to give you a sleeping pill.

2) so quickly / smoking / How / did / last year? / give / up / you

3) was / This / by / written / uncle / book / my

4) is / relaxing / The / I'm / CD / to / very / listening

CHAPTER 14: PARTICIPIAL CONSTRUCTIONS

Life is sometimes hard so I'm in favour of making it as easy as possible – and that includes English grammar! The expression *participial constructions* sounds complicated, but you'll see how easy they are.

As Carolin told us in the programme *participial constructions* are used to shorten parts of sentences or to connect sentences. Very often we can read such sentences:

The Prime Minister, **answering** a question **asked** by the MP (Member of Parliament) for Botherton, Mr Dudley Sanders, said that the law **passed** by the House of Commons was good for the future of education in Great Britain. The government could not afford to neglect (vernachlässigen) the field of education, **knowing** how important it was for the future of Great Britain.

The writer could say: The Prime Minister **who was answering** a question **which was asked** by the MP for Botherton, Mr Dudley Sanders, said that the law **which had been passed** by the House of Commons was good for the future of education in Great Britain. The government could not afford to neglect the field of education, **because it knew** how important it was for the future of Great Britain.

Der Premier, der eine Frage beantwortete, die vom Mitglied des Parlaments für (den Wahlkreis) Botherton, Herrn Dudley Sanders, gestellt wurde, sagte, dass das Gesetz, das vom Unterhaus verabschiedet wurde, gut für die Zukunft der Bildung in Großbritannien sei. Die Regierung könne es sich nicht leisten, den Bereich Bildung zu vernachlässigen, da sie wüsste, wie wichtig sie für die Zukunft Großbritanniens sei.

Eine nicht sehr elegante Übersetzung, aber Sie sehen, wie *participial constructions* Relativsätze ersetzen können!

Die *participial constructions* werden hauptsächlich in der Schriftsprache angewandt, um möglichst viele Informationen in einem Satz unterzubringen.

Wie immer werden wir mithilfe einiger Witze Carolins Erläuterungen wiederholen und im Nu – oder fast im Nu – werden die *participial constructions* für Sie keine Geheimnisse mehr sein. Wieder haben wir es mit Konstruktionen zu tun, die Sie nicht selbst verwenden müssen. Sie sollen sie bloß erkennen, wenn sie in einem geschriebenen Text vorkommen. OK. Ready, steady, go!

SHORTENED RELATIVE CLAUSES (VERKÜRZTE RELATIVSÄTZE)

a) The young man **learning** to drive was very nervous.
    "Quick – take the steering wheel (Lenkrad)!" he shouted to the driving instructor (Fahrlehrer) **sitting** next to him. "There's a tree **coming** towards us."

Hier haben wir uns jeweils zwei Wörter gespart – ein großer Vorteil in unserer schnelllebigen Zeit.

A Texan **photographing** the Niagara Falls is approached (sich nähern, ansprechen) by a local. "I'm sure you've got nothing like that in Texas!" "No, we haven't," the Texan says. "But we've got plumbers (Klempner) who could fix it."

The young man **who was learning** to drive	⇨	The young man **learning** to drive
the driving instructor **who was sitting**	⇨	the driving instructor **sitting**
There is a tree **which is coming** toward us	⇨	There's a tree **coming** towards us
A Texan **who was photographing**	⇨	A Texan **photographing**

Wie Sie sehen, wird das *present participle*, wie z. B. *sitting, coming, photographing* etc., verwendet, um Handlungen, Zustände und Vorgänge im Aktiv auszudrücken. Es wird sowohl in der Gegenwart als auch in der Vergangenheit benutzt.

b) Auch mit Passivkonstruktionen können wir den Nebensatz verkürzen. Dabei verwenden wir das *past participle* des Verbs (z. B. used, written, stolen):

A clock is a thing **used** to wake people up who haven't got young children.
A clock is a thing **which is used**   ⇨ A clock is a thing **used**

After these examples this exercise won't be difficult for you.

Exercise A.

Translate these sentences:

1) The man playing the banjo is really getting on my nerves.

   Der Mann, der das Banjo spielt, geht mir wirklich auf die Nerven.

2) I really admired the man singing in the choir.

3) This house built over four hundred years ago, is still in good condition.

4) The people working in this firm aren't content with their working conditions.

5) Of those thousands of books published every year, only a few become bestsellers.

Participial Constructions to Express Reasons
(Partizipialkonstruktionen zum Ausdruck des Grundes)

"Dad," says Jill, "I had a strange dream. I dreamt that you had given me $5!"
"Well," says her father, "**being** so honest you can keep the $5."

"I'm writing a book. **Having written** the page numbers, I can now start writing the text."

Hier haben wir wieder eine Verkürzung des Satzes.

As° (Since°) you're so honest	⇨ **being** so honest
As° (Since°) I've written the page numbers	⇨ **Having written** the page numbers

°*Since* und *as* haben hier die Bedeutung von „da".

Now it's your turn!

Exercise B.

Translate these sentences:

1) Living in two different continents, my sister and I don't see each other very often.

   Da wir auf zwei verschiedenen Erdteilen leben, sehen meine Schwester und ich uns nicht sehr oft.

2) Having eaten seven plates of spaghetti, Julia felt rather sick.

3) Knowing how many trouser pockets he had, Charles decided not to buy the pocket calculator.

4) Brunhilde was very sad, not having heard a word from Max for the last seventy years.

5) Being very generous, Naomi bought all of us an ice-cream.

Participial Constructions as a Substitute for *and* or *and so* (Partizipialkonstruktionen als Ersatz für *and* und *and so*)

A husband and his wife entered a dentist's surgery. The husband said: "I want a tooth out. We don't want an injection because we're in a hurry. Just pull the tooth out, **taking** as little time as possible, please."
"You're a brave man," said the dentist, **shaking** his hand, "Now which tooth is it," he asked, **looking** into the man's mouth. The husband said. "No, no – it's not my tooth that's the problem. Show the doctor your bad tooth, darling," he said to his wife.

Colin took his girlfriend to a really expensive restaurant in New York and ordered the whole meal in perfect French, **impressing** (beeindrucken) his girlfriend enormously. The waiters in the restaurant were also very impressed as it was a Chinese restaurant and they had just arrived from Shanghai to take up their new jobs.

In diesen beiden Witzen haben wir uns das *and* bzw. *and so* gespart.

and take as little time as possible	⇨	**taking** as little time as possible
and shook his hand	⇨	**shaking** his hand
and he looked into the man's mouth	⇨	**looking** into the man's mouth
and so impressed his girlfriend enormously	⇨	**impressing** his girlfriend enormously

Participial Constructions to Express Time (Partizipialkonstruktionen zum Ausdruck der Zeit)

Wir können *participial constructions* einsetzen, um eine Handlung zu beschreiben, die zur gleichen Zeit wie eine andere Handlung oder vor dieser Handlung stattfindet. *Participial constructions* werden auch benutzt, wenn es um zwei kurze aufeinanderfolgende Handlungen geht.

Gleiche Zeit wie andere Handlung:
Seeing a man in the courtroom, the judge asked: "Are you the defence lawyer?"
"No," the man replied, "I'm the man who robbed the bank."

Vor einer anderen Handlung:
Having hurt himself while he had been drinking milk, Mr Smith had to go to hospital. The cow had sat on him.

Zwei kurze aufeinanderfolgende Handlungen:
A motorist stopped at a ford. He asked a man sitting near the river how deep the water was. "About six or seven centimetres," the man said. **Hearing** this, the man drove into the river
and the car sank and disappeared (verschwinden) under the water. "Funny," the other man said to himself, "the water only goes up six centimetres on those ducks."

One last thing: Manchmal gibt es zwei Subjekte in einem Satz. Nehmen wir Carolins Beispiel:
I was driving on the motorway, when the baby started to cry.

Wenn wir sagen würden *Driving on the motorway, the baby started to cry*, würden wir den Eindruck erwecken, das Baby sei sehr begabt und könne sogar ein Auto fahren! In diesem Fall müssen wir auf eine *participial construction* verzichten. In anderen Fällen muss man das Subjekt explizit erwähnen (siehe Nr. 4 in exercise C.)

A few more examples? OK, here you are:

EXERCISE C.

I would like **you to translate** these sentences – please!

1) Walking into the room he saw his ex-girlfriend.

    Als er das Zimmer betrat, sah er seine ehemalige Freundin.

2) Having eaten the ice cream, I bought myself a pizza.

3) Susan hurt her foot playing football.

4) The computer having broken down, we had to think for ourselves!

5) Relaxing during my lunch break, I often manage to do a few exercises for Telekolleg.

6) Looking himself in the mirror, Gerry understood why so many women liked him. (A very vain (eitel) man!)

Knowing how little time you have, I have only discussed most of the important *participial constructions*. However, **having done** the exercises above, you should be able to understand sentences with other kinds of *participial constructions*:

Exercise D.

Can you replace these *participial constructions*?

1) When entering the concert hall, please talk quietly.

   When you enter the concert hall, please talk quietly.

2) Although not knowing much French, Jim could at least say "je t'aime" to his French girlfriend.

3) If broken your lamp will, of course, be replaced.

4) While operating this machine please wear a safety helmet.

5) Used carefully, this machine will never break down.

6) With his mouth stuffed (hier: vollstopfen) with apple strudel, Tim started to sing an Austrian folk song.

TIPP:
Die gute Nachricht ist, dass Sie, wie eingangs erwähnt, die *participial constructions* nicht selbst anwenden müssen, sondern nur erkennen und verstehen sollen. Ob Sie z. B. sagen *Many of the people living in my town work in Munich* oder *Many of the people who live in my town work in Munich*, ist völlig unerheblich. Außerdem werden diese Strukturen hauptsächlich in der englischen Schriftsprache verwendet. Im gesprochenen, informellen Englisch klingen sie manchmal etwas geschwollen.
Deshalb gebe ich Ihnen den Rat, *participial constructions* nur dann anzuwenden, wenn Sie sich absolut sicher sind, dass sie richtig und angemessen sind.

Let's look at words

Ich habe oft darauf hingewiesen: Wenn man ein englisches Wort gelernt hat, kann man die Bedeutung sehr vieler anderer Wörter leicht erraten. Mithilfe von Nachsilben kann man z. B. eine Vielzahl neuer Wörter bilden. Aus *accomplished* und *honest* in „Into the English World"14A können wir z. B. die Wörter: *accomplishment* (Leistung) und *honesty* (Ehrlichkeit) bilden. In der folgenden Übung geht es darum, passende Nachsilben (*suffixes*) für Wörter aus „Into the English World" 14A und 14D zu finden.

Exercise E.

Bilden Sie neue Wörter mithilfe passender Nachsilben. Was bedeuten die neuen Wörter?

Word-building clouds with bases: size, settle, help, consider, forget, origin, recover, success, remain, rely, agree, complain; and suffixes: -ation, -able, -al, -ful, -der, -t, -less, -y, -ment.

reliable (zuverlässig)

Vorsilben – *prefixes* – (un-, dis-, extra, mis-, etc.) können uns ebenso helfen, weitere Wörter zu bilden oder zu erkennen.

Exercise F.

Die unterstrichenen Wörter sind Wörter aus „Into the English World" 14A und 14D „angereichert" mit Vor- oder Nachsilben. Übersetzen Sie diese.

1) There have been <u>complaints</u> about your daughter. I hope she will <u>reconsider</u> her <u>inconsiderate</u> behavior to pupils and teachers.

   complaints = Beschwerden; reconsider = noch mal überdenken
   inconsiderate = unbedacht, rücksichtslos

2) Eating fish and chips with my boyfriend outside Buckingham Palace will always remain an <u>unforgettable</u> experience. It was a great <u>disappointment</u>, however, that the Queen didn't come out to chat with us.

3) We reached a <u>satisfactory agreement.</u>

4) I hope this exercise helps you to <u>enlarge</u> your vocabulary.

5) The two firms agreed on a <u>joint</u> project.

_____

6) This desert region in Australia is absolutely <u>uninhabitable</u>.

_____

DO YOU STILL REMEMBER?

Before we finish, I **would like** you **to do** a few exercises on grammar: one on *gerunds* and *infinitives* and one on *reflexive pronouns*. I'm sure that you won't mind do**ing** them. They will **let** you **see** how much you have remembered from the last chapters!
Before attempt**ing to do** exercise G, **it is worth** read**ing** the lists of verbs (chapter 13) requir**ing** a) *infinitives* with *to*, b) *infinitives* without *to*, c) *gerunds* and d) *gerunds* with *to*.
Read about Graham Harris' strange hobby and you'll see many of these *gerunds* and *infinitives* again:

Graham Harris was fascinated by owls (Eulen) and was **interested in** find**ing** out all he could about these lovely birds. One day he had the **idea of** communicat**ing** with them so he went into his garden and started **to hoot**/hoot**ing** as loudly as he could. Unfortunately he **failed to get** a reply. But he didn't **give up** try**ing** to communicate with the owls. He even **asked** his son **to help** him and every evening they **spent** happy hours
5   hoot**ing** in their garden – something they really **enjoyed** do**ing**.
Graham's wife was not very happy about all this. She didn't **want to make** him **give** up his hobby but she **tried to persuade** her husband **to spend** more time in the evenings with her. Graham, however, **refused to make** any compromises.
One evening **after** hav**ing** hooted/hoot**ing** for half-an-hour, Graham and his son were excited to hear five
10 hoots in the distance. From then on, every evening when they hooted they heard the reply. Every evening at seven o'clock, Graham and his son **looked forward to** "talk**ing**" to the owl. Graham bought an exercise book **to write** a record of his "conversations" with the owl. He even **thought of** publish**ing** (veröffentlichen) a book about the language of owls. He was, after all, **the most competent man to write** such a book.
One afternoon, his wife was in the supermarket and met Mrs Clark, who lived a few streets away. "My
15 husband **spends** most of the evening hoot**ing** like an owl in the garden," Mrs Harris complained. "That's funny," said Mrs Clark, "so does mine. He's so happy because he's even **succeeded in** mak**ing** contact with two owls in the neighbourhood."

EXERCISE G.

Jetzt sind Sie an die Reihe! Können Sie den Inhalt dieser Sätze mithilfe der angegeben Verben und einer passenden Infinitiv- oder *ing*-Konstruktion ausdrücken?

1) Perhaps we'll go to Spain for our holidays. (think)

   We're thinking of going to Spain for our holidays.

2) I'm sorry, but I won't work on Sundays. (refuse)

   I refuse to work on Sundays.

3) I watched an American movie yesterday but it was really boring. (worth)

   _____

4) At first I didn't want to go to the theatre, but after my wife had spoken to me I agreed to go with her. (persuade)

_____

5) Sam eats fish and chips every day. (enjoy)

_____

6) Great! Tomorrow we are going to see my cousin Terry. (look forward)

_____

7) John answered emails for five hours yesterday. (spend)

_____

8) We had a wonderful meal at an English restaurant in Munich and then we went home. (after)

_____

_____

9) "You mustn't come home after ten o'clock, Paula." (let)

Yesterday, Paula's mother _____

10) "Fantastic! David and June have just constructed their own computer by themselves!" (succeed)

_____

_____

11) John, please would you close the window? (would like)

John's mother _____

12) Every day of the week we travel to work by helicopter. (accustomed)

_____

Exercise H.

Put in *myself, yourself, ourselves*, etc. and *each other* where necessary.

1) After her mouse had died, Eva couldn't forgive __herself__ for letting her cat come near it.
2) He apologized _____ for coming late.
3) We really can't afford _____ to go on holiday this year.
4) Mary and Fred phone _____ every day. Fred phones in the morning and Mary phones in the evening.
5) Mary and Fred hurt _____ when their car crashed into the wall.
6) We did the homework all by _____ .

7) Hello, you guys! Please help _____ to tea and biscuits. I'll be with you in a moment.

8) Father: "Can you do your homework by _____, or shall I help you?"

   Son: "No thanks Dad. I can get it wrong by _____."

9) They complained _____ about the terrible service in the hotel.

10) I can't remember _____ his name, can you?

11) The two sisters haven't spoken to _____ for years.

12) Timmy concentrated _____ on the maths problem and eventually he was able to solve it _____ without the help of his father.

13) Sally and I made _____ comfortable on the sofa and played chess.

EXERCISE I.

Drücken Sie die Inhalte dieser Sätze anders aus.

1) Darling Henrietta. I'm sitting with you in the moonlight. I'll never forget this moment

   I'll always remember _sitting with you in the moonlight._

2) It's not as warm today as it was yesterday.

   Yesterday it was _____

3) I started playing the piano twenty years ago and I still play it.

   For the last twenty years _____

4) I phone my girlfriend every day and she phones me every day, too.

   We phone _____

5) I saw the woman. You like her daughter.

   I saw the woman wh_____

6) "Why do the female members of the Royal Family wear such strange hats, Charles?"

   Mary asked Charles why_____
   _____

7) We came to this town in 2007. We are still here.

   We _____ since 2007.

8) Despite the heavy rain, they still went out for a picnic.

   Although it _____

9) They haven't sent off the catalogues yet.

   The catalogues _____

Well, you have worked hard! So now please relax with a crossword puzzle with lots of *infinitives* and *gerunds* and two last jokes with *participial constructions*!
So now, please try this crossword puzzle: It will **help** you **to remember** many *infinitives* and *gerunds*.
Tip: Answer the easiest questions first!

EXERCISE J.

A crossword with a lots of *infinitives* and *gerunds*:

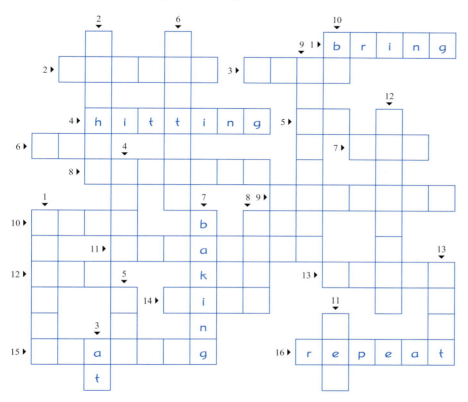

Across:
1) John was the only one to __bring__ flowers for the secretary's birthday.
2) "We _____ an hour <u>for</u> John to come, yesterday. Finally at 8 o'clock he arrived."
3) "I saw the thief _____ away on my motorbike."
4) __Hitting__ each other won't solve problems. Kids should talk about their problems together!
5) Successful children are interested _____ learning everything about the world.
6) He'd rather _____ than tell the truth and make his girlfriend unhappy.
7) "Mummy, please _____ me stay out to midnight on Saturday. I promise not to come home later!"
8) _____ to the railway station every day is Stuart's only sport.
9) He enjoys just _____ on the sofa for hours. He calls it "meditation".
10) He's accustomed to going everywhere on his _____.
11) He keeps _____ of getting a better job, but he doesn't want to work hard for it!

Chapter 14: participial constructions | 155

12) Many people in England are accustomed to drinking a cup of _____ at 5 pm.
13) Some pupils _____ most of their free time playing computer games.
14) My son managed to make a _____ with just two pieces of wood!
15) Our son dislikes _____ and we can't get him to even look at one page of a book.
16) What a horrible teacher! At the end of every lesson he makes us _repeat_ what he has said.

Down:
1) "You'd _____ take an umbrella, John. I'm sure it's going to rain."
2) "Would you like to go to the cinema?" "No, thanks. I'd _____ go to the theatre."
3) He isn't good _at_ working himself - but he's good _at_ telling you how to do it!
4) It's 10 o'clock and we're still here in the firm! I'm not _____ to working so late.
5) Philip enjoys hearing his own voice, but he's _____ at listening to others speak!
6) Daniel succeeded in _____ a prize for his invention.
7) I'm looking forward to _baking_ the cakes for the Christmas party.
8) I would _____ all the colleagues to come to the meeting next Friday afternoon.
9) _____ too much alcohol can be very bad for your liver.
10) We expect a representative of your firm to _____ here for the meeting.
11) I haven't got much time and I don't know when to _____ the customer in Tunbridge.
12) Sue has such a bad memory, so I _____ her again to download the software.
13) It's OK. I'll take the rubbish out. I _____ mind going out in the rain!

Hier sind nun die zwei Witze, die ich Ihnen versprochen habe!

A young man was showing his apartment to his friends. One of them saw an enormous gong and a hammer **placed** near the wall. "What are the big gong and the hammer for?" he asked. "Oh, that's a special talking clock," replied the man. **Saying** this, he hit the gong as hard as he could with the hammer. They heard a scream, **coming** from the other side of the wall: "Stop it, you idiot. It's two o'clock in the morning!"

An Italian with a parrot **sitting** on his shoulder went into a bar and ordered a glass of grappa.
The barman, **looking** admiringly at the parrot, said: "That's really beautiful. Where did you get him?"
"In Italy," the parrot replies. "There are millions of them."

(which was placed; After he had said this; which came; which was sitting; looked)

Chapter 15: conditional sentences

Sehr viel von dem, was wir tun oder getan haben, ist mit Bedingungen verknüpft: Falls es morgen regnet, werden wir zu Hause bleiben. Wenn ich vor vierzig Jahren nicht nach München gekommen wäre, hätte ich meine Frau nicht kennengelernt … Diese Sätze sind die berühmten *conditional sentences* (Bedingungssätze) oder die *If*-Sätze. Da die Bedingungen im Leben sehr wichtig sind, sollten Sie diese Formen nicht nur passiv verstehen können, sondern selbst in der Lage sein, sie anzuwenden.

> **WATCH OUT! (1)**
> Wenn wir von *If*-Sätzen sprechen, müssen wir berücksichtigen:
> a) *If* kann auch, wie wir gesehen haben, die Bedeutung von „ob" haben:
>   I don't know **if** he can come.
>   Solche Sätze sind keine „If"-Sätze!
> b) Manchmal können andere Wörter statt *if* im *If*-Satz verwendet werden, z. B.:
>   unless = wenn nicht   as long as = solange, sofern
>   provided that = vorausgesetzt dass in case = für den Fall dass
>   supposing that = angenommen dass
> Tipp: Wenn Sie nur die Formen mit *if* aktiv beherrschen, aber die anderen passiv verstehen, reicht dies im Moment aus.

If-Clauses (*If*-Sätze / Wenn-Sätze)

a)   *If*-clause type 1 (*If*-Satz Typ 1)

Wie Carolin erklärt hat, bezieht sich der *If*-Satz Typ 1 auf die Zukunft. Es wird etwas geschehen, wenn eine bestimmte Bedingung erfüllt ist:

> If it **snows** tomorrow, we**'ll make** a snowman.
> If you **don't eat** onions, I **will kiss** you.
> I**'ll go** to the cinema with you if you **pay** for the tickets.

If you **look** carefully, you **will see** that we only need a comma if we **begin** the sentence with an *if*. Viel wichtiger ist aber, sich einzuprägen, dass wir das *present simple* im *If*-Teil des Satzes verwenden und das *future simple* im anderen Teil.
If I **tell** you a joke, you **won't have** problems with this structure, I'm sure!

Hank: "Can you lend me $5 until tomorrow?"
Sam: "But you already owe me $3."
Hank: "Well, *if* you **lend** me $8, I**'ll give** you back the $3."

Bei Aufforderungen im *If*-Satz Typ 1 werden häufig beide Verben ins *present simple* gesetzt:

> *If* I **am** not downstairs at 7 am, please **wake** me up.

You **will** soon **learn** the structure if you **do** the following exercise!

Exercise A.

Put the verbs in the right forms:

1) If you __send__ (send) me the packet before Saturday, that __will be__ (be) OK.

2) If Sue _____ (not stop) eating so much, she _____ (put) on too much weight.

3) You can stay out later as long as you _____ (not be) here later than midnight.

4) If they _____ (offer) you the car for 500 euros, _____ (you/buy) it?

5) Susan _____ (be able to talk) to the Italians on her holiday in Italy next year if she _____ (learn) Italian before.

6) You _____ (catch) the train, Terence, if you _____ (not hurry).

7) _____ (we/get) to the meeting on time if we _____ (miss) the next train?

8) Graham _____ (go) to the concert tomorrow unless he _____ (have) too much work.

9) If you _____ (see) Jimmy, _____ (not tell) him where I've hidden his Christmas presents.

10) Please _____ (wash) your hands if they _____ (be) dirty.

b) IF-CLAUSE TYPE 2 (IF-SATZ TYP 2)

Dieser *If*-Satz wird verwendet, um eine theoretische Möglichkeit in der Gegenwart zu beschreiben oder eine Bedingung, die entweder unmöglich oder mit sehr hoher Wahrscheinlichkeit nicht eintreten wird:

After a rainy holiday in England, an Australian tourist says:

"England is great, but *if* there **were** a roof over it, it **would be** even better."

Wie Sie sehen, verzichtet man in der englischen Sprache auf eine neue Form (könnte, müsste, hätte, wäre etc.). Stattdessen verwendet man im *If*-Teil des Satzes das *past simple* und im anderen Teil des Satzes *would* + Infinitiv. Obwohl man das *past simple* hier zu Hilfe nimmt, beschreibt es im *If*-Satz Typ 2 nicht einen Vorgang oder einen Zustand in der Vergangenheit.

EXERCISE B.

Write down the appropriate *if-clauses*.

1) Malcolm doesn't do enough sport, so he's not very fit.

   If Malcolm did enough sport he would be very fit.

2) Rachel doesn't speak to her colleagues at work so she isn't very popular.

   If _____

   _____._

3) Bill doesn't live in a quiet area. That's the reason he doesn't sleep well at night.

   _____ if _____.

4) This Rolls Royce is so expensive that we cannot buy it.

   If _____.

5) Samantha always catches a cold because she doesn't wear a coat in winter.

   If _____.

6) Philip is always bored because he spends every evening watching DVDs.

   _____

   if _____.

7) My little son is often sick because he eats worms from the garden.

   If _____

   _____.

8) Michaela goes to the disco every evening, so she doesn't get to bed very early.

   _____ if _____.

9) Hannah isn't very happy in her job because it isn't very interesting.

   If _____.

10) We know the if-clauses so well, because we practise them so often.

    _____

    if _____.

WATCH OUT! (2)

In der überwiegenden Mehrzahl der Fälle darf *will* oder *would* nicht im *If*-Teil des Satzes stehen:

Statt: If it ~~will rain~~ tomorrow, we'll stay at home.   If it rains tomorrow, we'll stay at home.
Statt: If it ~~would be~~ sunny now, we'd go for a walk.   If it were sunny now, we'd go for a walk.

c) IF-CLAUSE TYPE 3 (IF-SATZ TYP 3)

Er beschreibt eine Bedingung <u>in der Vergangenheit</u>, die nicht eingetreten ist:

Tania: "Oh, David, my darling! What beautiful roses you've brought me!"
David: "I **would have brought** you more roses **if** Mrs Smith **hadn't seen** me in her garden."

Aber Frau Smith hat David doch gesehen! Of course, **if** David **had bought** the roses at a florist's, he **wouldn't have had** to steal the roses from poor Mrs Smith. He's lucky that Mrs Smith knows young David's mum and didn't call the police. **If** she **had called** the police, David **would have got** into trouble. I suppose the police **would have informed** his parents and **if** the police **had informed** his parents, they **would have been** very angry indeed. But, thank Goodness, Mrs Smith didn't phone the police and the police didn't inform his parents.

Wie Sie sehen, wird dieser Bedingungssatz nach folgendem Muster gebildet:

    if + had + *past participle* ... ...would + have + *past participle*

Hier eine Übersicht über die drei *If*-Sätze:

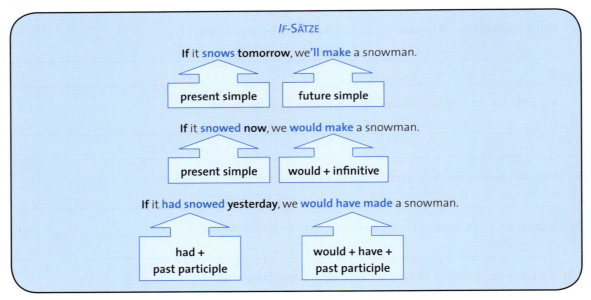

Now see if you can make some *if-clauses* (type 3) yourself:

Exercise C.

Write down the corresponding *if-clauses*.

1) I left the house late this morning and so I missed the train.

   *If I **hadn't left** the house so late this morning, I **wouldn't have missed** the train.*

2) We didn't get a ticket for the concert because we didn't book early.

3) I really felt ill yesterday after I had eaten nine pizzas in twenty minutes.

4) I didn't phone you yesterday because I didn't know you were here in London.

5) I didn't send you an email last Sunday because my computer broke down.

6) We didn't have enough money last summer, so we couldn't spend a holiday in the States.

7) I went to a party forty years ago and met my future wife.

8) It rained the whole day yesterday so we didn't go out for a picnic.

9) I didn't come to your birthday party on Saturday because you forgot to invite me.

10) Mr Green drove into another car last night because he didn't see the red lights.

_____

_____.

TIPP: Lernen Sie bitte die drei Merksätze und versuchen Sie, *If*-Sätze zu Ereignissen aus dem eigenen Leben zu bilden: Wie haben Sie Ihren Ehemann/Ihre Ehefrau oder Ihren Freund /Ihre Freundin kennengelernt? Warum wohnen Sie nicht an Ihrem Geburtsort? Wie sind Sie zu Ihrem Hobby gekommen? Warum besuchen Sie das Telekolleg? Hinter all diesen Fragen stecken *If*-Sätze:

    If my firm hadn't sent me to Augsburg, I wouldn't have looked for a flat here.
    If my friend hadn't asked me to play football, I wouldn't have become interested in this sport.
    If my girl-friend didn't go to Telekolleg, I wouldn't be here.
    If I lived in Memmingen, I would be nearer my parents.

EXERCISE D.

Look at the table above with the three *if-clauses* and then put the verbs in this exercise into their correct forms:

1) If I *had been* in Nuremberg last weekend, I *would have seen* my friend Martin.

2) If we _____ (not reduce) our consumption of energy, we'll have great problems in the near future.

3) If I _____ (live) nearer my job, I would have a much less stressful life.

4) We _____ (get) to work earlier yesterday if the train _____ (not be) late.

5) If I _____ (not have to go) to a conference last week I _____ (go) skiing.

6) What _____ (we/do) next week if the new software doesn't arrive?

7) Would you accept it if they _____ (offer) you a job in their firm?

8) If I _____ (not have to work) overtime so often, I'd stay in the firm.

9) We _____ (all/be) enormously happy if the economic climate remains positive next year.

10) The fish _____ (be) fresh if we _____ (come) to this restaurant six weeks ago.

11) John _____ (have) more chances with Mary if he didn't kick her while he was dancing with her.

12) If John _____ (learn) to dance when he was young, he

_____ (kick) Jane on her legs so often at the disco in the last few weeks.

13) If sales _____ (not improve) in the coming months, we'll have to decide

on a plan of action.

d) IF-CLAUSE – OTHER TYPES (*IF*-SATZ – ANDERE TYPEN)

Der Vollständigkeit halber werden hier einige zusätzliche Möglichkeiten aufgeführt. Im Moment reicht es jedoch, wenn Sie diese Formen in schriftlichen und mündlichen Äußerungen erkennen. Im Telekolleg-Hauptkurs werden Sie sicherlich die Möglichkeit haben, sich mehr damit zu beschäftigen.

- Wie im Deutschen lassen sich *If*-Sätze vom Typ 2 und 3 kombinieren, um Mischformen zu bilden:
  If I **spoke** Italian, I **would have got** the job in Rome.
  (Wenn ich Italienisch sprechen würde, hätte ich die Stelle in Rom bekommen).
  If I **hadn't met** my wife forty years ago, I **wouldn't be** so happy now.
- Wenn eine Bedingung automatisch zu einem bestimmten Ergebnis führt, können wir das *present simple* in beiden Teilen des *If*-Satzes verwenden:
  If you boil water, it turns into steam.
  (Wenn Sie Wasser kochen, verwandelt es sich in Dampf.)
  If someone works hard, he or she is successful.
- Statt *will* können Sie manchmal auch *can* oder *might* verwenden, statt *would* manchmal *could* oder *might*:
  If you had come to my party yesterday, you could have met my cousin.
  (hätte … treffen können)
  If you hurry, you might catch the train. (werden Sie vielleicht erwischen)
  If you hadn't got up late, you might have caught the train.
  (hätten Sie vielleicht … erwischt)

Let's look at words

Exercise E.

These words and expressions come from the book "Into the English World" text 15A (I and II) and 15D. They also fit into this dialogue. Where?

`virtually` `unless` `hospitable` `hassle` `supposing` `short notice` `invited` `recovered`

Samantha: Victor, I know it's rather _short notice_, but Marvin is holding a Christmas party tomorrow and he has _____ us to come.

Victor: He's a wonderful guy, so _____: he always makes everyone feel welcome, but I'm not sure that I can go.

Samantha: That's a shame. Why not?

Victor: Well, I only got back from Europe yesterday and I still haven't quite _____ from the jet lag yet. I'm afraid that _____ I feel better tomorrow, I won't be able to come.

Samantha: To tell you the truth, I'm not feeling too well, myself. It's such a _____ going to town to buy all the Christmas presents with all those crowds of people everywhere. _____ everyone seems to buy their presents at the last moment. Look, I'll tell you what – _____ we tell him the situation and go to his party next year. What do you think?

Victor: That's a good idea. I'm sure he'll understand.

EXERCISE F.

Which words fit together? You can find these expressions in "Into the English World" 15A (I and II) and 15D. What do they mean?

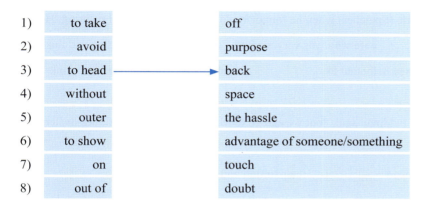

1) to take — off
2) avoid — purpose
3) to head — back
4) without — space
5) outer — the hassle
6) to show — advantage of someone/something
7) on — touch
8) out of — doubt

DO YOU STILL REMEMBER?

EXERCISE G.

The American constitution guarantees the right of everyone to carry a gun. Not everyone in the USA thinks this is a good idea. For our first revision exercise, please read this true story. Can you replace the *participial constructions*? The first one has been done for you as an example.

An old woman parked her car on a parking lot **situated** _(which was situated)_____ near a supermarket. **Having locked** _____ her car, she went into the supermarket. She returned to the car, **having finished** _____ her shopping.
She was rather surprised to see four men **sitting** _____ in the car, **drinking** _____ cola.
She quickly took out a gun from her bag and **pointing** _____ it at the four men told them to get out of the car. **Seeing** _____ the anger in the old woman's face and **not wanting** _____ to be shot by her, the four men rushed out of the car as quickly as they could.
The old woman got into the car, but **putting** _____ the key into the ignition, she found out that it didn't fit. It wasn't her car! In the meantime, the police having been **informed** _____ by the four men, arrived.

And now a small exercise on *pronouns*:

Exercise H.

Put in the missing *pronouns* (*our, us, ours, ourselves*, etc.) into this text:

Mr Feldman was looking in the attic (Speicher) when he found an old violin and an old oil painting. He showed _them_ to _____ wife who was very excited. "I remember this painting and this violin," she told _____, "they belonged to _____ grandfather. How much do you think they're worth?"

"I don't know _____," Mr Feldman said, "but we can go to Mrs Daly. She's an antiques dealer (Händler). I'm sure she can tell _____."

So they went to Mrs Daly and showed _____ the painting and the violin.

"Good Heavens!" she said, "These things of _____ are interesting. You've got a Picasso and a Stradivarius there!"

"Great!" said Mr Feldman. "They must be worth millions of dollars. Just think," he said to Mrs Feldman, "now we can buy _____ a big house in the country!"

"I'm sorry to tell _____ this," said the antiques dealer, "but unfortunately they're not worth much. Stradivarius painted the picture and Picasso made the violin."

One last exercise – this time on *question forms*.

Exercise I.

Write *questions* to find the missing information:

1) I saw John at the concert on

   When did you see John?

2) Salina is quite talented. She plays quite a few different musical instruments.

   How many _____?

3) Cedric has to do a few things before he leaves the office this evening.

   What _____?

4) The sales manager is going to the meeting next week.

   Where _____?

5) We've been working on this problem for a very long time.

How long _____?

6) Mr Peat worked in one of our other branches.

Which _____?

That was hard work, wasn't it? Now it is time to relax. **If** you **read** this story, you **will see** examples of the *if-clauses* again. I'm sure you**'ll** also smile **if** you **read** it.

A bank robber was sent to prison, but he refused to tell the police where he had hidden the money. One day he received a letter from his wife. She wrote: "I really need to plant the potatoes in the back garden, but first I have to dig up the back garden. **If** you **weren't** in prison, you **could dig** up the back garden and I **wouldn't have to do** it by myself."
The bank robber wrote back: "Don't dig up the back garden. That's where I hid the money. **If** you **dig** up the back garden, the police **will** immediately **find** the money!"
A week later, he received another letter from his wife. "You won't believe this," she wrote, "yesterday I had just started to dig up the back garden, when suddenly ten policemen came. They dug up the whole garden for me! Afterwards, they looked very disappointed (enttäuscht) and they left. **If** they **hadn't dug** up the garden for me I **would have needed** hours to do it myself!" The bank robber wrote back: "Now plant the potatoes."
If you **think** a while, you **can find** an answer to most problems. That's also true for bank robbers in prison!

We have now come to the end of this trainer. **If** I **were** you, I **would go** through all the chapters again. If you **look** at the next page, you**'ll find** a test on many of the things we have looked at in these past 15 chapters. If you **do** the test, you **can see** which chapters you should look at again!

TEST YOUR GRAMMAR!

A. Put the right *pronouns* in these sentences, where necessary.

1) "Philip, is this one of _your (my)_ pens or is it _____?"
2) Richard and I injured _____ very badly in a road accident last year.
3) Some very young children cannot concentrate _____ on a task for longer than five minutes.
4) Tony and Gillian send _____ love letters every day. They really can't afford _____ the time to do this, because they have very busy jobs.
5) "Peter, darling, your two children are having difficulties with _____ maths homework. Can you help _____?"
6) "I'm sorry but they'll have to do the homework _____. I could never understand maths!"
7) The coal industry in Germany has many problems. That's one reason why the government supports _____ financially.
8) Mrs Deakin has to attend the meeting and I think this report is _____. Mr Donnelly isn't working on the project, so it can't be _____.

B. Put the verbs in their correct forms.

1) Most of the time Jenny _doesn't use_ (not use) her laptop, but today she _____ (use) it because the computer has broken down.
2) This is terrible! We _____ (work) on this problem for the last two hours and we _____ (not find) an answer yet.
3) If Stuart _____ (not always come) to the office so late every day, he would finish his work before five o'clock.
4) After we _____ (wait) for two hours, Peter finally came. He _____ (not apologize) for being late.
5) We'll inform our neighbours before we _____ (leave) for our holiday tomorrow.
6) Our firm _____ (sell) more of the new washing machines last year if there _____ (be) a better marketing campaign before the products came onto the market.

7) Too much pollution _____ (cause) nowadays by cars and lorries.

8) Don't worry! Maybe we won't finish the job on Thursday or even on Friday, but by Saturday at the latest we _____ (finish) it.

C. Put the words in the right order to make sensible sentences.

1) we'll / nearer / Sheffield / we / If / move / be / my / sister. / to

   _If we move to Sheffield ..._____

2) during / train / the / comes / The / late / usually / week.

   _____

3) weren't / letters / you / you! / The / for / read

   _____

4) been / buildings / floods. / by / destroyed / Many / the / have /

   _____

D. Put in *although, because, how, what, whether, which, who* or *whose*.

1) The colleague _who_____ is working in the next room is our new sales assistant.

2) They went for a walk _____ it was raining very heavily.

3) I didn't agree with Malcolm's idea _____ I thought it was too impractical.

4) These papers _____ are lying on my table don't belong to me.

5) I didn't understand _____ he was trying to say.

6) I'm afraid I don't know _____ to operate this machine. Can you show me?

7) The colleague _____ email address I've given you will help you if you have any problems.

8) We aren't sure _____ to go to Oxford or to Brighton for our outing (Ausflug).

E. Finish the second sentence so that it has a similar meaning to the first sentence.

1) A professional photographer photographed us at our wedding.

   We _were photographed_____ at our wedding _____ a professional photographer.

2) "Will you be in Munich tomorrow?"

   Peter asked me _____ the next day.

3) My wife and I started working for this company twenty years ago.

   For the last twenty years _____.

15

4) William thinks that card games aren't as interesting as chess.

   William thinks that chess _____.

5) Josephine didn't work hard enough last year so she didn't pass her exams.

   If Josephine _____, she _____ her exams.

6) It's silly to switch on the TV now because we have to leave in five minutes.

   It's not worth _____.

7) Oh that's great! I'm going to see my cousins on Saturday!

   I'm really looking forward _____!

8) Turkish is a fascinating language, but unfortunately I don't have the time to learn it.

   I _____ if _____.

9) "Mary, please don't smoke in the house."

   "Mary, we would like _____."

10) Nobody except for Giovanni began the work on time.

    Giovanni was the only one _____.

11) "Did you go to the computer fair in Hamburg last week?"

    One of our colleagues asked her _____
    _____ the week before.

12) Louisa doesn't drink as much beer as I do.

    Louisa drinks _____.

F. Read these sentences and if there are mistakes in them, please correct them.

1) We've been living here since many years.

   We've been living here **for** many years.

2) Claudia, three friends of you are waiting to play with you!

   _____

3) We had a wonderful holiday in California before three years.

   _____

4) Where you work?

   _____

5) I didn't see your brother yesterday.

   _____

6) I can't remember me his face.

7) I really find this grammar rules easy to understand.

8) We'll be eating a wonderful meal at the Ritz hotel this time tomorrow.

9) We don't have an own car – we borrow our brother's one when we drive into town.

10) The Harry Potter books were written from J. K. Rowling.

11) He has to wear an uniform in his job.

12) We always on Tuesdays go to our club.

G. Write down the *short answers*.
1) "You didn't see Frank's presentation yesterday." "Oh yes, _I did_____."
2) "Terry and Sue speak good German." "I'm sorry, but unfortunately _____."
3) "James owns a blue Aston Martin." "Really, I don't think _____."
4) "Janet really should give up smoking." "You're right, _____."
5) "Diana has been fired from her job." "I'm pleased to say that, thank Goodness, _____."
6) "I think we can get the eight o'clock if we leave now." "Of course, _____!
It's already 7.56 and the station is two miles away!"

H. Write down the *question tags*.
1) Your sisters didn't bake this cake, _did they_____?
2) Simon and I can come to your party a little later, _____?
3) Brian doesn't feel too well in his new job, _____?
4) I'm too late for the presentation, _____?
5) Daniella hasn't understood the instructions, _____?
6) Mrs Dubovie, you will be at our meeting tomorrow, _____?

I. Put the verbs in brackets into their correct forms. Add *prepositions* where necessary.

1) Harry always succeeds _in winning_ (win) at chess. He seems _____ (do) it without _____ (concentrate) much on the game!

2) I really can't manage _____ (get) up so early in the morning. I'm used _____ (sleep) until about 8 o'clock.

3) It's rather late, I think we should _____ (leave) now.

4) Jean promised _____ (knit) me a pullover. I've been waiting _____ her _____ (do) it for ages. She always has difficulty _____ (remember) her promises.

5) My boss wants me _____ (take) my holiday in August, but I don't like the idea _____ (spend) my holiday _____ (lie) on beach with thousands of sunbathers. I'll try to persuade him _____ (let) me _____ (have) my holidays in April or May.

6) I really don't know whether _____ (leave) my job or not. I certainly don't enjoy _____ (have to do) the same monotonous tasks day after day. However, I'm worried _____ (not find) another job so easily. So I suppose. I'll stay in my present job for a while. Maybe the management will agree _____ (give) me a better job in this firm.

J. Replace the *participial constructions*:

1) All those people living near the main road complain about the noisy traffic.
   All those people **who live** near the main road complain about the noisy traffic.

2) The strategy decided on turned out (sich herausstellen) to be rather unsuccessful.
   _____
   _____

3) Not having much money we had to walk home instead of taking a taxi.
   _____
   _____

4) If required, I can come into the office over the weekend.
   _____
   _____

5) Many people working with asbestos in the past had – and still have – serious health problems.

_____

_____

K. Put in the right *adjectives* or *adverbs*.

1) I don't understand why, but _lately_____ (late) my train has always arrived ten minutes

   _____ (late).

2) We'll have to work _____ (hard) if we want to send off all the catalogues before

   5 pm.

3) Have you got a sore throat (Halsweh)? Your voice sounds a bit _____ (funny).

4) Robert is an _____ (extreme/dangerous) driver. He doesn't drive

   _____ (careful) at all.

TEST YOUR VOCABULARY!

Ich hoffe, dass Sie mithilfe der Sendungen und Bücher Ihren englischen Wortschatz ausgebaut haben – auch wenn diese wichtige Arbeit selbstverständlich im Telekolleg-Hauptkurs fortgesetzt werden muss. Die folgenden Übungen werden Ihnen helfen, einiges in Erinnerung zu rufen und zu verfestigen.

A. Which words from "Into the English World" chapters 1–15 do not fit?

1) huge (6A), vast (12D), enormous, ornate (5D)

   Huge, vast und _enormous_ haben die Bedeutung von „sehr groß".

   Ornate bedeutet „verziert".

2) recreation (11D), intersection (12A), relaxation (2D), vacation (7A)

   _____

   _____

3) celebrity (13D), graduate (13F), degree (14A), university (2D)

   _____

   _____

4) mortgage (13D), revenues (7D), tax (11D), outskirts (11D)

   _____

   _____

5) crazy (13A), picturesque (12D), freaky(6A), weird (9A)

6) boarding school (2D), boundaries (8D), curriculum (2D), primary level (2D)

7) magnificent (5D), awesome (14A), flamboyant (6D), enduring (11D)

B. Word building: Form the right words!

1) Good Heavens! This view is really _spectacular_ (spectacle).
2) After the all-night party, Hugh's _____ (appear) looked quite strange.
3) You can pay for the goods after _____ (deliver).
4) Tania is a really _____ (mess) person. You should see her bedroom!
5) Forty _____ (employ) of the firm work in this department.
6) The _____ (major) of the tourists who come to Cardiff visit the castle.
7) _____ (immigrate) to Germany has increased recently.

C. Write in the right *prepositions*:

| up | of | on | to | up | ~~from~~ | to | off | to | of | for | to |

1) The English Channel separates Britain _from_ France.
2) Twenty seven countries at present make _____ the European Union.
3) In contrast _____ many other countries, the number of graduates in this country is quite high.
4) Our country is in danger _____ falling behind if we don't invest more in education.
5) Some animals have a surprising way of adapting _____ their environment.
6) Bill wanted _____ study physics but he ended _____ studying engineering.
7) Instead _____ sending off dozens of emails, Jack prefers to write old-fashioned letters.
8) I'm looking _____ somebody who can talk to me in English. But I can't find anyone.
9) Pete's really keen _____ learning languages.

10) We're looking forward _____ trying out our English with our guests from Nigeria.

11) Maurine's new dress triggered _____ a long discussion!

D. Which words and expressions fit together?

1) Last June I had to attend a _course_ in business management in San Francisco.

2) I took a flight from Munich and it took me ages to reach my _____.

3) What's more – after my flight to America it took me a few days to recover from my jet _____.

4) I couldn't stand up straight – let _____ walk to the bathroom.

5) I was so ill that I just wanted to head _____ to Munich.

6) Without _____ that was one of the worst flights I have ever had.

7) I recovered after a few days and wanted to _____ a car and see the sights before the course started.

8) I thought I had remembered to take everything with me, but I hadn't paid enough _____.

9) I had forgotten to take my driver's _____ with me!

| ~~course~~ | doubt | destination | lag | alone | back | attention | license | rent |

E. How many words from the book "Into the English World" chapters 1–15 can you find here?

o	d	u	m	p	w	o	r	t	h	s	o	b	a	t
v	e	n	t	w	c	o	m	p	u	l	s	o	r	y
e	p	a	t	t	e	n	d	o	u	g	h	t	a	o
r	o	e	n	a	r	i	i	n	v	r	a	a	n	d
l	s	l	n	a	x	c	r	o	a	a	r	f	n	e
o	i	a	o	s	i	u	b	d	l	b	k	l	o	p
o	t	r	i	l	a	n	d	l	i	n	e	a	y	a
k	p	o	e	a	d	a	p	t	d	i	e	t	e	r
u	b	d	r	e	p	u	t	a	t	i	o	n	d	t

F. Which words from the word search (exercise E) fit into this story? You may need to change them a little!

Mr and Mrs Feldman had been __attending__ singing lessons for a year, but unfortunately they didn't have the best of _____ for their singing. In fact, when they practised their duets in their living room every evening, for their neighbours, it sounded really _____ – rather like a frightened cat.

5 One evening Mr and Mrs Feldman had just left their _____ and were on their way to their singing lesson when Mr Feldman suddenly shouted out to his wife: "Oh, no!"

"What's the matter?" Mrs Feldman asked.

"I've _____ something really important. What an idiot I am! It's my mum's birthday today. We haven't sent her a birthday card. She'll be quite sad and _____."

10 "I know," said Mrs Feldman, "When we come back from the lesson, I'll make her a nice, __delicious__ cake and we'll take it to her."

"It really isn't _____ doing that," said Mr Feldman, "have you forgotten? For the past few weeks my mum has been on a _____. She certainly won't want to eat one of your cakes. And maybe she'll be in bed when we get home. I think we _____ to

15 phone her here and now and wish her a Happy Birthday."

176 | Test

"O.K.," his wife said, "you can use my mobile phone – yours isn't working." Mr Feldman _____ the mobile phone his wife offered him and dialed his mother's number. As soon as somebody picked up the phone at the other end both Mr and Mrs Feldman started singing "Happy Birthday to you" as loudly as they could. Unfortunately, as usual, their singing sounded quite
20 terrible.

"Dr Hamilton speaking. Who's there? " the man at the other end asked.

"Oh, my Goodness," Mr Feldman said, "I'm sorry we've got the wrong number." "Don't worry," Dr Hamilton replied. "After listening to your terrible singing, I can hear that both of you need all the practice you can get!"

G. In this trainer and in "Into the English World" we have seen many words ("false friends") that are difficult for German learners of English. Find the right translations for the words in brackets:

Ruben and Leah are talking to each other in the _break_ (Pause) at school.

"I'm really worried," says Ruben, "my father works so hard – ten hours a day. And with the money that his _____ (Chef) gives him, he pays for our nice home and lots of food for me and my sisters. And my mum _____ (verbringt) the whole day cleaning and cooking for us. She
5 and dad _____ (sparen) the whole year to buy us birthday and Christmas presents. And on Christmas Day and on our birthdays we _____ (bekommen) wonderful presents – _____ (eventuell) the best presents in the world. Our granddad, who lives with us, gives me and my sisters extra pocket money every week, _____ (obwohl) he only has a small _____ (Rente). I'm really so worried, I can tell you!"
10 "Worried? Well, _____ (eigentlich) I don't understand you," says Leah. "I _____ (meine) your parents and granddad are great. I'm sure many kids would be _____ (glücklich) to live in such a family. In my _____ (Meinung) you live in a paradise. Why are you so worried?"

"Well," says Ruben, "what if they try to run away?"

15

Key to Exercises

Chapter 1

Exercise A.
2) He; 3) They; 4) We; 5) It; 6) They; 7) You; 8) I ; I;

Exercise B.
2) you; 3) me; 4) them; 5) them; 6) her; 7) us; 8) you;
9) it; 10) it;

Exercise C.
2) her; 3) She; 4) They; 5) It; 6) them;

Exercise D.
2) his; 3) her; 4) my; 5) your; 6) my; 7) his; 8) your;
9) my; 10) her; 11) their; 12) his; 13) her; 14) their; 15) my; 16) his;
17) his; 18) our; 19) my; 20) his; 21) mine; 22) yours; 23) mine;

Exercise E.
1) The patient in the waiting room is very nervous.
The dentist introduces **himself**: "Hello, I'm Dr Wilson, your dentist. Now, don't worry," he says. "It won't hurt you."
"I don't believe you," says the other man, "I'm a dentist **myself**."
2) "Please hurry and open the door," Bill says to his friend Fred.
Fred complains: "Can't you open the door **yourself**?"
"Of course I can open the door **myself**," says Bill, "but the paint is still wet."
3) Helen and Robert have got a telephone love affair: They talk to **each other** eight hours a day on their mobile phones. They can't, of course, really afford it, but they feel so happy!
4) Rachel and Tom looked at **each other** in the eyes. "I love you Rachel," Tom said.
"I love **myself**, too," Rachel replied, as she looked at **herself** in her pocket mirror.
5) Tim and his sister Sue are feeling hungry. "Look at the biscuits on the table!" Tim says. "Let's help **ourselves**." "We can't," says Sue. "They're dog biscuits."

Exercise F.
lives; children; students; cities; diets; toys; men; families; brushes; knives; women; difficulties; industries; steaks; feet; sheep; fish;

Exercise G.
am; is; am; are; is;

Exercise H.
2) I'm; 3) aren't ; they're; 4) I'm; I'm 5) We're; It's; 6) she isn't; She's;
or: she's; She isn't;

Exercise I.
1) Can you hear my sister? No, I can't hear her. But your brothers are in the next room and they are (they're) very noisy. You can hear them.
2) That's a book of ours.
3) We have our own method to learn words (of learning words).

Exercise J.
enthusiastic = begeistert (German: enthusiastisch)
medical service = Gesundheitswesen (The German words "medizinisch" and "Service" can help you here.)
return = zurückkehren (Look at the context!)
flexible = anpassungsfähig (German: flexibel)
maths = Mathe
unsporty/uncreative (No problem for speakers of German!)
written off = abgestempelt (abgeschrieben) (The same expression in German)
purely = rein (The German word "pur" can help here.)
theoretical = No problem for Germans!
excelling = sich auszeichnend, übertreffend (The German word "exzellent" can help you here.)
multicultural (The German word is very similar.)
origin = Ursprung

Exercise K.
2) famous (fame = Ruhm); natural (Natur = nature)
3) important (importance = Wichtigkeit)
4) varied (vary = sich unterscheiden, unterschiedlich sein, (sich) verändern)
5) countless (count = zählen)
The German words "natürlich" und "variieren" können Ihnen hier helfen.

Exercise L.

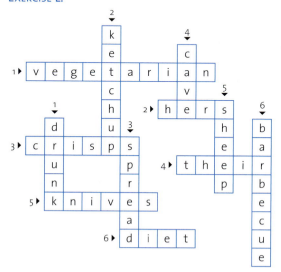

CHAPTER 2

EXERCISE A.
2) an English word
3) a barbecue
4) an umbrella
5) an organization
6) a computer
7) a useful book
8) a French town
9) an octopus
10) a European city
11) an address
12) an apple
13) an honour
14) a happy TK student
15) an office
16) an insect

EXERCISE B.
1) He's always in a hurry.
2) He's a smoker.
3) She's an English woman/She's English and a teacher.
4) For a change we can eat here.

EXERCISE C.
2) I liked George right from **the** beginning.
3) We need water to live. **The** water here is very rich in minerals.
4) I must go to bed early tonight.
5) Munich is **the** city which I live in.
6) Not everybody likes city life.
7) John is still at school. **The** school in our town is very big.
8) What can we eat for breakfast?
9) **The** second meal of the day is lunch.
10) **The** breakfast that they serve in this restaurant is not cheap.
11) I live in Lenham Road, near Jessam Avenue.
12) Westminster Abbey is near Trafalgar Square and Hyde Park.
13) In March we want to go to New York and see Central Park.

EXERCISE D.
2) **Those** houses in the next street are all very old.
3) **This** book here is very interesting.
4) Oh dear! Look at **those** black clouds. We can forget our picnic!
5) Hey – who left **these** letters here on my desk?
6) **This** car here is mine, but **that** car is hers.

EXERCISE E.
2) the twenty-first of March two thousand and ten
3) the fifteenth of October nineteen ninety-three
4) the thirty-first of December eighteen eighty-four
5) the fifth of February seventeen seventy-three
6) the eleventh of July two thousand and eight
7) the twenty-third of January nineteen seventy
8) the ninth of November nineteen eighty-nine
9) the twelfth of May eighteen seventy-one
10) the twenty-second of September two thousand and five

Exercise F.
2) 8.55 — eight fifty-five (in the morning); five to nine
3) 10.30 — ten-thirty; (a) half past ten (in the morning)
4) 11.35 — eleven thirty-five; twenty-five to twelve (in the morning)
5) 15.45 — fifteen forty-five; (a) quarter to four (in the afternoon)
6) 19.40 — nineteen forty; twenty (minutes) to eight (in the evening)
7) 5.59 — five fifty-nine; one minute to six (in the morning)
8) 17.09 — seventeen nine; nine minutes past five (in the afternoon)
9) 12.00 — twelve o'clock; midday
10) 13.27 — twenty-seven minutes past (after) one (in the afternoon)

Exercise G.
2) New Zealand and Australia **belong to** the Commonwealth.
3) The number of tourists here **keeps on** rising every year.
4) The region is **characterized by** sleeping volcanoes.
5) Every year I **look forward to** my holiday in Brighton.
6) London is **famous for** its many sights.
7) The Commonwealth **consists of** many countries in four continents.
8) Education is **divided into** four different types of education: primary, secondary, further and higher education.

Exercise H.
1) Mrs Smith's son comes home with dirty shoes. She looks at **him** and says: "Look at those dirty shoes. Why can't you clean **them** before you come in?" "Mummy," **her** son asks **her**: "You mustn't be angry with **me**. You've got a vacuum cleaner (Staubsauger). Why can't you get **it**, clean the floor **yourself** and laugh like the woman in the TV commercial for vacuum cleaners?"
2) The customs official (Zollbeamter) sees the two passengers and asks **them**: "Cognac? Whisky? Cigarettes?" The man says: "That's very nice of **you**, but no thank you." "Yes," says **his** wife. "**We** have already got **them ourselves**. Look at this bag. **They**'re in **it**."

Exercise I.
1) Stuart is a good friend of ours.
2) We write to each other every day.
3) Is this book yours?
4) Carol has got her own room.
5) I'm worried about my old aunt. She can't remember me.

Chapter 3

Exercise A.
2) c) Now I need to update the software.
3) c) Could you please repeat the last step?
4) a) We can buy the laptop in this shop tomorrow.
5) b) Tom usually works in London from Monday to Friday.

Exercise B.
2) Mr Smith doesn't always eat cornflakes for breakfast.
3) We play table-tennis together after work. (After work we play table-tennis together.)
4) I can see a red light on the router.
5) Our colleague is downloading the software onto the computer.
6) The secretary hardly ever sends her reports by e-mail.
7) Our partner Ms Maunders must send the catalogue today. (Today our partner Ms Maunders must send the catalogue.)
8) My girlfriend usually takes her cigarette out of her mouth before she kisses me.
9) I can use the laptop on Ray's desk now. (Now I can use the laptop on Ray's desk.)

Exercise C.
2) I eat an apple every day. (Every day I eat an apple.)
3) Peter and Mary are making breakfast now. (Now Peter and Mary are making breakfast.)
4) Mark can't install the new program.
5) We need to update the program.
6) I don't have the latest version of the software here.
7) You can always read the labels from the front.
8) I don't have the latest version of the firmware.
9) They don't usually work in the office on Saturdays. (On Saturdays they don't usually work in the office.)
10) Peter always goes on a diet every summer. (Every summer Peter always goes on a diet.)

Exercise D.
Lösung siehe Kapitel 3.

Exercise E.
2) Do you always eat a big breakfast?
3) Do you need my help?
4) Does Tom have the updated version of the software?
5) Does Miriam work with the new program?
6) Do the children in this English class read Harry Potter stories?
7) Do Mrs Jenkins and Mr Finch work in this room?
8) Do I need to download the software?

Exercise F.
2) **Can** you install the latest software?
3) **Is** Tom connecting the computer to the power supply?
4) **Can** you see a red light on the Router?

5) **Have** you installed the T-Box program?
6) **May/Can/Could** I help you?
7) **Could/Would** you connect the extension cord to the T-phone for me, please?
8) **Would** you like a cup of coffee?
9) **Are** those two colleagues flying to New York?

Exercise G.
2) a) Quick, our train leaves at 5 o'clock. We have to leave now.
3) b) Some people are able to remember a hundred numbers in 5 minutes.
4) a) Many doctors have to work at night.
5) b) My brother isn't able to read Spanish.

Exercise H.
2) a) Bill mustn't forget to buy a ticket for the train. I haven't got a ticket for him.
3) b) Bill doesn't have to buy a ticket for the train. I've got a ticket for him.
4) b) Yvonne mustn't park here. She's next to the bus stop!
5) b) We can eat here, but we needn't. There's another good restaurant in the next street.

Exercise I.
1) We needn't (don't need to/haven't got to/don't have to) buy a new computer.
2) We mustn't come home too late.
3) May I come again tomorrow?
4) They/You mustn't connect the laptop.
5) Could you come to me, please?

Exercise J.

neighbourhood:	Nachbarschaft; wir können das Wort von *neighbour* ableiten.
huge:	riesengroß; Rachel says: And the windows are huge, so there's always lots of light. Deswegen können wir schlussfolgern, dass *huge* „sehr groß" bedeutet.
bookshelves:	Bücherregale. Was könnte *shelves* sonst bedeuten!
utility costs:	Kosten für Strom, Wasser etc. Für eine Wohnung zahlt man in der Regel (as a rule!) nicht nur die Miete, sondern auch Nebenkosten wie Strom, Wasser etc. Die Kosten für den *caretaker* (Hausmeister), falls vorhanden, sind in der Miete enthalten.

Exercise K.
2) With a computer you **encounter** one problem after the other every day!
3) The Scottish kilt bears **witness** to the Scottish love of tradition.
4) **Apart from** Scotland, three other countries – England, Wales and Northern Ireland make up the United Kingdom of Great Britain.
5) The most **populated** parts of Scotland are the cities and towns.
6) Bars and cafés in Edinburgh are often old **converted** houses.
7) Not everybody drinks alcohol in **moderation**.
8) Life for the Scottish was often a life full of **hardship**.
9) Not many people in Scotland try to **cultivate** the traditional Scottish language, Gaelic.
10) The United Kingdom was **founded** over three hundred years ago.

Exercise L.
2) George has a book of **mine**.
3) Tamara has **her** own car.
4) Nobody in New Zealand is written **off** as unsporty.
5) John has **a** cold.
6) With **the** help of my Spanish wife, I am learning Spanish.
7) **Those** flowers in the next garden are lovely.
8) I'm looking forward **to** the next programme on TV.
9) I love most music but **the** music which my teenage son plays is terrible.
10) The car industry in this country is very strong. **It** is important for the economy.

Chapter 4

Exercise A.
2) I**'m having** breakfast now.
3) Today we **aren't working** in the office. We**'re swimming** in the sea.
4) "That machine is so noisy." "It's OK – I**'m stopping** it right now.
5) Hey Terry – you **aren't doing (you're not doing)** your homework!
6) Look at Harold and Meg: They**'re lying** on the wet grass.
7) We**'re seeing** the client next week.

Exercise B.
1) I **live** in a small town in Scotland, but my brothers **don't live** near me. They **live** in Oxford.
2) Betty **isn't** very happy in her new job. She **likes** to have a lot of colleagues around her.
3) **Do** you **drive** an old car?
4) We **cannot come** to the party tomorrow.
5) Malcolm **doesn't get** home early during the week. He seldom **gets** home before eight o'clock in the evening.
6) We **don't usually eat** in fast food restaurants.
7) **Do** you **speak** French?
8) Gerry **still plays** tennis, although he **is** 94 years old!
9) David and I **don't go** out very often but once a month we usually **watch** a film at the local cinema. Jane sometimes **watches** the film with us.
10) Alison always **brushes** her teeth before she **kisses** me, but I **don't often brush** my teeth.
11) **Does** your wife **smoke** cigarettes in bed? No, she **doesn't smoke** cigarettes in bed – she **smokes** a pipe.
12) Bill and Sue **shouldn't go** on a diet. They only **weigh** fifty kilograms each.

Exercise C.
1) "Why **do** birds **fly** south in winter?"
   "Because they **don't want** to walk."
2) "Waiter! What**'s** (What **is**) this fly **doing** on my ice cream?"
   "I **think** it**'s learning** to ski, sir."
3) "What **is** that woman **doing**?" "She**'s looking** for a one pound piece."
   "How **do** you **know**?" "Because **I'm holding** it here in my hand."
4) Mrs Simmonds: "Doctor, it's terrible. My husband **blows** smoke rings every day."
   Doctor Dobbin: "That's O.K., Mrs Simmonds. Many smokers **do** that."
   Mrs Simmonds: "But my husband **doesn't smoke**!"
5) Little four-year old Tania and her dad are in New York for the first time.
   They **are standing** in a lift in a skyscraper and the lift **is going** higher and higher.
   Tania asks her father: "Dad, **does** God **know** that we**'re coming**?"
6) "How many hours **do** you **sleep** every day?" "Four to five."
   "That isn't enough!" "It's enough for me. I **sleep** ten hours every night."
7) "You **need** glasses," the optician says.
   "But," says the patient, "**I'm wearing** glasses now."
   "Then I **need** glasses," says the optician.

Exercise D.
1) Please don't smoke in the bathroom.
2) Sam! Take your cat out of the fridge!
3) Norma, don't play with the tigers – that's dangerous!

Exercise E.
2) b) Where can we go now?
3) a) What are you doing at the moment, Bill?
4) b) Why must we leave so early?
5) a) Which student can give me the answer?
6) b) Who is coming to your party tomorrow?
7) b) Which country attracts the most tourists?
8) a) Who speaks Russian here?
9) a) How many people attended the knitting course last weekend?
10) a) Who plays golf in your family and how often does he play?
11) a) Where do all these people come from?

Exercise F.
1) Who visits Mr and Mrs Meier every weekend?
2) How often does Claudia visit her parents?
3) Who is speaking (talking) to Fred at the moment (right now)?
   (Im Prinzip ist die Ergänzung *at the moment* oder *right now* nicht unbedingt nötig. Indem wir die Verlaufsform verwenden, drücken wir aus, dass die Person <u>gerade</u> mit Fred spricht.)
4) What are they speaking about?
5) How many colleagues work here every day?
6) How many colleagues do you meet here every day?
7) Who can help me – and when can he help me?

Exercise G.

1) How many colleagues are going hiking?
   When are the colleagues going hiking?
2) Which country is famous for this product? (Wales)
   Which product is this country famous for? (sheep)
3) Which animals populate the lush pastures of this country? (sheep)
   Which country do these animals populate? (Wales)
4) Who have to learn this subject? (pupils in Welsh schools)
   Which subject do they have to learn? (Welsh)
5) Whose brother is trying out the new software?
   Which software is he (my brother) trying out?

Exercise H.

1) Ich sende Ihnen das Dokument per E-mail. Es befindet sich (ist) im Anhang.
2) Diese Insel ist unbewohnbar.
3) Peter trennte die Adresse vom Brief(-kopf) ab.
4) Der Sturm entwurzelte viele Bäume.
5) Jeremy ist gegenüber anderen Meinungen ziemlich intolerant.
6) Marshalls Brüder sind nicht sehr nett. Sie schließen den armen Marshall von ihren Spielen aus.
7) Donalds Vater ist dumm: Er zwingt seinen Sohn, siebzig lateinische Vokabeln jeden Tag zu lernen.
8) Mein Verdienst in diesem Job ist nicht sehr hoch.

Exercise I.

2) Many old people in the centres of our towns cannot pay the high **rents** for flats because their **pensions** are so low.
3) I **think** that my little son doesn't know what the word "quiet" **means**!
4) I can **save** money this month but unfortunately I can't **spare** the time to go to the bank today.
5) Darling – you weigh more than 95 kilograms. You're too **heavy** for me to carry! And I feel so tired after my maths exam. It was so **difficult/hard**.
6) This is really **heavy** rain and the wind is so **strong**, but I can't run home faster. I'm a **heavy** smoker!
7) I can't find my glasses so I can't **drive** my car or even **ride** my motorbike. But I can always **go** by bus.
8) Tony **attends** an English course at an evening institute. After the course he always **visits** his uncle.
9) What a **nice** sister you have! She is always so **sympathetic** when I tell her about my problems.
10) I'm **surprised** Tony isn't here. I **wonder** where he is.

Exercise J.

1) Michael is a vegetarian.
2) We can stay at home for a change. (For a change we can stay at home.)
3) Mr Stanley needn't work today.
4) Helen is always in a hurry.
5) I often drink a cup of tea in the garden after work.
6) We can't buy the furniture today – it's Sunday!
7) Susan, you mustn't come home too late.

Exercise K.
2) You mustn't always go to school so late.
3) Do you often learn English words before work?
4) Simon needn't download the report onto his computer.
5) We can give him the printed version next week.
6) Mr Hindly occasionally leaves his firm before 3 pm on Friday.

Exercise L.
2) those hobbies   3) people (two persons)   4) profits   5) potatoes   6) women

Exercise M.
2) Does Fred (he) eat sauerkraut **for breakfast?**
3) Does she attend an **English course** every Tuesday?
4) Is she visiting **her parents**?
5) Yes, but can he finish it (the work) **before 8 o'clock**?
6) Really? Do they work in the **same company**?
7) Oh, and does **this earring** belong to her, **too**?
8) Did she watch the **"Titanic"** last night?
9) But, are they allowed to go to the disco **at the weekend**?

Chapter 5

Exercise A.
2) Gillian's boyfriend can cook very well, **can't he**?
3) Her children shouldn't eat so much, **should they**?
4) Malcolm doesn't answer many e-mails, **does he**?
5) That information is very useful, **isn't it**?
6) Ronald has got three children, **hasn't he**?
7) Your wife works in our firm, **doesn't she**?
8) There are lots of tourists in Munich, **aren't there**?
9) Tania's brother could help us to move the piano, **couldn't he**?
10) I mean, he's got strong muscles, **hasn't he**?
11) You don't live near us, **do you**?
12) Rebecca and Simon know a lot about Scottish history, **don't they**?
13) The weather is so nice. Let's have a picnic, **shall we**?
14) I'm not too late, **am I**?
15) Christine, please answer the phone, **will you**?
16) I'm too early, **aren't I**?

Exercise B.
2) "Does Tom use the latest version of the BR–10–12 TK software?" "**No, he doesn't**. It's too expensive."
3) "Must you go now?" "**Yes, (unfortunately/I'm sorry/I'm afraid) we must**. We must be at the office at 2 pm."
4) "Have you got a brother?" "**Yes, I have**. In fact I've got a sister, too."
5) "Do you speak French?" "**Yes, I do**. But only a little."
6) "Are Harry and Maude interested in swimming?" "**No, they aren't**. Harold and Maude hate all sports!"
7) "Is Stephanie a good cook?" "**No, she isn't**. She eats in a restaurant every day!"

8) "Are the prices rising?" "**Yes, (unfortunately) they are**. Everything is so expensive."
9) "Is English food wonderful?" "**Yes, it certainly is!** Especially the fish and chips – I could eat that every day!"

Exercise C.
1) I am **inspired** (begeistert; in anderen Zusammenhängen auch: inspiriert) by the natural beauty of Ireland's landscape.
2) Most people do not go to a **grocer** (Inhaber eines Lebensmittelgeschäfts) to buy their groceries – they go to a supermarket.
3) In 2011 there is the 80th anniversary of the **founding** (Gründung; foundation: Grundlage) of the Republic of Ireland.
4) John has a really **annoying** (ärgerliche) habit. He's always late.
5) The **surroundings** (Umgebung) of Dublin are really spectacular.
6) Are these your **belongings** (Sachen, Besitz), Christina?
7) Your husband **appears** (scheint) to be a little overworked.
8) Despite (trotz) the **division** (Teilung) of Ireland into two parts it is now easy to travel from the Republic of Ireland to Northern Ireland.

Exercise D.
2) "You're English, but you don't seem to be interested in the **current** situation in English politics." "Well, **actually** I'm not English, I'm Irish."
3) "Helmut, why are you **carrying** ten pairs of 'Lederhosen'?" "Well, my friends from America and I want to **wear** them at the Oktoberfest."

Exercise E.
1) **telephone;** *delicious*, *chips* and *barbecue* have something to do with food.
2) **It's chilly;** You say *Don't mention it*, *You're welcome* or *It's my pleasure* if someone says *Thank you* to you for something. You say *It's chilly* if it's cold.
3) **fortresses**; *mountains, pastures,* and *hills* are natural parts of a landscape, a *fortress* (Festung) isn't.
4) **capital**; *government*, *parliament* and *House of Commons* are parts of the British system of government.
5) **landscape**; *inhabitants, people,* and *population* are all people!
6) **ceiling**; you have to pay a *deposit*, your *rent* and for the *heating* when you rent a flat.
7) **farmstead**; *boarding school, (school) uniform* and *secondary level* are expressions which have to do with education.
8) **curriculum**; *internet access, disconnect* and *download* are "computer words".
9) **opportunity**; *hiking, knitting* and *open air sports* are leisure activities.
10) **backyard**; you can find a *fridge, wardrobe* or *walk-in closet* in a flat.

Exercise F.

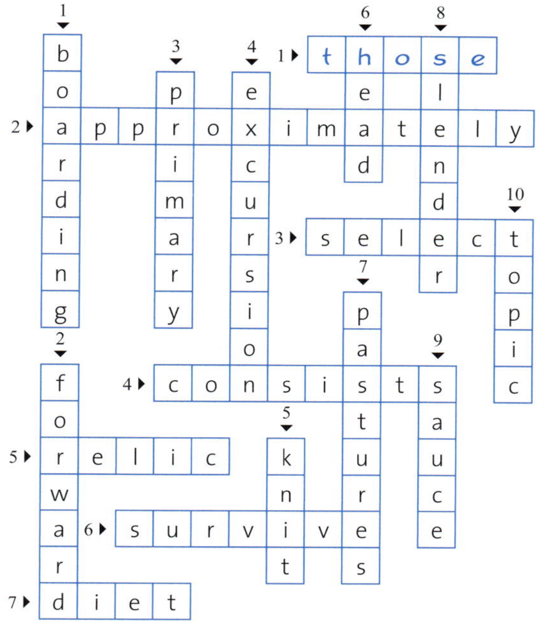
1 those
2 approximately
3 select
4 consists
5 relic
6 survive
7 diet
1 boarding
2 forward
3 primary
4 excursion
5 knit
6 head
7 pastures
8 slender
9 sauce
10 topic

Exercise G.

ahead of him = vor ihm; overtake = überholen; he accelerates = er beschleunigt, gibt Gas; alongside = auf seiner Höhe; amazing = erstaunlich; caught (hier) = eingeklemmt;

Exercise H.

2) “Bill, is this **your** sandwich?” “No, it isn’t **mine**. I don’t like cheese sandwiches, but one moment – there’s Rose. Perhaps it’s **hers**.”
3) “Look – three bottles of lovely English wine. Would you like one of **them**, Pat?” “No thanks. I’ve got enough bottles of **my** own.”
4) “Bertha and I like Julia. **She**’s a good friend of **ours**.”
5) “Where are Sue and her brother? Can you see **them**?” “No, I can’t. But I can see **their** dog, so **they** can’t be far away.”
6) “Mr McCullough, I think this report is **yours** and that is **your** diary, too.” “Oh, thanks. Can you give **them** to **me**, please.” “There’s the report.” “Oh, put **it** over there on the table, please.”

Exercise I.

2) We **can’t come** to the office early tomorrow.
3) Mr Collins **doesn’t use** the latest software.
4) We **don’t need to** (We **needn’t**) install the new firmware.
5) Ms Kerry **isn’t finishing** the report now.
6) Our customers **aren’t waiting** for the new catalogue.
7) This firm in America **doesn’t want** to work with us.

EXERCISE J.
2) Julia doesn't usually drink vodka before breakfast.
3) We're seeing your brother in Rome tomorrow.
4) Samantha wants to find a new job in the neighbourhood next year.
5) Philip often reads the sales reports at home before work in the morning.
6) Are you phoning from home now?

EXERCISE K.
"Hello John, this is Harry. Can you **hear** me? Good. At the moment I**'m sitting** in the InterCity to Birmingham. I **don't usually phone** from trains, but this problem is urgent. **I'm going** to my girl-friend's party in Birmingham this evening but I **don't have** (**haven't got**) a present for her. I **mustn't come** without a present. I would like to buy some flowers for her, but the shops **shut** at seven o'clock and it's 6.40 pm now. Could you **buy** some flowers for me to give her? You **needn't buy** an expensive bunch of flowers. £2 are enough. Oh – and please **don't buy** tulips. She only **likes** roses – she **doesn't like** tulips or other flowers. Oh, one moment – the train **is just coming** into Birmingham and it's only 6.45 now. Maybe I have the time to buy the roses myself!"

CHAPTER 6

EXERCISE A.
2) I **waited** for you for two hours yesterday.
3) We **wanted** to go to the cinema on Saturday.
4) We **went** to Italy last year.
5) Billy **left** the house at 6 am.
6) Mrs Simmonds **arrived** at the airport very early.
7) Two years ago I **was** in Buenos Aires and my sisters **were** in New York.
8) On Monday I **drove** to work, but yesterday I **walked** there because I **had** more time.
9) Gordon **drank** three litres of coke at Joe's 100th birthday party three days ago.
10) Peter and Mary **finished** work early on Friday.

EXERCISE B.
2) They **gave** me a job, but unfortunately they **didn't give** my friend one.
3) I **didn't take** the bus to work yesterday. I **took** the train.
4) My daughter **broke** three glasses this morning. Thank Goodness, she **didn't break** my expensive ones.
5) We **met** Mr Symonds last week, but unfortunately we **didn't meet** his colleagues.
6) The software **didn't cost** much, but the T-box **cost** a lot.
7) I **didn't know** his exact address but I **knew** the name of the street.
8) The profits of the firm **rose** last year but they **didn't rise** the year before.
9) Our sales **didn't grow** much last year, but in the first three months of this year they **grew** very fast.
10) Fred **came** to the conference yesterday but his boss **didn't come**.

EXERCISE C.
2) **Where did you spend** your holiday? In Norway.
3) **Did you go** there alone? No, we didn't. We went with our kids.
4) **Did they like** Norway? Oh, very much.
5) **How long did you stay** in Norway? Oh, for three weeks.

6) **Why did you choose** to go there? Because we wanted to see the beautiful landscape there.
7) **Did you see** the fjords? Of course we did. They came so close to the car that we could feed them!

EXERCISE D.
2) Ms Dubovie **didn't send** me the report last week because she **couldn't find** it.
3) I **didn't read** your e-mail yesterday because I **wasn't** in the office.
4) We **had to work** hard yesterday because the computer **was** broken and nobody **could repair** it.
5) **Did** George **leave** his laptop on the train when he **came** home from work yesterday? Yes, he **was** so tired and when he **got** off the train he **left** the laptop on the seat. He **forgot** about it until he **arrived** home. When he **went** back to the train station it **wasn't** there any more.
6) **Could the electrician repair** the new DVD player before the football match **started**? No, he **couldn't**. He **didn't have** all the necessary components.

EXERCISE E.
2) Yesterday **was** a hard day. I **was working** in the office the whole day. (Mit der Verlaufsform wird die Arbeit als Tätigkeit hervorgehoben.)
3) Mary **was** just **leaving** the house when her mother **asked** her to do the washing up.
4) They **were working** on the computer when suddenly there **was** a power cut (Stromausfall).
5) Terry **was eating** his hamburger during the film when his dog **took** it out of his hand and **ate** it in three seconds!
6) "What **were** you **doing** when I **saw** you in the street yesterday?" "Oh, I **was** just **looking** at shop windows."
7) Now I'm working in the office, but this time last week I **was lying** on the beach at Brighton.
8) I **didn't get** a telephone call from the client while I **was working** in the office yesterday afternoon.
9) Last night we **watched** a horror film on TV from beginning to end.
10) Mrs Thompson **was writing** an e-mail to the client when her boss told her it **wasn't** necessary. The client **was** already in his office.

EXERCISE F.
2) London machte auf Tony einen riesigen **Eindruck**.
3) Die **Eroberung** Englands durch die Normannen im Jahr 1066 (oder nur: 1066) ist ein wichtiges Datum in der englischen Geschichte.
4) Bill litt sehr unter der **Trennung** seiner Eltern.
5) Normas **Vorschlag** wurde von allen akzeptiert. Oder: Normas Vorschlag wurde von jedem akzeptiert.
6) Ist John jetzt in der Arbeit? Das ist sehr **unwahrscheinlich** – es ist erst sechs Uhr in der Früh!
7) Es ist **zweifelhaft**, dass er seine Arbeit mit so viel **Hingabe** macht! Oder: Es ist zweifelhaft, dass er sich seiner Arbeit so hingibt!
8) Wir hatten eine **unterhaltsame (amüsante)** Zeit auf der Party, aber ich muss sagen, dass Dereks Benehmen ziemlich **taktlos/geschmacklos** war.
9) Die **Vielfalt** der architektonischen Stile in diesen Häusern ist sehr beeindruckend.

Exercise G.

2) My wife came up with a great idea – a holiday in Ireland.
3) Too many people are addicted to alcohol.
4) The Irish Republic doesn't belong to the United Kingdom.
5) In Irish pubs you come across many good musicians.
6) Ireland is divided into the Irish Republic and Ulster.
7) The people in Bavaria are attached to their Bavarian roots!
8) The farmhouse was converted into a pub.

Exercise H.

2) Does John help his mother every day?
3) Can Mr Feldman install the new program tomorrow?
4) Do the two firms work together on this project?
5) Could they use a different software?
6) Is the new colleague connecting the computer to the power supply?
7) Do Mr Bentley and the new secretary eat in the canteen together?
8) Are our boss and the new client in the park?
9) Would she like a cup of tea?

Exercise I.

1) We needn't finish the work today.
2) We mustn't use the old software.
3) Tomorrow I'm driving to Bristol.
4) He usually eats in an expensive restaurant, but (right) now he's sitting in a cheap fast food restaurant, although he doesn't actually like fast food.
5) In London many people have their own car.

Exercise J.

2) Peter never comes home before seven o'clock in the evening.
3) (Please) Could you help me with this new program, please?
4) Our colleague always eats toast for breakfast in the morning.
   In the morning our colleague always eats toast for breakfast.
5) We are (We're) flying to London next week.
6) This firm seldom sells many sandals in the Antarctic in winter.
7) Do many people usually go to the museum during the week?
8) The manager doesn't often check the sales reports before Friday.

Chapter 7

Exercise A.
1) One moment, please. **I'll** (just) **close** the window.
2) These bags are too heavy. **We'll help** you.
3) It's your birthday – **I'll pay** for the drinks.
4) (Which would you like – the Italian grappa or the French wine?) **I'll take** the French wine, please.
5) **I'll call** (phone) you tomorrow.
6) Next week **I'll be** 94 years old.
7) **Will you paint** a picture for me?

Exercise B.
2) There are three flies in Tom's beer. I'm sure **he isn't going to drink** it.
Or: I'm sure **they aren't going to drink** it! (Unless they're thirsty flies!)
3) It's 10 o'clock and the bus isn't here. **I'm not going to wait** any longer.
4) Do they have a train ticket to Brighton? No, they don't. **They're going to cycle** there.
5) At present there aren't any shops here, but next year they**'re going to open** a supermarket in the town centre.
6) Look at all that work on Helen's desk. I don't think **she's going to leave** early this evening!
7) It's 10 o'clock and the bus isn't here. We**'re going to be late**.
8) Oh dear. Look at those black clouds. I think **it's going to rain**.
9) My phone isn't working so **I'm going to write** Bob an e-mail.
10) Our daughter is ill so **she's going to stay** at home today.
11) I know you're late for work, but **aren't you going to have** breakfast before you go?

Exercise C.
1) Our plane **departs** at 4.30 pm. At 4.35 we**'ll (we will) be sitting** in our seats and I**'ll (I will) be drinking** a cup of coffee.
2) Just think! This time next month we**'ll be lying** on the beach in the Bahamas.
3) I'm sorry, but I**'m** definitely **not going to do** your homework for you. You must do it without my help.
4) Before we **go** out, we must do the washing up.
5) I usually start my breakfast at 7 am, so if you phone me a little after 7 am, I**'ll be eating** my toast!
6) The new shopping centre **opens** at 8 o'clock tomorrow morning. Believe me – a few minutes after the opening, thousands of shoppers **will be searching** for good bargains.
7) Look at Tony. He's walking on the wall, but I'm absolutely sure he**'s going to fall** off it in a moment.
8) When you **get** off the bus, you'll see the Houses of Parliament in front of you.

Exercise D.
1) The travel agent can **provide** you with information about the arrivals and **departures** of all flights.
2) Many people decide to **settle** in London because of all the **leisure** possibilities in this great city.
3) I can **assure** you that it is not always a good idea to go to a **real estate** agent's to find a flat.
4) An **ancestor** of my wife's made this **ornate** wrought iron (Schmiedeeisen) gate.
5) There was an **uproar** when Kate spilled the **ketchup** all over Clive's new jacket.
6) The **vendors** always **arrive** very early to sell their goods.
7) Paul had to fill in a **questionnaire** about the **revenues** from his new business.

Exercise E.
2) The Maoris are now a **minority** group in New Zealand society.
3) One of the **employees** who works for the company showed us the way to the **production** line.
4) Can you tell me the **departure** times of the **flights** to London Heathrow, please?
5) My **advice** to you is not to rent a flat in the **surroundings** of Heathrow Airport!
6) Mr Grove's **collection** of water colour paintings is on **display** at the Sheffield Art Gallery.
7) People say that Peter is a hard-working colleague, but I have my **doubts.**

Exercise F.
2) Did you spend a lot of money at the market yesterday? Yes, **I (we) did**.
3) Could you help me, please? Yes, of course, **I (we) could**.
4) Does your son have difficulties at school? Thank Goodness, **he doesn't**.
5) Can you speak Russian? Unfortunately **I can't**.
6) Are you tired? No, **I'm not.** Are you?
7) Did they leave work early yesterday? **Yes, they did**. They left at midday.
8) Was your son at school yesterday? **No, he wasn't**. He was ill.
9) Are you and Jenny coming to our party tomorrow? **Yes, we are.** When does it start?
10) Were your brothers watching TV when I phoned yesterday? I'm afraid **they were.**

Exercise G.
2) Sally doesn't work here, **does she**?
3) Your sister speaks English fluently, **doesn't she**?
4) Your husband didn't feel well yesterday, **did he**?
5) You're flying to America next Monday, **aren't you**?
6) We can go now, **can't we**?
7) Please put the bags down here, **will you**?
8) Ben and Julia sold the car, **didn't they**?

Exercise H.
Mrs Douglas **doesn't like** opera, but she **loves** pop songs. Every day she **sits** in the bath and **sings** old songs by the Beatles and Rolling Stones. In fact, right now I can **hear** her.
She **is singing** "I Can't Get No Satisfaction". So her neighbours **don't need to buy/needn't buy** a CD player to listen to the songs. The problem is that they **don't like** her singing so much.
One evening last January something terrible **happened**. Mr Douglas **was watching** "Who Wants to be a Millionaire" on TV in the living room, when his wife **rushed** into the room. She **didn't show** any interest in Mr Douglas's programme.
"George," she **shouted**. "Our neighbour Mr Henry **threw** a stone through the window while I **was singing** 'She Loves You Yeah, Yeah, Yeah'."
"What an idiot," George **said**. "Now he can **hear** you even better."

Exercise I.
2) Mary didn't drink any alcohol at the party. She **drank** orange juice.
3) I didn't sleep the day before yesterday but I **slept** a lot last night.
4) We didn't sell much last Saturday but we **sold** a lot at the market yesterday.
5) Mr and Mrs Cheeseman didn't choose a holiday in Spain, they **chose** a holiday in Scotland.
6) I didn't catch the mouse. Our cat **caught** it.

7) Stella didn't pay for the drinks. Who **paid** for them, then?
8) They didn't build the house in the centre of the town. They **built** it outside the town.
9) What a stupid thief! He didn't hide the money in the wood. He **hid** it in the bank!
10) What did Mr Stanly bring with him yesterday? He **brought** a memory stick.

Chapter 8

Exercise A.
2) **since** my birthday
3) **since** the fourth of June
4) **for** three months
5) **since** 3 o'clock
6) **since** September
7) **for** a few seconds
8) **for** five weeks
9) **since** Christmas
10) **for** 200 years
11) **for** a century
12) **since** I last saw you

Exercise B.
1) I haven't played table tennis **for the last two years**.
2) We haven't watched television **since Sunday**.
3) Peter **came** here last week.
4) My mother-in-law didn't visit us **at Easter**.
5) Have you finished the work **yet**?
6) **Did your husband make** the reservation in February?
7) Mr Peters hasn't painted the living room **for** many years.
8) When **did you build** that beautiful house? (Es handelt sich um eine Frage nach einem bestimmten Zeitpunkt in der Vergangenheit!)
9) Rachel and I got married **in 1999**.

Exercise C.
2) Last year Timmy **didn't grow** so much. He only **grew** by 1 millimetre. Then last December, the doctor **gave** him some special pills. Since the beginning of the year, Timmy **has grown** by 12 centimetres and he **hasn't stopped** growing yet.
3) Prices **have risen** enormously since January. Before that they **didn't rise** much at all, although last September they **rose** by 3 % because of the increase in the price of oil.
4) "Mary, somebody has **taken** the car!" "It's OK, our son **took** it to the disco a few hours ago. He'll be back before midnight."
5) "That's the fourth glass that you**'ve broken** since the beginning of the week!"
"That's not true. I **didn't break** any glasses on Tuesday. I only **broke** nineteen glasses on Wednesday and Thursday and in the last two days I **haven't broken** any at all."
6) Mandy **hurt** her boyfriend after the party on Saturday. She **didn't take** the cigarette out of her mouth when she **kissed** him and it **burned (burnt)** a hole in his lips. Poor Bill **has been** in hospital for the last three days and he **hasn't drunk** or **eaten** anything up to now.

Exercise D.
1) In summer 2008 we went (drove) to Italy but since then we haven't been there.
2) Three years ago we saw Harry but since then we haven't heard anything from him.
3) Did you meet Jacob yesterday?

Exercise E.
2) I**'ve been lying** in bed with the flu since Monday.
3) He**'s been practising** the banjo for thirty-eight hours now.

4) My wife **has been working** in a youth club since 1950. (My wife's been working ...)
5) Graham **has been learning** to cook for many years now. (Graham's been learning ...)
6) Up to now they've **been playing** the piano all the time.
7) Since the beginning of 1997 my brother and I **have been living** in New York.

EXERCISE F.
1) Mr Martin will get his pension before his wife (does).
2) I must check the bill for my mobile phone.
3) It's no fun to be (being) addicted to alcohol.
4) I attend a skiing course and have no time to visit my aunt.

EXERCISE G.
2) The people in this part of Ottawa are **immigrants**.
3) We have checked all the **items**.
4) John is only fourteen and he drove his dad's car without a **driver's licence**.
5) Many buildings in Canada are **reminiscent** of nineteenth century British architecture.
6) The Maoris were **assured of** their civil rights. After all they are the **indigenous** population.

EXERCISE H.
2) John **doesn't usually smoke** in the living room.
3) This newspaper is **mine**. **It's** very interesting.
4) **Did** you **go** to the party yesterday?
5) I occasionally **work** in the office, but right now **I'm working** at home.
6) We have **our** own car.
7) Our colleague didn't **get** to work early yesterday.
8) Gerry has two **sisters.** I like **them** very much.
9) **There's (There is) an** interesting film in the cinema.
10) Tom **lives** near his work.
11) It's too warm in here – **I'll** open the window.
12) Our boss **often meets new clients in the firm on Mondays.**
                    1   2   3   4   5
13) **While** I was working yesterday, the computer **broke** down three times.
14) Before we **start** our work we'll have a cup of coffee.

EXERCISE I.
2) **Didn't** Neville **meet** us at the station on Wednesday?
3) Jennifer **often forgets** names.
4) We **didn't understand** everything the maths teacher taught us.
5) Harry **didn't keep** a cool head in the exam.
6) **May** Graham **come** in now?
7) Sue and Pat **bought** a present for the host and **brought** a bottle of wine to the party. They **left** the party early and **caught** the last bus home.
8) **Were** you **watching** me when Ron's dog bit me and hurt my leg?
9) **Will** Malcolm **be sleeping** in his office when we come in?
10) When **are** Simon and his wife **going to emigrate** to the USA?
11) How many e-mails **did** George **have** to write yesterday?

Exercise J.

It **was (2)** 4 pm in the afternoon of July the fifteenth, 2006. Mr and Mrs Rose and the other passengers in the aeroplane **were enjoying (1)** their flight. Mr Rose **drank (2)** a small glass of champagne in only a few seconds. His wife **didn't drink (2, 5)** champagne as she **didn't like** alcohol, but she **took (2)** a cup of coffee from the stewardess. "Just think," Mrs Rose **said (2)** to her husband, "we **land (3)** at Los Angeles airport at 12.30. Before we **get (4)** out of the airport it will be 1.30 pm. But then – this time in ten hours – **we'll be lying (6)** on the beach at San Barbara. Don't you **feel (5)** excited?!"

Suddenly, while they **were talking (1)**, the engines of the aeroplane **stopped (2)**. The passengers **screamed (2)** when they **saw (2)** the pilot of the aeroplane with a parachute on his back.

"What **is** he **doing (7)** here?" Mr Rose **asked (2)** his wife. "He should be in the cockpit!"

"Don't worry," the pilot **shouted (2)**, "everything is OK. I **'m going to jump (8)** out of the aeroplane and get help."

(1) Vorgänge/Zustände, die nicht abgeschlossen waren, als die Motoren ausfielen!
(2) Handlungen, die in der Vergangenheit abgeschlossen wurden.
(3) Die beste Lösung (*timetable future*). Auch möglich: We**'re going to land**/We**'re landing**
(4) *Present simple* in Nebensätzen: We'll wait here until he **comes**. When we **have** time, we'll visit you.
(5) Infinitiv nach **do, don't, does, doesn't, did, didn't**.
(6) Das *future continuous* wird verwendet, um Handlungen zu beschreiben, die zu einem bestimmten Zeitpunkt in der Zukunft nicht abgeschlossen, sondern im Verlauf sind.
(7) Nicht *What **does** he **do** here?*, sondern *What **is** he **doing** here?* – Die Frage bezieht sich auf seine Handlung in diesem Moment.
(8) Eine feste (wenn auch problematische!) Absicht wird zum Ausdruck gebracht.

Chapter 9

Exercise A.
2) My mother is a very **careful** driver.
3) I **hardly** know that boy, but he hit me so **hard**.
4) Jeremy is not very **polite**. He always interrupts his teacher **impolitely**.
5) What a **slow** car! Well, the car isn't **slow**. It's just that Mr Gilbert prefers to drive **slowly**.
6) Oh Gladys, my darling. Your voice is so **wonderful** and you sing so **beautifully**. I want to kiss you **passionately** on your **lovely** lips.

Exercise B.
1) Mr and Mrs Douglas are **late** for the opera. The usherette says to them: "Please walk to your seats **extremely quietly**. The opera is just beginning." "Why should we be so **quiet**?" Mr Douglas asks. "Is everyone sleeping already?"
2) "Is this milk **fresh**?" "Yes, madam. Two hours ago it was still grass."
3) "Waiter! The kitchen in this restaurant must be **exceptionally clean**."
"Thank you, sir. That's **really** kind of you to say that. But how do you know how **clean** our kitchen is?" "Well, the soup tastes very **strange** – it tastes of soap!"
4) Mark asks his girlfriend: "Am I your first boyfriend?" She replies: "Maybe. You look **familiar**."
5) My husband is so **helpful**. He knows that I have many jobs to do in the garden and in the house and he knows that I forget important things very **easily**. So yesterday, before the football match on TV he spent ten minutes for me. I was **completely** surprised this morning when I saw a long list on the table. It was a **useful** list of all the things I had to do. What a **thoughtful** husband! And he never gets **angry** with me when I clear up the living room while he's watching a football match on TV.

Exercise C.
2) My husband worked very hard in his firm yesterday. (Yesterday my husband …)
3) Brian doesn't usually come late to important meetings.
4) Sue hardly ever works hard during the week. (During the week Sue …)
5) He often sends extremely urgent emails to the clients before he leaves the office. (Before he leaves the office he …)

Exercise D.
2) I've got even **less** time than you. I have to finish two reports before midday.
3) Travelling by train is **less** expensive than going by taxi. But the **least** expensive way to travel is to walk.
4) So **many** people came to the party, but so **few** stayed after the party to clean up. That's why it looks a big mess!
5) **Fewer** people live in Ireland than in Germany.
6) The **most** people live in China.
7) There are too **many** cars on the street and they cause too **much** pollution.

Exercise E.
2) The Cabriolet **is more expensive than this old car.**
3) The vegetables taste much **better than the meat.**
4) Philip **was as successful as Jane.**
5) The film "Dirty Dancing" **was more popular (successful) than** (the film) "Clean Dancing".
6) My sister **is as old as my brother.** (My sister isn't younger or older than my brother.)
7) Terry **was more successful (in the exams) than Camilla.**
8) My mother **is younger than my father.** (My mother isn't as old as my father.)
9) Mrs Collins is a **worse** driver **than Mrs Blake.** (She isn't as good a driver as Mrs Collins. She doesn't drive as well as Mrs Collins.)

Exercise F.
2) I have a big problem: I have the **most beautiful** wife. And I buy her the **finest** jewellery that I can find.
3) We live in the **most expensive** house in a suburb of Bristol. My six children go to the **best** boarding schools in Switzerland. My problem is that I earn only 500 euros a month which is not **as** much **as** I need to pay for all this!
4) I speak English quite well – **as** well **as** my brother. My wife, however, worked in New Zealand for three years so she speaks **better** English **than** I do. However, she thinks that people from Oxford speak **the best** English of all.
5) This pencil costs fifty cents. That pencil is a little **more expensive** – it costs eighty cents. The gold plated pencil over there is **the most expensive** of all: It costs eight hundred euros.
6) Man in a restaurant: "Waiter, this coffee is **worse than** the one you gave me yesterday. In fact it is **the worst** cup of coffee that I have ever drunk. I don't think you've used **as** much coffee **as** usual. Waiter: "That's not true, sir, but I've used more water **than** I did yesterday."
7) **The safest** way to use a hammer is to ask another person to hold the nails!
8) I play chess quite well, but my wife plays much **better** than me and our five-year-old son, however is **better** than his brothers, sister, dad or mum. He plays **the best** of all of us – a new Bobby Fisher.

Exercise G.
1) This school is one of the most modern (ones) in town.
2) The cinema is nearer than the school.
3) Is this car cheaper or more expensive than your old car?
4) The milk tastes worse than the lemonade.
5) He drives less carefully than his wife.
6) A Harry Potter book is (just) as interesting as a television programme for many children.

Exercise H.
2) I don't really want to drive today. **Let's** go by train.
3) Have you seen my mobile phone? I'm sure I **left** it in this room.
4) The teacher **let** the pupils hand in their homework a day later.

Exercise I.
2) Arsenic is a dangerous **poison**.
3) It is not important for John where he lives. He can **adapt** to all situations.
4) **Although** Raimund speaks good English he is too shy to speak it.
5) Oh no! Mary is wearing one of her **weird** hats again. It looks so silly.
6) We must remember that many countries do not have such **abundant** supplies of water as we do.
7) The weather looks **pretty** bad today.
8) **Antiques** at a flea market are generally less expensive than in a shop.

Exercise J.
1) The conditions in this part of Canada are quite **harsh.** It's not easy to survive when it is so very cold.
2) Some animals can **adapt** to any conditions.
3) Canada is a country with **abundant** supplies of water.
4) I didn't leave the party until three o'clock in the morning **although** I was tired.
5) **Perhaps** he will come to the party tomorrow but I'm not sure.
6) **Pardon** – I can't hear you very well – there's too much noise here!
7) The private car seems to be the most popular **means** of transport in our country.
8) **Despite** the bad weather we decided to go out for a walk.

Exercise K.
2) My girlfriend and I love **each other**. She phones **me** twenty times a day and I phone **her** thirty times a day.
3) Why are you looking at **me** in such a funny way? I like the hat you are wearing. The Queen wears rather strange hats and your hat looks just like one of **hers**.
4) Mary and Robert live here and Henrietta – a friend of **theirs/ours** – lives in the flat above them. They have known **each other** for many years now.

Exercise L.
2) When did the firm make a profit of $3?
3) Who(m) is Mr Smedley going to contact next Monday?
4) Whose personal assistant will be accompanying him to the meeting next week?
5) Which department of the firm does Mrs Simon work in?
6) How many firms have opened in this region since last year?

7) Who attends a management course every Monday evening?
8) What was Terence doing in his office?

Exercise M.
Darling Sally,
We last ~~have seen~~ ¹ **saw** each other two years ago. Since then I ~~am~~ ² **have been** so unhappy and I now ~~am knowing~~ ³ **know** that you are the only woman I can love. ~~Remember you~~ ⁴ **Do you remember** that day when I first kissed you? You ~~smoked~~ ⁵ **were smoking** your pipe when I ~~was taking~~ ⁵ **took** it out of your mouth and ~~was giving~~ ⁵ **gave** you a big kiss. I ~~have been~~ ¹ **was** so silly two years ago. When I left you I really ~~knew not~~ ⁶ **didn't know** how much I loved you. For the last two years I ~~thought~~ ² **have been thinking (have thought)** about you. Right now – at this very moment I ~~look~~ ⁷ **am looking** at your picture and tears are in my eyes. Why ~~I was~~ ⁸ **was I** so stupid to leave you? Please come back to me. Next weekend I ~~drive~~ ⁹ **am driving** to Manchester and I hope we can meet.

      Lots of love,
      Martin

P.S. I ~~have watched~~ ¹ **watched** you on television yesterday and saw you in "Who Wants to be a Millionaire". I was so happy when you ~~were answering~~ ⁴ **answered** the million pound question correctly. Congratulations!

1) Wir können diese Form nie benutzen, wenn eine Zeit in der Vergangenheit angegegeben wird: *two years ago, yesterday, when I was 16 years old, last Christmas, in 1999*, etc.
2) Wenn der Zeitraum in der Vergangenheit anfing und sich bis in die Gegenwart hineinstreckt, nehmen wir das *present perfect*: **Since last week (Up to now, so far, for the last three years) I have phoned** my girlfriend three hundred times. Wenn die Tätigkeit selbst weiterhin andauert, nehmen wir das *present perfect continuous (= Verlaufsform).* Vergleichen Sie die folgenden Sätze: *For the past two years I* **have been thinking** about you. I **have thought** of you twice in the last two decades. John **has been working** as a carpenter since 1998. John **has made** many nice tables and chairs since 1998. Es ist jedoch nicht das Ende der Welt, wenn Sie sagen: *John has worked as a carpenter since 1998*. Schlimmer ist es, eine Gegenwartsform statt *present perfect* zu verwenden: ~~We live here since 1980.~~
3) Bestimmte Verben, die auch für die Zukunft weiterhin Gültigkeit haben (Verben des Glaubens, Besitzes usw. – *know, believe, own, love, hate* etc., siehe „Into the English World", Kapitel 4) werden nie in der Verlaufsform verwendet. Es ist anzunehmen, dass Martin auch morgen wissen wird, dass Sally die Frau seines Lebens ist!
4) Fragen im *present simple* und *past simple* werden mit *do/does* oder *did* gebildet!
5) Wenn eine Handlung zu einem bestimmten Zeitpunkt in der Vergangenheit nicht abgeschlossen ist, benutzen wir das *past continuous*; wenn sie abgeschlossen ist, kommt in der Regel das *past simple*. Hier muss Martin also die Zeiten wechseln:

*You **were smoking** your pipe when I **took** it out of your mouth and **gave** you a big kiss.*

| Diese Tätigkeit wird nicht abgeschlossen, wird unterbrochen. | Diese Tätigkeit wird abgeschlossen. | Auch diese Tätigkeit wird abgeschlossen. |

6) Ein schlimmer Fehler: Bilden Sie bitte die negativen Aussagesätze im *present simple* und *past simple* immer mit *don't/doesn't/didn't*!

7) Wenn eine Handlung gerade in diesem Moment ausgeführt wird, benutzen wir das *present continuous*. Wenn eine Handlung regelmäßig, z.B. einmal im Monat, stattfindet, nehmen wir dagegen das *present simple*. Vergleichen Sie diese Sätze:
<u>At the moment</u> I'**m looking** at your picture.
I **look** at your picture every day (once a week/every Thursday/when I'm lonely, etc.)
8) Vorsicht mit den Frageformen!
9) Die „informelle Zukunft" wird mit dem *present continuous* gebildet!

Chapter 10

Exercise A.
2) Mr and Mrs Simmonds **had been** very happy in life – and then they **met**.
3) Agatha **gave** her boyfriend a big kiss, but he **didn't find** it very romantic because, unfortunately, Agatha **had eaten** half a kilogram of garlic a few hours before.
4) My girlfriend **hadn't phoned me or written** to me for twenty-five years, so I **took** the decision to get in touch with her again.
5) When I **got** to my car yesterday, I **realized** that I **had left** my car keys at home.
6) The thief **forgot** where he **had hidden** the money which he **had stolen** from the bank.
7) I **suffered** from terrible jet lag after we **had flown** from Munich to San Francisco.
8) We **managed** to get the train but we **had had to run** two kilometres to get to the station
9) As soon as we **had watered** the flowers it **started** to rain.

Exercise B.
1) After Sam **had been studying** archaeology and Chinese for twenty-two semesters, he **decided** that it **was** time to leave the university and look for a job. Before he **left** the university he'**d taken** only one exam: the test for his driver's licence.
2) On Saturday evening I **visited** my girlfriend Myrtle. She l**ooked** tired because she **had been working** in the kitchen for two hours . She **had made** us a huge meal. First we **started** with the salad. I **had been eating** for only about two minutes when I suddenly **felt** sick. I **looked** at the salad and **saw** three snails. Myrtle **had forgotten** to wash the lettuce before she **gave** it to me and I'**d eaten** one of the snails.
3) We'**d been running** to the station for about an hour when I **felt** out of breath. We'**d run** about 6 kilometres and we still **had** another three kilometres to run.
4) George suddenly **got** up from his armchair and **switched** off the television. He was very angry because he'**d been watching** television for five hours and none of the programmes **had been** really good.

Exercise C.
2) Go to the library in Katharine Street at 10. 15 am. **I'll be waiting** for you there.
3) Before you **kiss** me **you'll have** to take the chewing gum out of your mouth.
4) Else and I have decided something important: **We're going to emigrate** to Australia.
5) I think **I'll be** home tomorrow at five thirty or six, or maybe even six thirty. So, if **you phone** at seven o'clock, **I'll have arrived** home.
6) Bob tells me that **he'll have installed** the new software by Saturday at the latest, unless he **has** to fly to America this week.
7) **We're seeing** our American cousin Christine tomorrow. Her flight **leaves** Miami at 4.15 am, so at 4.20 she'll be in her seat and **she'll be watching** movies. Before **she lands** in Frankfurt she **will have watched** at least three movies.

Exercise D.

(crossword solution)

Across: 1) polite, 2) pity, 3) occasionally, 4) during, 5) cut, 6) reliable, 7) going, 8) least, 9) risen

Down: 1) fo(r), 2) until, 3) see, 4) thought, 5) casual, 6) essential, 7) chie(f), 8) cushion, 9) c, 10) ally

Exercise E.

2) inauguration
3) landmarks
4) to hold session
5) Global Positioning System (GPS)
6) to commemorate

Exercise F.

Brian Davis was very **tired** and **while** he **was sleeping peacefully** in his office, Mr Parks, his boss came in.

"Good morning, Mr Davis, I can see you **aren't working** very **hard** at the moment" he said. "And I'm afraid I must complain: You **have come** late to work four times since the beginning of the week. If I remember **correctly** your working day begins at nine o'clock, not ten o'clock. Why don't you come early for a change?"

"I'm **extremely** sorry, sir," Mr Davis said, "but since Monday I **have had to make** arrangements for my holiday in Miami next week."

"Holiday! What holiday?" Mr Parks shouted.

"Oh, I am spending five weeks in Florida in the biggest and most expensive hotel in Miami. My plane **leaves** London Heathrow airport at 7 pm tonight. This time next week, I **will be lying** on the beach."

"But I don't understand," Mr Parks said. "How can you afford such a holiday. And another thing: That car of **yours** – it's much bigger and more expensive **than** mine. You **have only been working** with us **for** three months and you only earn $500 a month. That isn't as much **as** you need for such a holiday and such a car!"

"Well," Brian said, "I'll tell you the secret. There are 800 employees in your firm, Mr Parks and at the end of each month I sell a raffle ticket to each employee for $5. The winner **gets** my salary of $500."

Exercise G.

Last year Mr Brady, a manager of an American oil firm, and his wife **flew** to Europe to spend their holiday. They **had already seen** Rome, Madrid and Munich and now they wanted to see the capital of France.
On the second day of their stay in Paris, they **were walking** along the River Seine when Mr Brady **said** to his wife: "We **have been walking** along the Seine for the last ten minutes and we **haven't seen** anything interesting yet." "What **do** you **mean**?" his wife **said**. "We**'re walking** along one of **the most interesting** rivers in Europe now! And you…" Suddenly, while Mrs Brady **was speaking**, they **saw** a big tower. "Look," Mrs Brady **shouted excitedly**. "That tower looks **funny** – it's made of iron! It's **higher** and **more interesting** than any tower that I know."
"Huh!" her husband **replied impatiently**. "That's the Eiffel Tower. The French are **really slow**. They **built** that derrick over a hundred years ago but so far, not a drop of oil **has come** out of it."

Exercise H.
2) Ms Finch's office isn't as large as **mine (is)**.
3) James's car is more expensive than **ours**.
4) My sister-in-law is older than **him**.
5) Our house is nearer the town centre than **theirs (is)**.
6) I've got much less time than **them**.
7) His computer is more reliable than **his (is)**.
8) I really think that your wife works more than **you**.
9) She can play the piano better than **him**.
10) Our car breaks down as often as **yours (does)**.
11) Geraldine doesn't live in the same house as **her**.
12) Raphael speaks as many languages as **us**.
13) John's job isn't as exhausting as **hers (is)**.

Exercise I.
1) While we were sleeping in the garden yesterday, it began to rain.
2) I didn't work yesterday, either. (I also didn't work yesterday.)
3) For three hours (now) she has been playing football with her son. (Vorsicht mit dem Satzbau!)
4) Why does he use less water for his garden than we do (than us)?
5) His voice sounded strange and I couldn't hear him so well.
6) Fewer and fewer people drive/go/travel by car in London. The fewer people travel by car the better the air is (the less air pollution there is).

Chapter 11

Exercise A.
2) Potatoes **were** first **grown** in Peru.
3) The Eiffel Tower **has been visited by** over two million people since it was built.
4) The birth of a child **is** usually **celebrated by** the people in Afghanistan six days after its birth.
5) On this day a name **is given** to the baby.
6) In Algeria it **is considered** impolite to point at people or objects.
7) The Statue of Liberty **was** actually **built** in France and then (it was) **transported** to America as a present.
8) Eight hundred different languages **are spoken** in Papua New Guinea.

9) In Malaysia, when a tooth **is lost by** a child it **must be buried**. The Malaysians think (It is thought by the Malaysians) that the tooth **should be given** back to the Earth, because it is a part of the human body.
10) In future new nuclear power stations **won't be built** in Germany.
11) Each of the employees **has been offered** a new job (by the firm).
A new job **has been offered** to each of the employees (by the firm).

Exercise B.
2) A big shopping centre **will be built/is going to be built** in the town next year.
3) This house **hasn't been painted** since we bought it.
4) This computer **cannot be repaired** so easily.
5) At present, the engines of our cars **are manufactured** in our factory in Belgium.
6) I **was told** the good news last week.

Exercise C.
2) Wendy is the attractive woman **who** wants to marry my brother.
3) BMW is the name of the car **which/that** is easiest to spell.
4) This swimming pool is the one **which/that** only good swimmers can use.
5) And the empty swimming pool is for people **who/that** can't swim.
6) The students for **whom** this course is aimed at can already speak some English.
7) Dr Smith, **whose** patient was sitting nervously in front of him, was very happy:
"I've got some good news for you, Mr Davis," he said. "It wasn't your pulse **which/that** stopped. It was your watch!"
8) "Darling, you're the only woman **whom** I love. Will you always remember me?" "Of course, I will. You're the man **whose** name I always forget."

Exercise D.
2) Mary Collins, **whose husband you know**, works hard for her family.
3) This book, **which/that I borrowed from the library**, is very interesting.
4) "I can do something **which/that the other children in my class can't do**, "says Sally proudly," I can read my handwriting."
5) This book, **which I bought for my husband**, is about doing repairs in the house.
6) Fred, **who jumped into the river and saved the little girl's life**, deserves a medal.
7) The letter, **which/that Cedric wrote to his grandmother**, was very long. Cedric wrote a letter to his grandmother, **which/that was very long**.
8) This car, **which/that would be best for our needs,** is unfortunately too expensive. This car, **which is unfortunately too expensive**, would be best for our needs.
9) We have informed the employees, **some of whom live far from the factory**.
10) This horse, **which belongs to Humphrey**, is really beautiful. This horse, **which is really beautiful**, belongs to Humphrey.
11) The woman **whom you saw yesterday** is my English teacher in Telekolleg.
12) My neighbour, **whose dog is looking at you very strangely**, is an aggressive man.

Exercise E.
2) The professor said many things **which** I didn't understand.
3) I'm sorry, I didn't hear **what** you just said.
4) The beautiful little girl **who's** standing there is my daughter.
5) The things **which** come your way in life are not always **what** you are expecting ...

6) Children **whose** parents speak different languages often learn foreign languages more quickly.
7) I don't know **who's** making so much noise in the street.
8) Do you know **whose** car this is? George's or Miriam's?

Exercise F.
2) The exhibition we went to has works by local painters.
3) The woman you talked to yesterday is an expert on Paul Revere.
4) Glenda has already read about the film we saw at the cinema.
5) We went to one of the restaurants my wife likes so much.
6) That newspaper you're reading isn't very objective.
7) Tim didn't know that the road we were walking on was once a Roman road.
8) Those seeds you planted last autumn have become beautiful flowers.
9) I'm sure that the bus we're waiting for is going to be late.
10) He never listens to the advice his friends give him.

Exercise G.
2) It's not a **sensible** thing to argue with John – he's too **sensitive**!
3) **Actually**, I don't think this problem is **of much importance** nowadays.
4) He can't afford to pay the **rent** for his flat because his **pension** is too low.
5) This town is a nice **place**, but unfortunately, there's not much **room** to build new houses in it.
6) Marjorie bought some **land** in a far-away **country**.

Exercise H.

a	l	s	u	f	f	e	r	n	i	o
p	s	e	p	a	r	a	t	e	g	u
r	c	d	e	p	e	n	d	e	n	t
o	a	b	o	m	x	o	p	d	a	s
t	m	d	g	u	i	d	e	s	s	k
e	n	u	o	k	e	i	u	t	n	i
c	e	m	e	t	e	r	y	o	y	r
t	e	p	a	n	f	i	j	r	e	t
e	v	o	l	u	n	t	e	e	r	s
u	l	s	r	o	s	h	a	r	e	s
f	k	t	u	i	r	e	l	x	h	a
b	c	o	r	n	e	r	e	l	i	b

Exercise I.
2) European countries are **dependent** on other countries for the import of raw materials.
3) The secretary of this environmental organisation gets a regular salary but the others who work here are unpaid **volunteers**.
4) Miriam has a **separate** bedroom in the flat, but she **shares** the bathroom and kitchen with two other students who live in the flat.
5) The rent is quite low but unfortunately the flat is on the **corner** of two busy roads.

6) It's really terrible! Some people **dump** their old furniture in this wood. They must think this beautiful wood is their own rubbish **dump**!
7) In some countries people have to pay a lot of **tax** from their salaries.
8) People who live on the **outskirts** of big cities often need a very long time to get to their work in the centre.

Exercise J.

1) In Monaco nearly 33,000 people live in **less (fewer) than** two square kilometres. That means 16,500 people per square kilometre. England is not as densely populated **as** Monaco. There are only 246 people per square kilometre in England. So Monaco is one of the **most (highly) populated** countries in the world.
2) There are **more kangaroos than** people in Australia.
3) There are six times **as many** sheep in the United Kingdom **as** there are in the USA.
4) Canada has the **highest** proportion of left-handed people.
5) The United Kingdom is **more expensive** to live in **than** Germany. Japan is perhaps one of the **most expensive** countries in the world.
6) Vatican City is 0.44 square kilometres – Hyde Park is **three times as large (big)**. Only 800 people live in Vatican City so it is **the least populated** country on earth.
7) The **smallest** and **least comfortable** church in the world is in Kentucky, USA. In this church there is much **less room than** in any other church. Actually there is room for only three people inside the church!

Exercise K.

2) On the one hand the cost of living **is extremely** high in England. However, on the other hand, **there are always** a lot of interesting things to see in the English countryside.
3) We stayed in a small hut in the Alps **a few years ago**. (**A few years** ago we stayed in a small hut in the Alps.)
4) Georgette and Raymond Rowley played Hector Millstein's concerto for mouth organ and bagpipes **beautifully** at the concert on Sunday.
5) I've **seldom** had to travel abroad in these last few years.

Exercise L.

1) You**'ve been working** in this firm **for** many years, **haven't you**? (Falls Sie die *question tags* nicht so gut beherrschen: You've been working in this firm for many years, right?)
2) Although Alexander **doesn't** usually (normally) **like** Hollywood films he**'s watching** a James Bond film at the moment.
3) Seventy years **ago** I **kissed** my wife for the first time.
4) George **became** (got) impatient because he **had to** wait four hours for the train.

Chapter 12

Exercise A.

2) Dr Gray's personal assistant told us (that) **he was away on business**.
3) The manager was sorry that **they hadn't found the client's new address.**
4) My colleague thought (that) **we should hold the meeting there in our office.**
5) I was told that **they could not supply the goods before the end of the following month.**
6) The patient complained that **the nurse had given him his sleeping pill at 4 o'clock in the morning after she had woken him up to do it.**
7) Our son claimed that although **his computer beat him at chess, it didn't beat him at** kick boxing.

8) Little Sue told us that **her dad had just got a new car and that the night before (the previous night) he had painted it and (had) changed the number plates.**
9) The production manager assured us **they were working on our new order that week.**
10) The silly man told the police **that while the thief had been driving away in his car he had noted down the number of the car.**

Exercise B.
2) The sales manager asked us **if/whether we could install the computer that (same) day.**
3) Mr Dykes asked his colleague **where he had bought the mobile phone.**
4) George enquired **if/whether Mr Clark was the person responsible for security in their firm.**
5) Our neighbour asked Mr and Mrs Skiffle **when they were going on holiday.**
6) Chaim asked his teacher **if/whether there was a synonym for the word** *synonym*.
7) The angry passenger asked the train driver **why he hadn't informed his passengers** that there would be a delay.
8) Peter asked Rose **if/whether there would be many guests at her party the next day.**
9) Mrs Samuels asked her teenage daughter **what time she had got home the previous night.**
10) Mrs Roe was a bit disappointed and asked her grandson **if/whether they really had to leave the party right away.**

Exercise C.
2) The customer told the waiter to take the snails out of his salad immediately.
3) The boss asked Ms O'Connell to wait in his office.
4) Mrs Smith asked her husband not to play the saxophone in bed.
5) Sheila's mum told her to remove the paper before she ate the chocolate.
6) Terry's dad asked him not to eat so much.

Exercise D.
1) They told me not to come too late.
2) Our boss asked us to send the clients a catalogue./Our boss asked us to send a catalogue to the clients.
3) Alan asked her (them) to write the letter quickly.
4) Miranda asked us to repair her mobile phone/cell phone/mobile.
5) The teacher told Philip not to copy from the other pupils.

Exercise E.
1) ~~will~~ would have; if he ~~wishes~~ wished
2) ... boyfriend **if** he thought; (to know **if** her boyfriend thought ...); ~~are~~ were vain
3) ~~from~~ by Terry; ~~borrowed~~ had borrowed his pen
4) could say ~~her~~ ; Terry told **her** that

Exercise F.
2) Customer: "I'd like to order (to have) a pizza, please."
   Waiter: "(Certainly, sir). Shall I cut the pizza into six pieces or into twelve?"
   Customer: "Please cut it into six. I could never eat twelve."
3) Patient: "Can (Could) you cure my sleepwalking?"
   Doctor: "Take this."
   Patient: "Are there sleeping pills in this packet?"
   Doctor: "No, there aren't. They're drawing pins. Put them on the floor near your bed every night."

Exercise G.

It was my first day in London. This great city is often (thought) **considered** to be one of the most confusing cities in the world and now I understand why!
I hadn't (stayed in contact) **kept in touch** with my friend Tim and now that I was in London I had arranged to meet him under Big Ben, the famous clock near the Houses of Parliament. Anyway, I had probably (not noticed) **overlooked** a sign or notice and taken the wrong road because I was completely lost!
I was standing at a busy (place where a number of streets came together) **intersection** and I (really didn't know) **had no clue** how to get to Big Ben. Then I saw a (man who was walking along the road) **passer-by** and I hoped that he (lived in the area) **was a local** and could help me.
I went up to him and asked him how I could get to (the place I wanted to go to) **my destination**.
"Oh, it's easy," he said: "Just go down this road, turn left at the traffic lights and walk down the road to the end. Then you'll see Big Ben in front of you. You can't miss it – it's opposite the fast food restaurant on the corner of the street."

Exercise H.

2) This room is in a big **mess**. My son hasn't cleared it up for months!
3) Those lobsters don't look so fresh and frankly, I don't think that they are **worth** so much money.
4) This is a **vast** area! There is room to build lots of houses here.
5) This hotel doesn't **offer** a good service.
6) The **staff** in the hotel were not very helpful. We had to carry our luggage into our rooms by ourselves.
7) Mr Soames is a multi-millionaire and is always on Forbe's list of the **wealthiest** people in the world.

Exercise I.

1) Mr and Mrs Collins **have been living** in New England **for** many years.
2) **While** her daughter **was reading** "Alice in Wonderland" in bed at midnight, Mrs Simmonds **came** into the room.
3) The **rent** for this flat is very **high**.
4) Many lobsters **were caught by** the fishermen.
5) I don't know **what** I can do to help him.
6) Lewis Carroll is the author **of** "Alice in Wonderland".
7) We aren't very **happy** with our new neighbour. She sings much too **loudly** in the bath at one o'clock in the morning.
8) Many people drink too **little** water **during** the day.
9) Prices are in general higher in Japan **than** in many European countries.
10) Although the title of the book "Bees in your garden" doesn't **sound** very **interesting** it is actually **extremely** fascinating.
11) **I was given** twenty-four hours to decide whether I wanted to accept the job.
12) **We're visiting** our grandmother tomorrow.

Exercise J.

1) Sie wurden über den neuen Vertrag informiert./Man hat sie über den neuen Vertrag informiert.
2) Das Buch, das du mir gegeben hast, ist ziemlich langweilig.
3) Seit drei Stunden versuchen wir, eine Lösung für dieses Problem zu finden.
4) Normalerweise (Gewöhnlich) steht er nicht so früh auf. Aber heute steht er um sechs Uhr auf, weil er einen wichtigen Termin hat.

Exercise K.
3) I got up late, ~~what~~ **which** meant that I missed the train.
4) The music I like isn't played very often on the radio. ✓
5) The secretary **who** usually arranges the appointments is ill today.
6) They told me about their financial problems, something ~~what~~ **which** I already knew.
7) Henrietta didn't know ~~which~~ **what** she could do.
8) Do you know whose car this is? ✓
9) I didn't know that you ~~many years ago in Italy lived.~~ **lived in Italy many years ago**.
10) The clients ~~which~~ **who** came to the presentation were very impressed.
11) All those customers who have used our software are very satisfied. ✓
12) The students, all of ~~who~~ **whom** live in the suburbs, have a long way to the university.

Exercise L.
2) **an** interesting book 3) **a** nice aunt 4) **an** uncle 5) **a** cake
6) **an** appointment 7) **an** explanation 8) **a** solution

Chapter 13

Exercise A.
2) We have dozens of things **to talk** about.
3) Don't worry, if you come a little late – I've got a letter **to write**.
4) We really need something **to open** this bottle with.
5) Tony is the most intelligent man **to try** to solve the problem.
6) Can you tell me how often **to give** the cat its food?
7) He gave me a book **to read** on the long train journey.
8) Sally was the only one in the school **to be accepted** for a place at Oxford University.

Exercise B.
1) "Let me **help** you with your maths homework." "Sorry, but I'd really rather **do** it alone."
"Really? I always prefer **to do** my homework with friends." "Oh, I'm sure I can manage **to finish** the homework alone. I know how **to solve** quadratic equations. I watched my brother **do** his homework and he had **to do** the same sort of exercise."
2) "Well, all I can do is offer **to help** you. If you don't want **to accept** my help, I can't force you **to take** it! Nobody can make anyone **do** something he or she doesn't want to."
3) "Don't get me wrong, Clive, I don't usually refuse **to accept** your help, but today I'd like **to try to solve** the problems by myself. Next week, there's a maths exam and I can't afford **to fail** for the second time. In the exam I won't have an expert like you **to help** me! Anyway, please excuse me, but I really should **concentrate** on my homework now, because I want **to watch** the football match at 6 o'clock." "OK, I get the message! I'd better **leave** you alone then!"

Exercise C.
2) You should persuade her to do her homework.
3) I would like you to close the window.
4) Your dad and I don't want you to make so much noise (... to make less noise/... to stop the noise).
5) John, please can you help us to repair this computer (it)?
6) I hope he's going to invite (will invite/invites) me to come to it (his birthday party).

7) Mrs Collins, I'd like you to inform her about the meeting next Thursday.
8) We're expecting them to ask for an estimate soon."
9) We don't want you to work so hard.
10) We're waiting for them to send us the contract.
11) I'll get him to send the fax.
12) Miss Harper, please ask her to come in.

Exercise D.
2) She's **used** to smoking 50 cigars every day.
3) Last Saturday Amy **avoided** meeting (talking to) her ex-boyfriend.
4) Margaret **suggested** going to the theatre instead of the cinema.
5) "I really must **practise** playing (this Beethoven sonata on) the mouth organ more."
6) "Ugh! I'm not **looking** forward to seeing her. She **keeps** giving me horrible, wet kisses."
7) "I don't **mind** waiting for him/staying a little longer/standing here until he comes."
8) "I really **fancy** drinking a glass of lemonade."
9) "Oh I can't **imagine** working/living in Alaska. It's much too cold for me there."
10) "Yesterday somebody stole an elephant from the circus. We've found a suspect but she **denies** stealing it/ having stolen it"
11) "I'm sure I won't **finish** baking them (the cakes) before midnight!"

Exercise E.
1) I have great difficulty **in getting** out of bed in the morning. I just can't get used **to waking** up before 7 o'clock, but my wife wants me **to make** her breakfast so early.
2) "I really don't want you **to come** home so late, my son."
"But Dad you know how much I enjoy **going** to the disco on Saturdays and I'm the only one among my friends **to leave** so early. I really am sick **of having** these silly discussions every weekend. After all, dad, I am forty-five years old."
3) At the library:
   Customer: "Good morning madam, I would like you **to give** me ten thick books."
   Librarian: "Ten thick books! I'd like you **to tell** me why you need thick books."
   Customer: "Well, my son is very interested **in playing** soccer and his teacher has encouraged him **to practise** football as much as he can. He thinks he'll succeed **in making** it to the top. And my wife, unfortunately lets him **practise playing** soccer in the living room. Well, yesterday he kicked the ball at our television table and managed **to break** the table. I don't know what **to do**. I don't mind **missing** television dramas, but I'm really looking forward **to watching** the football match between Albania and Syria tonight. I need the thick books **to put** my TV on."
   Librarian: "Well, I'm sorry but I'd better **talk** to the director of the library before **taking** a decision on the matter. He's at lunch at the moment, so we'll have to wait **for him to come** back."

Exercise F.
2) Is there a possibility **of you finishing the work soon**.
3) We're worried **about them missing their flight**.
4) It's really worth **her staying in an English family for six months**.
5) My parents are sorry **about you/me having to wait four hours for your flight**.
6) I don't mind **him listening to his radio programme while I'm typing this letter**.
7) My boss can't imagine **us ever getting married**.

Exercise G.
Beispielsätze finden Sie in Kapitel 13, Exercise G.

Exercise H.
2) coverage = Berichterstattung (cover = bedecken)
3) remarkable = bemerkenswert (mark = markieren)
4) globalization = Globalisierung (global = global)
5) powerful = mächtig (great power status = Großmachtstatus)
6) permission = Erlaubnis (to permit = erlauben)
7) ridiculous = lächerlich (ridiculed = verspottet/lächerlich gemacht)
8) ragged = zerlumpt, abgerissen (rags = abgerissene Lumpen)
9) enlarge = erweitern, vergrößern (large = groß)

Exercise I.
While the barber **was cutting** his hair six months **ago**, George **told** him about his plans for a holiday in England. "I **have always wanted** to spend a holiday in England, ever since I was a child," George said. "Who knows? Maybe I**'ll see** the Queen when I**'m** (I **am**) in England in July."
"That's impossible," the barber said. "She only meets people who are **more** important **than** you – like other queens, kings or politicians."
Two months later George **came** back to the barber's shop and asked the barber **if/whether** he could remember what he **had said** two months previously. The barber said he **could.**
"Well," said George, "you're going to be **extremely surprised** to hear this. I **was walking** in the gardens of Buckingham Palace, when suddenly the Queen saw me, invited me for a cup of tea and asked me a question."
"Good Heavens!" the barber said **excitedly**. "What **did she ask** you?"
George replied: "She asked me **who gave me** my terrible hair cut!"

Exercise J.
2) Mrs McDonald said that her husband was really good at woodwork. He had just bought some shelves and now he was writing some books to put on them.
3) The poet T.S. Eliot once asked where the wisdom was that people had lost in knowledge and where the knowledge was that they had lost in information.
4) The statistician told the audience not to believe what statistics said until they had carefully considered what they did not say.

Exercise K.
2) How did you give up smoking so quickly last year?
3) This book was written by my uncle.
4) The CD I'm listening to is very relaxing.

Chapter 14

Exercise A.
2) Ich habe den Mann, der im Chor gesungen hat, wirklich bewundert.
3) Dieses Haus, das vor über vierhundert Jahren gebaut wurde, ist immer noch in gutem Zustand.
4) Die Leute, die in dieser Firma arbeiten, sind mit ihren Arbeitsbedingungen nicht zufrieden.
5) Von den Tausenden von Büchern, die jedes Jahr veröffentlicht werden, werden nur wenige zu Bestsellern.

Exercise B.
2) Da (Nachdem) Julia sieben Teller Spaghetti gegessen hatte, fühlte sie sich krank (wurde es ihr schlecht).
3) Da Charles wusste, wie viele Hosentaschen er hatte, entschied er sich, den Taschenrechner nicht zu kaufen.
4) Brunhilde war sehr traurig, da sie seit siebzig Jahren nichts von Max gehört hatte.
5) Da Naomi sehr großzügig ist, kaufte sie uns allen ein Eis.

Exercise C.
2) Nachdem ich das Eis gegessen hatte, kaufte ich mir eine Pizza.
3) Als Susan Fußball spielte, verletzte sie sich am Fuß.
4) Da (Nachdem) der Computer abgestürzt war, mussten wir selbst denken!
5) Während ich mich in der Mittagspause entspanne, schaffe ich es, ein paar Aufgaben für das Telekolleg zu machen.
6) Als Gerry sich im Spiegel betrachtete (sah), verstand er, warum so viele Frauen ihn mochten.

Exercise D.
2) Although he didn't know much French Jim could at least say "je t'aime" to his French girlfriend.
3) If it is broken your lamp will, of course, be replaced.
4) While you operate this machine, please wear a safety helmet.
5) If you use it carefully, this machine will never break down.
6) Tim's mouth was stuffed with apple strudel and he started to sing an Austrian folk song.

Exercise E.

reliable (zuverlässig); remainder (die übrigen ...); successful (erfolgreich); original (ursprünglich, originell); consideration (Überlegung, Erwägung, Rücksicht); considerable (beträchtlich); settlement (Siedlung); sizeable (ziemlich groß, beträchtlich); helpful (hilfreich); helpless (hilflos); forgetful (vergesslich); forgettable (man kann es getrost vergessen!); recovery (Erholung, Wiederfindung); complaint (Beschwerde); agreement (Abmachung, Übereinkunft, Übereinstimmung, Einwilligung); agreeable (angenehm);

EXERCISE F.
2) unforgettable = unvergesslich; disappointment = Enttäuschung
3) satisfactory = befriedigend; agreement = Abmachung, Übereinkunft, Abkommen
4) enlarge = erweitern
5) joint = gemeinsam
6) uninhabitable = unbewohnbar

EXERCISE G.
3) It wasn't worth watching the American movie/The American movie wasn't worth watching.
4) My wife persuaded me to go to the theatre.
5) Sam enjoys eating fish and chips (every day).
6) We're (I'm) looking forward to seeing my cousin Terry tomorrow.
7) John spent five hours answering emails yesterday.
8) After having a wonderful meal at an English restaurant in Munich we went home.
9) Paula's mother didn't let her (Paula) come home after ten o'clock.
10) David and June have succeeded in constructing their own computer by themselves!
11) John's mother would like him (John) to close the window.
12) We are accustomed to travelling to work by helicopter every day of the week.

EXERCISE H.
2) He apologized for coming late.
3) We really can't afford to go on holiday this year.
4) Mary and Fred phone **each other** every day. Fred phones in the morning and Mary phones in the evening.
5) Mary and Fred hurt **themselves** when their car crashed into the wall.
6) We did the homework all by **ourselves**.
7) Hello, you guys! Please help **yourselves** to tea and biscuits. I'll be with you in a moment.
8) Father: "Can you do your homework by **yourself** or shall I help you?"
   Son: "No thanks Dad. I can get it wrong by **myself**."
9) They complained about the terrible service in the hotel.
10) I can't remember his name, can you?
11) The two sisters haven't spoken to **each other** for years.
12) Timmy concentrated on the maths problem and eventually he was able to solve it **himself** without the help of his father.
13) Sally and I made **ourselves** comfortable on the sofa and played chess.

EXERCISE I.
2) Yesterday it **was warmer than (it is) today.**/Yesterday it **wasn't as cold as it is today.**
3) For the last twenty years **I have been playing the piano.**
4) We phone **each other every day.**
5) I saw the woman **whose daughter you like.**
6) Mary asked Charles why **the female members of the Royal Family wore such strange hats.**
7) We **have been in this town** since 2007.
8) Although it **was raining heavily, they still went out for a picnic.**
9) The catalogues **haven't been sent off yet.**

EXERCISE J.

(crossword puzzle solution)

CHAPTER 15

EXERCISE A.
2) If Sue **doesn't stop** eating so much, she**'ll put** on too much weight.
3) You can stay out later as long as you **aren't** here later than midnight.
4) If they **offer** you the car for 500 euros, **will** you **buy** it?
5) Susan **will be able to talk** to the Italians on her holiday in Italy next year if she **learns** Italian before.
6) You **won't catch** the train Terence if you **don't hurry**.
7) **Will** we **get** to the meeting on time if we **miss** the next train?
8) Graham **will go** to the concert tomorrow unless he **has** too much work.
9) If you **see** Jimmy, **don't tell** him where I've hidden his Christmas presents.
10) Please **wash** your hands if they are dirty.

EXERCISE B.
2) If Rachel spoke to her colleagues at work, she would be (more) popular.
3) Bill would sleep well at night if he lived in a quiet area.
4) If this Rolls Royce wasn't (weren't) so expensive, we could buy it.
5) If Samantha wore a coat in winter, she wouldn't always catch a cold.
6) Philip wouldn't always be so bored if he didn't spend every evening watching DVDs.
7) If my little son didn't eat worms from the garden, he wouldn't often be sick.
8) Michaela would get to bed early if she didn't go to the disco every evening.
9) If Hannah's job was (more) interesting, she would be happy in her job.
10) We wouldn't know the if-clauses so well if we didn't practise them so often.

Exercise C.
2) If we had booked early, we would have got a ticket for the concert.
3) If I hadn't eaten nine pizzas in twenty minutes yesterday, I wouldn't have felt ill yesterday.
4) If I had known you were here in London yesterday, I would have phoned you.
5) I would have sent you an email last Sunday if my computer hadn't broken down.
6) We could have spent our holiday in the States last summer if we had had enough money.
7) I wouldn't have met my wife if I hadn't gone to a party forty years ago.
8) We would have gone out for a picnic yesterday if it hadn't rained the whole day.
9) I would have come to your birthday party on Saturday if you hadn't forgotten to invite me.
10) If Mr Green had seen the red lights last night, he wouldn't have driven into another car.

Exercise D.
2) If we **don't reduce** our consumption of energy, we'll have great problems in the near future.
3) If I **lived** nearer my job, I would have a much less stressful life.
4) We **would have got** to work earlier yesterday if the train **hadn't been** late.
5) If I **hadn't had to go** to a conference last week I **would have gone** skiing.
6) What **will** we **do** next week if the new software doesn't arrive?
7) Would you accept it if they **offered** you a job in their firm?
8) If I **didn't have to work** overtime so often, I'd stay in the firm.
9) We**'ll** all **be** enormously happy if the economic climate remains positive next year.
10) The fish **would have been** fresh if we **had come** to this restaurant six weeks ago.
11) John **would have** more chances with Mary if he **didn't kick** her while he was dancing with her.
12) If John **had learned** to dance when he was young, he **wouldn't have kicked** Jane on her legs so often at the disco in the last few weeks.
13) If sales **don't improve** in the coming months, we'll have to decide on a plan of action.

Exercise E.
Samantha: Victor, I know it's rather **short notice**, but Marvin is holding a Christmas party tomorrow and he has **invited** us to come.
Victor: He's a wonderful guy, so **hospitable**: he always makes everyone feel welcome, but I'm not sure that I can go.
Samantha: That's a shame. Why not?
Victor: Well, I only got back from Europe yesterday and I still haven't quite **recovered** from the jet lag yet. I'm afraid that **unless** I feel better tomorrow, I won't be able to come.
Samantha: To tell you the truth, I'm not feeling too well, myself. It's such a **hassle** going to town to buy all the Christmas presents with all those crowds of people everywhere. **Virtually** everyone seems to buy their presents at the last moment. Look, I'll tell you what – **supposing** we tell him the situation and go to his party next year. What do you think?
Victor: That's a good idea. I'm sure he'll understand.

Exercise F.
to take advantage of someone/something (jemanden/etwas ausnutzen); avoid the hassle (den Ärger vermeiden); to head back (zurückeilen); without doubt (zweifellos); outer space (Weltraum); to show off (angeben mit); on purpose (absichtlich), out of touch (ohne Kontakt)

Exercise G.

An old woman parked her car on a parking lot **which was situated** near a supermarket. **After she had locked** her car, she went into the supermarket. She returned to the car**, as/after she had finished** her shopping.
She was rather surprised to see four men **who were sitting** in the car **and drinking** cola. She quickly took out a gun from her bag, **she pointed** it at the four men and told them to get out of the car.
As they saw the anger in the old woman's face and **did not want** to be shot by her, the four men rushed out of the car as quickly as they could.
The old woman got into the car, but **when she put** the key into the ignition, she found out that it didn't fit. It wasn't her car! In the meantime, the police **who had been informed** by the four men arrived.

Exercise H.

Mr Feldman was looking in the attic when he found an old violin and an old oil painting. He showed **them** to **his** wife who was very excited. "I remember this painting and this violin," she told **him**, "they belonged to **my** grandfather. How much do you think they're worth?"
"I don't know **myself**," Mr Feldman said, "but we can go to Mrs Daly – she's an antiques dealer. I'm sure she can tell **us**."
So they went to Mrs Daly and showed **her** the painting and the violin.
"Good Heavens!" she said, "These things of **yours** are interesting. You've got a Picasso and a Stradivarius there!"
"Great!" said Mr Feldman. "They must be worth millions of dollars. Just think," he said to Mrs Feldman, "now we can buy **ourselves** a big house in the country!"
"I'm sorry to tell **you** this," said the antiques dealer, "but unfortunately they're not worth much. Stradivarius painted the picture and Picasso made the violin."

Exercise I.

2) How many instruments does Salina play?
3) What does Cedric have to do before he leaves the office this evening?
4) Where is the sales manager going (to) next week?
5) How long have we been working on this problem?
6) Which branch did Mr Peat work in?

Grammar Test Solutions

Geben Sie sich für jede richtig ausgefüllte Lücke (z.B. Übung A) oder für jeden richtig gebildeten Satz (z.B. Übung C) einen Punkt.

A.

1) "Philip, is this one of **your** (**my**) pens or is it **mine** (**yours**)?"
2) Richard and I injured **ourselves** very badly in a road accident last year.
3) Some very young children cannot concentrate on a task for longer than five minutes. ✓
4) Tony and Gillian send **each other** love letters every day. They really can't afford the time to do this, because they have very busy jobs. ✓
5) "Peter, darling, your two children are having difficulties with **their** maths homework. Can you help **them**? "
6) "I'm sorry but they'll have to do the homework **themselves**. I could never understand maths!"
7) The coal industry in Germany has many problems. That's one reason why the government supports **it** financially.
8) Mrs Deakin has to attend the meeting and I think this report is **hers**. Mr Donnelly isn't working on the project, so it can't be **his**.

B.
1) Most of the time Jenny **doesn't use** her laptop, but today she **is using** it because the computer has broken down.
2) This is terrible! We**'ve been working** (also acceptable: **have worked**) on this problem for the last two hours and we **haven't found** an answer yet.
3) If Stuart **didn't** always **come** to the office so late every day, he would finish his work before five o'clock.
4) After we **had been waiting** (also possible: **had waited**) for two hours, Peter finally came. He **didn't apologize** for being late.
5) We'll inform our neighbours before we **leave** for our holiday tomorrow.
6) Our firm **would have sold** more of the new washing machines last year if there **had been** a better marketing campaign before the products came onto the market.
7) Too much pollution **is caused** nowadays by cars and lorries.
8) Don't worry! Maybe we won't finish the job on Thursday or even on Friday, but by Saturday at the latest **we'll have finished** it.

C.
1) If we move to Sheffield, we'll be nearer my sister.
2) The train usually comes late during the week. (Auch möglich: During the week ...)
3) The letters you read weren't for you!
4) Many buildings have been destroyed by the floods.

D.
2) They went for a walk **although** it was raining very heavily.
3) I didn't agree with Malcolm's idea **because** I thought it was too impractical.
4) These papers **which (that)** are lying on my table don't belong to me.
5) I didn't understand **what** he was trying to say.
6) I'm afraid I don't know **how** to operate this machine. Can you show me?
7) The colleague **whose** email address I've given you, will help you if you have any problems.
8) We aren't sure **whether** to go to Oxford or to Brighton for our outing.

E.
1) We **were photographed** at our wedding **by** a professional photographer.
2) Peter asked me **whether/if I would be in Munich** the next day.
3) For the last twenty years **my wife and I have been working for this company.**
   For the last twenty years **my wife and I have been in this company.**
4) William thinks that chess **is more interesting than card games.**
5) If Josephine **had worked harder last year**, she **would have passed** her exams.
6) It's not worth **switching on the television now.**
7) I'm really looking forward **to seeing my cousins on Saturday!**
8) **I would learn Turkish** if **I had the time (to learn it).**
9) "Mary, we would like **you not to smoke in the house, please.**"
10) Giovanni was the only **one to begin the work on time.** (Auch möglich: ... one who began the work on time.)
11) One of our colleagues asked her **if she had gone to the computer fair in Hamburg** the week before.
12) Louisa **drinks less beer than I do (than me).**

F.
2) Claudia, three friends of ~~you~~ **yours** are waiting to play with you!
3) We had a wonderful holiday in California ~~before~~ three years **ago**.
4) Where **do** you work? (Where **are** you **working** now?)
5) I didn't see your brother yesterday. ✓
6) I can't remember ~~me~~ his face.
7) I really find ~~this~~ **these** grammar rules easy to understand.
8) We'll be eating a wonderful meal at the Ritz hotel this time tomorrow. ✓
9) We don't have ~~an~~ **our** own car – we borrow our brother's one when we drive into town.
10) The Harry Potter books were written ~~from~~ **by** J. K. Rowling
11) He has to wear ~~an~~ **a** uniform in his job.
12) We always ~~on Tuesdays~~ go to our club **on Tuesdays**. (Oder: **On Tuesdays** we always go to our club.)

G.
2) "Terry and Sue speak good German." "I'm sorry, but unfortunately **they don't**."
3) "James owns a blue Aston Martin." "Really, I don't think **he does**."
4) "Janet really should give up smoking." "You're right, **she should**."
5) "Diana has been fired from her job." "I'm pleased to say that, thank Goodness, **she hasn't**."
6) "I think we can get the eight o'clock if we leave now." "Of course **we can't**! It's already 7.56 and the station is two miles away!"

H.
2) Simon and I can come to your party a little later, **can't we**?
3) Brian doesn't feel too well in his new job, **does he**?
4) I'm too late for the presentation, **aren't I**?
5) Daniella hasn't understood the instructions, **has she**?
6) Mrs Dubovie, you will be at our meeting tomorrow, **won't you**?

I.
1) Harry always succeeds **in winning** at chess. He seems **to do** it without **concentrating** much on the game!
2) I really can't manage **to get** up so early in the morning. I'm used **to sleeping** until about 8 o'clock.
3) It's rather late, I think we should **leave** now.
4) Jean promised **to knit** me a pullover. I've been waiting **for her to do** it for ages. She always has difficulty **in remembering** her promises.
5) My boss wants me **to take** my holiday in August, but I don't like the idea **of spending** my holiday **lying** on the beach with thousands of sunbathers. I'll try to persuade him **to let** me **have** my holidays in April or May.
6) I really don't know whether **to leave** my job or not. I certainly don't enjoy **having to do** the same monotonous tasks day after day. However, I'm worried **about not finding** another job so easily. So I suppose I'll stay in my present job for a while. Maybe the management will agree **to give** me a better job in this firm.

J.
2) The strategy **which/that was decided** on turned out to be rather unsuccessful.
3) **As/Since we didn't have** much money we had to walk home instead of taking a taxi.
4) If **it is required**, I can come into the office over the weekend.
5) Many people **who worked** with asbestos in the past had – and still have – serious health problems.

K.
1) I don't understand why, but **lately** my train has always arrived ten minutes **late**.
2) We'll have to work **hard** if we want to send off all the catalogues before 5 pm.
3) Have you got a sore throat? Your voice sounds a bit **funny**.
4) Robert is an **extremely dangerous** driver. He doesn't drive **carefully** at all.

What is your score?

POINTS

95–85	Excellent	Well done! You could, I'm sure, help some of the other students in the class! I'm sure they will be happy if you offer them your help.
84–70	Good	You have a good basis in English grammar which will help you in the Telekolleg main course.
69–55	Satisfactory	Your command of English grammar is OK, but it would be a good idea for you to repeat some of the grammar in this book and in the programmes.
54–45		You have understood many aspects of English grammar, but for you, too, it would be a good idea to look at the explanations and do some of the exercises again.
Less than 45		There is no need to panic because in the Telekolleg main course we will repeat a lot of the grammar. However, it would be a good idea for you to do a number of the exercises in the last 15 chapters again before the Telekolleg main course begins. Then you will be well prepared!

VOCABULARY TEST SOLUTIONS

Geben Sie sich für jede richtige Antwort (z. B. Übung A) einen Punkt. Geben Sie sich beim Kreuzworträtsel für jedes gefundene Wort einen Punkt.

EXERCISE A.
2) recreation (11D), **intersection** (Kreuzung) (12A), relaxation (2D), vacation (7A)
   Die anderen Wörter beziehen sich auf unsere Freizeit.
3) **celebrity** („Promi", Berühmtheit) (13D), graduate (13F), degree (14A), university (2D)
   Ein *graduate* (Absolvent) bekommt seinen *degree* (akademischen Grad) von der *university*.
4) mortgage (13D), revenues (7D), tax (11D), **outskirts** (Außenbezirke) (11D)
   Die anderen Wörter haben mit Geld und Finanzen zu tun.
5) crazy (13A), **picturesque** (malerisch) (12D), freaky (6A), weird (9A)
   Die anderen Wörter haben die Bedeutung von „sehr sonderbar"/*very strange*.
6) boarding school (2D), **boundaries** (Landesgrenzen) (8D), curriculum (2D), primary level (2D)
   Die anderen Wörter beziehen sich auf das Bildungswesen in Großbritannien.
7) magnificent (5D), awesome (14A), flamboyant (6D), **enduring** (andauern) (11D)
   Die anderen Wörter bedeuten „prächtig, herrlich".

EXERCISE B.
2) After the all-night party, Hugh's **appearance** looked quite strange.
3) You can pay for the goods after **delivery**.
4) Tania is a really **messy** person. You should see her bedroom!

5) Forty **employees** of the firm work in this department.
6) The **majority** of the tourists who come to Cardiff visit the castle.
7) **Immigration** to Germany has increased recently.

EXERCISE C.
2) Twenty seven countries at present make **up** the European Union.
3) In contrast **to** many other countries, the number of graduates in this country is quite high.
4) Our country is in danger **of** falling behind if we don't invest more in education.
5) Some animals have a surprising way of adapting **to** their environment.
6) Bill wanted **to** study physics but he ended **up** studying engineering.
7) Instead **of** sending off dozens of emails, Jack prefers to write old-fashioned letters.
8) I'm looking **for** somebody who can talk to me in English. But I can't find anyone.
9) Pete's really keen **on** learning languages.
10) We're looking forward **to** trying out our English with our guests from Nigeria.
11) Maurine's new dress triggered **off** a long discussion!

EXERCISE D.
2) I took a flight from Munich and it took me ages to reach my **destination**.
3) What's more – after my flight to America it took me a few days to recover from my jet **lag**.
4) I couldn't stand up straight – let **alone** walk to the bathroom.
5) I was so ill that I just wanted to head **back** to Munich.
6) Without **doubt** that was one of the worst flights I have ever had.
7) I recovered after a few days and wanted to **rent** a car and see the sights before the course started.
8) I thought I had remembered to take everything with me, but I hadn't paid enough **attention**.
9) I had forgotten to take my driver's **license** with me!

EXERCISE E.

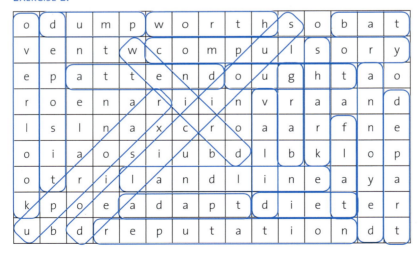

EXERCISE F.

Mr and Mrs Feldman had been **attending** singing lessons for a year now, but unfortunately they didn't have the best of **reputations** for their singing. In fact, when they practised their duets in their living room every evening, for their neighbours, it sounded really **weird** rather like a frightened cat.
One evening Mr and Mrs Feldman had just left their **flat** and were on their way to their singing class when Mr
5 Feldman suddenly shouted out to his wife: "Oh, no!"
"What's the matter?" Mrs Feldman asked.
"I've **overlooked** something really important. What an idiot I am! It's my mum's birthday today. We haven't sent her a birthday card. She'll be quite sad and **annoyed**."
"I know," said Mrs Feldman, "when we come back from our lesson, I'll make her a nice, **delicious** cake and we'll
10 take it to her."
"It really isn't **worth** doing that," said Mr Feldman, "have you forgotten? For the past few weeks my mum has been on a **diet**. She certainly won't want to eat one of your cakes. And maybe she'll be in bed when we get home. I think we **ought** to phone her here and now and wish her a Happy Birthday."
"O.K.," his wife said, "you can use my mobile phone – yours isn't working." Mr Feldman **grabbed** the mobile
15 phone his wife offered him and dialed his mother's number.
As soon as somebody picked up the phone at the other end Mr and Mrs Feldman both started singing "Happy Birthday to you" as loudly as they could. Unfortunately, as usual, their singing sounded quite terrible.
"Dr Hamilton speaking. Who's there? " the man at the other end asked.
"Oh, my Goodness," Mr Feldman said, "I'm sorry we've got the wrong number."
20 "Don't worry," Dr Hamilton replied. "After listening to your terrible singing, I can hear that both of you need all the practice you can get!"

EXERCISE G.

Ruben and Leah are talking to each other in the **break** at school.
"I'm really worried," says Ruben, "My father works so hard – ten hours a day. And with the money that his **boss/ employer** gives him, he pays for our nice home and lots of food for me and my sisters. And my mum **spends** the whole day cleaning and cooking for us. She and dad **save** the whole year to buy us birthday and Christmas
5 presents. And on Christmas Day and on our birthdays we **get** wonderful presents – **perhaps/possibly/maybe** the best presents in the world. Our granddad, who lives with us, gives me and my sisters extra pocket money every week, **although** he only has a small **pension**. I'm really so worried, I can tell you!"
"Worried? Well, **actually** I don't understand you," says Leah. "I **think** your parents and granddad are great. I'm sure many kids would be **happy** to live in such a family. In my **opinion** you live in a paradise. Why are you so
10 worried?"
"Well," says Ruben, "what if they try to run away?"

What is your score?

70 – 60	Great!	You've built up a good basis.
59 – 50	Good!	
49 – 35	Satisfactory	
34 – 20		Well, O.K., but I hope that you go through the chapters before the main course starts!
19 – 0		Don't panic! However, it would be good to reread the chapters again to refresh your vocabulary.

Weiteres Begleitmaterial zu den Grundkursen im Telekolleg

Buch „Into the English World – Grundkurs Englisch"
Autor: Günther Albrecht
Format: 19 x 24 cm
Umfang: 288 Seiten
Preis: 17,95 EUR [D]
ISBN: 978-3-941282-25-4
Erhältlich über www.telekolleg-info.de

„Into the English World – Grundkurs Englisch" ist das Begleitbuch zu den Sendungen „Grundkurs Englisch" des Bayerischen Rundfunks. In 15 Kapiteln geht es um die Erlebnisse des Amerikaners Eric in Deutschland und den USA. Anhand lebensnaher Themen wird dem Leser die englische Grammatik und Sprache unterhaltsam und leicht verständlich nähergebracht. In jedem Kapitel wird zudem ein englischsprachiges Land oder Gebiet vorgestellt.
Im Sprachlaboratorium werden sprachliche Missverständnisse und die englische Aussprache humorvoll erklärt sowie auf den Unterschied zwischen amerikanischem und britischem Englisch aufmerksam gemacht.
Keine Angst vor englischsprachiger Literatur – mit Auszügen aus Original-Werken möchte das Buch dem Leser Freude an bekannten Werken vermitteln.

Buch „Worte haben Bedeutung – Grundkurs Deutsch"
Autor: Stefan Bagehorn
Format: 19 x 24 cm
Umfang: 222 Seiten
Preis: 15,95 EUR [D]
ISBN: 978-3-941282-11-7
Erhältlich über www.telekolleg-info.de

Die Kapitel 1–5 befassen sich mit der mündlichen Sprachkompetenz: Zwischenmenschliche Kommunikation; Recherchieren; Mediennutzung; Besser Reden; Formulieren und Mitreden.
In den Kapiteln 6–11 geht es um die Lese- und Schreibkompetenz: Texte beurteilen; Lesen und Verstehen; Lesen, Verstehen, Zusammenfassen; Texte analysieren und verarbeiten; Erörtern; Grammatik und Rechtschreibung.
Die Kapitel 12–15 fördern die Literaturkompetenz: Prosatexte untersuchen; Eine gute Geschichte: Der Vorleser; Literatur und Liebe; Literatur und die Welt draußen.

**Buch „Grundkurs Mathematik
Vom Rechnen zu Algebra und Trigonometrie"**
Autor: Ferdinand Weber
Format: 19 x 24 cm
Umfang: 204 Seiten
Preis: 16,95 EUR [D]
ISBN: 978-3-941282-10-0
Erhältlich über www.telekolleg-info.de

In 15 Lektionen vermittelt der Autor einfach und verständlich mathematisches Grundwissen in Algebra und Trigonometrie. Das Buch ist eine fundierte Einführung in das Fach Mathematik, und richtet sich an alle an Grundbildung interessierte Lernende der verschiedenen Schulstufen und Schulformen.

Themen: Mengen, Schnittmengen, Zahlengerade; Terme und Termumformungen; Multiplikation von Summen; Binome; Gleichungen und Ungleichungen; Lineare Gleichungssysteme; Proportionalitäten; Relationen − lineare Funktionen; die reellen Zahlen; quadratische Gleichungen; quadratische Funktionen; Schnittmengen von linearen und quadratischen Funktionen; Sätze am rechtwinkligen Dreieck; Sinus-, Kosinus- und Tangensfunktion; Winkelfunktionen im rechtwinkligen Dreieck; Sinussatz; Kosinussatz.

Der Grundkurs Mathemathematik ist auch auf DVD erhältlich:

**DVD „Grundkurs Mathematik
Vom Rechnen zu Algebra und Trigonometrie"**

Umfang: 15 Sendungen des Bayerischen Fernsehens auf 3 DVDs
Preis: 49,95 EUR [D]
ISBN: 978-3-941282-43-8
Erhältlich über www.telekolleg-info.de